The Birth of a First Child
towards an understanding of femininity

The Birth of a First Child
towards an understanding of femininity

DANA BREEN

TAVISTOCK PUBLICATIONS

First published 1975 by
Tavistock Publications Limited
11 New Fetter Lane, London EC4P 4EE

© 1975 Dana Breen

Printed in Great Britain by
Butler & Tanner Ltd, Frome and London
ISBN 0 422 74340 2
ISBN 0 422 75900 7

To my mother

To my daughter Sasha,
may she enjoy being a woman

and to the memory of my father
who taught me to appreciate the
world of books

Contents

Acknowledgements

I would like to express my gratitude to the women who participated in this study. My contact with them has been personally enriching.

I am also indebted to Mr Melville, to the doctors and hospital staff who made this study possible by offering their co-operation and their time.

A number of people carefully read the draft or parts of it and offered their constructive criticisms: Dr Barbara Lloyd, Dr Peter Smith and Dr Anthony Ryle at an earlier stage of the work; Dr Fred Shadforth and Ms Susan Lipshitz at a later stage. I would like to thank them for this. I am indebted to Professor Marie Jahoda for her invaluable help at all stages of the book. I am also grateful to Mr Ian Birksted without whose encouragement and help the book would probably not be.

My warmest thanks to Nan Lurie who contributed to this book with her artistic talent.

Professor Dunn and the Australian Council for Educational Research have kindly agreed to let me reproduce parts of the Franck Drawing Completion Test.

Acknowledgement is made to Herbert A. Brant, M.B., Ch.B. (N.Z.), M.R.C.O.G., F.R.C.S.(Ed.), M.R.C.P.(Ed.) and Margaret Brant, Dip. Phys. Ed. (Otago University, N.Z.), for extracts from their book, *Pregnancy, Childbirth and Contraception—All you need to know*. Copyright © Herbert and Margaret Brant 1971, published by Transworld Publishers Ltd.

Preface

This book is about one of the most profound and most commonplace experiences in the life of a woman: a first pregnancy and confinement. Both these aspects explain – perhaps paradoxically – why we know so very little about it. Birth, sex and death form the inevitable basis of our experience in being alive; they are taken for granted as not needing further explanation. Indeed there are many who feel that the study of such experiences may be dangerous; they are too close to the question of the meaning of our existence, a question which only those can face with equanimity who find comfort in the impossibility of understanding through their religious faith. They are diminishing in numbers. But when these profound and commonplace events occur in the life of an individual nothing is taken for granted. In the privacy of personal experience every woman pregnant for the first time struggles for meaning, comes to terms with her fate or fails to do so, just as her ancestors have done for untold generations.

Dr Breen has here undertaken to trace significant aspects of this private experience. This raises questions: can it be done and should it be done?

The answer to the first question every reader will undoubtedly give for himself; in my opinion it is yes. The processes of adaptive and maladaptive experiences of a first pregnancy are here made explicit thanks to Dr Breen's special stance in psychological research; special in the combination of three elements which much of academic psychology regards as incompatible. First, and quite uncontroversially, she relies on empirical evidence marshalled and analysed with as much accuracy as appropriate. Second, she refuses to treat her 'subjects' as 'objects'. The young women who shared their experiences with her were not only put into the position of collaborators and fully informed of the research purposes but, what is at least of equal importance, Dr Breen used research instruments designed to elicit as data subjective experiences without manipulation. In both these respects she was enormously helped by the ideas and methods of George Kelly whose great distinction lies in the fact that he found ways and means of according the persons he studied both dignity and freedom. Third, her approach to psychological research is informed by the complex image of man which psychoanalysis provides. The unending controversy about the place of psychoanalysis in psychological research is often conducted by both sides from false premises. Psychoanalysis is not a psychological theory in the established sense of the term. It is a conception of man in depth, not just as the pawn of circumstances, not just as the victim of his past history and its conscious and unconscious residues, but as both plus an ego engaged in the business of living with whatever degree of harmony between his desires and the real world he can achieve. To do research with such an orientation in mind requires more than collection of evidence; there must be interpretation. Psychologists can, of course, prefer to stay at the surface of overt behaviour describing what people do and say in operationalized concepts; and much useful work has been done in that manner. But this remains outside a psychology concerned with meaning and experience, conflict, intentions and purposes. Interpretation in such terms is what sets apart this study from a mechanistic, natural science approach to psychology, and not the false dichotomy between 'experimental' and 'humanistic' psychology.

But should private experiences be made the subject of systematic study? What are the ethical and intellectual justifications for such an enterprise? Academic psychologists who shun research into private experiences could claim, but have de facto not done so, that a delicacy of feeling prevented them from such undertakings. Is not the privacy of personal experience the last safeguard against overwhelming pressures to reinforce us into a wholesale conformity of outlook, thought and feeling? I believe that such arguments rest on a misunderstanding of how we acquire individuality and the nerve to have our own experiences. We become ourselves through encounters with others, not in splendid isolation. Experiences and feelings are all too easily repressed or thwarted if one makes the assumption that everybody else manages to go through life without inner turmoil – or ecstasy, for that matter. Awareness of the variety of human experiences in similar circumstances undermines conformity, if for no other reason than because one cannot conform to all of them at once. We become individuals in distinction from others, not by imitation. If we do not know how others feel and experience, the distinction is more difficult to make. If we do know, it is no guarantee, of course, for success in our own private world, but it gives us a better chance, and this is all we can hope for.

Dr Breen's study is not a prescription of how to become a happy mother, but it does enlarge our awareness of many aspects of this most personal experience. I hope that she and others will continue on the way toward a humane and systematic psychology, in all our interests.

Marie Jahoda
November, 1973

. . . I feel almost as if I were going to die, as if the only thing that would make the pattern correct would be to have the woman part kill off the child who so resisted being a woman. And, in a sense, it will *be a death – and a birth, too. The defiant tomboy that was me will be finally and irrevocably lost, but someone else will be born, though not so apparently as the baby is born. Or at least I hope so. I can't go on resenting. One must learn to change with changing circumstances or it is death indeed.* Abigail Lewis

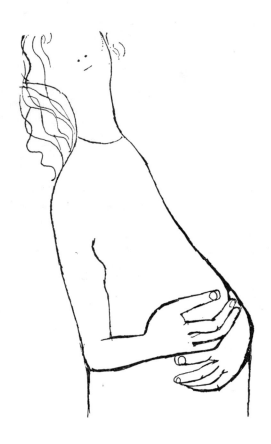

Chapter 1
Introduction

L'homme est ce qu'il se fait. J.-P. Sartre

Flux and order are equally necessary to the existence of anything.
George Santayana

*The life of a healthy individual is characterized by fears, conflicting feelings,
doubts, frustrations, as much as by the positive features.* D. W. Winnicott

This book is concerned with psychological changes in women
with the birth of a first child, in other words with the impact on a
woman of becoming a mother, with all the social and personal meaning this new state may have for her. It is centred around some research I conducted a few years ago.

The roots lie in my desire to study femininity and understand
myself as a woman, and my fascination with a psychoanalytic type
of thinking. About the former I would say that, sociologically this is
part of the increased awareness of women of their situation in our
society, their realization that they themselves must study femininity
and reject old male-made models if they are to bear children while at
the same time fulfill themselves as individuals.

About the latter I would like to point out my commitment to a
psychoanalytic type of interpretation of phenomena (in taking the
word fairly loosely to refer in particular to concern with unconscious
meaning) though I will at times attack a strictly Freudian analysis.
These roots have continually fed my curiosity, helping me over the
tedium which is part of any empirical research.

Understanding and new discovery in the human and social sciences
requires the combination of intuition (one's own and other people's)
and empirical research. Without the former it is difficult to uncover
new ground; without the latter it is easy to assert anything. Empirical
research, the testing of specific hypotheses, is essential if we are to

rule out certain assumptions and confirm others. It does mean certain limitations – for example it is only possible or practicable to test certain hypotheses at a particular time (historically).

A number of people have read or heard me talk about my research; depending on their background or orientation (psychoanalysts, non-psychoanalytically oriented psychologists, non-psychologists, mothers, etc.) the findings which are obvious to some people are puzzling to other people and vice versa. This is probably because I combine different approaches and combine psychoanalytic thinking with non psychoanalytic methods.

No research is value free. The researcher must be aware of and take responsibility for the values implicit in his work, since the way he works and reports his findings may be one prestigeful factor involved in the making of society. Every way of tackling a problem presents only one of many possible approaches. This is no reason for despair, but a reason to become aware of what is being masked or avoided. Are we leaving out the potentially creative and fulfilling aspects of human beings and thereby contributing to the development of a mechanical and rigid society? The choice is ours in what we set out to describe, how we describe it, and by the same token in the kind of society we are working to promote. The choice of a topic, of the research methods and of the theoretical background employed are the ways in which the values of the researcher are expressed. For example, do we want to emphasize the innate, immutable aspects of human nature thereby accepting its static elements, or do we want to emphasize the changing, creative, non deterministic aspects of ourselves thereby taking responsibility for our actions?

Some social scientists try to study people and society 'objectively', by which they mean that they are not involved in the process of knowing; they feel either that their work will have no influence on the development of society, or, if it does, that they are not responsible, since they have only described what already existed. Because I feel that we *are* involved and *are* responsible, I believe that it is necessary to become aware of and make explicit our own value judgements. I hope to make my values explicit throughout this book. The interpretation of findings is also coloured by values. For this reason I have set out the actual findings of my research in the Appendix. The interested reader can refer to the raw data which I describe and interpret in the book.

I am interested in the making of a certain kind of society, a society in which people can express and fulfil themselves. I look at people as potentially able to 'grow'. I look at their creative aspects. Fairly frequently people come up to me and say: I hear that you are doing work on 'personality and pregnancy' – this is precisely what I am *not* doing! 'Personality and pregnancy' suggests to me something very static, far removed from the complexity of a lived experience. Besides which the actual pregnancy is not the major emphasis of my research. I will come back to this later.

Included in my values is the importance to me of combining intuition, introspection, artistic expression with empirical validation if we are to come to grips with any real psycho-social problem. A constant use of these different areas should keep us aware of the importance of the problem we are tackling, its implication, its personal and social meaning while helping us to grasp the range and variety of its expression.

Finally I put a particular value on being in touch with one's feelings. To reduce conflicts and difficult times which are characteristic of human existence to 'neuroticism' is a serious and dangerous misunderstanding. The healthy person is aware of and able to tolerate a very wide range of feelings and conflicts.

The central theme of my research concerns changes in a woman's 'self-concept' with the birth of her first child. This means the way in which a woman modifies her perception of herself in relation to other important people in her life. I choose the word self-concept to describe not only the more conscious or potentially conscious aspect of the self, but also to include elements which may or may not be retrievable into consciousness. Many people are important in the world of the woman at the time of having a child; I have not studied them. The role of the husband[1] at this time is particularly crucial: his feelings about the baby, his relationship with his wife, his changed perception of his wife. The couple's economic and social situation are also influential. My particular focus though has been the woman's perception of herself and others, the meaning she gives to her world (which of course is coloured by these other factors). Meaning takes into account herself and the outside world, meaning is where objectivity and subjectivity intersect. As Giorgi puts it 'meaning is the

---

[1] When I refer to 'husband' and 'wife' I use the terms without necessarily implying a legal marriage.

result of the encounter between man and the world, an encounter in which both are essentially involved' (1970).

More specifically three important and related perspectives converge in my research topic: the person, mental health and femininity. I shall discuss these separately. These three areas are closely linked by my orientation towards a conception of the mature healthy person as one who is able to develop, to become aware of and integrate the positive and negative elements within himself[1] and take responsibility for his actions.

When I say that my concern is with changes in a woman's self-concept with the birth of her first child, I am taking up a stance from the start since this statement implies that changes *do* occur at this time. But more than that, it reflects a general theoretical approach: it is more productive when studying the person to emphasize process, change, development, than to concentrate on static, immutable features. Linked to this idea of continual change is the idea that there is never a return to a previous state; even a regression would always be coloured to some extent by the intermediary period. Looking at changes occurring with the birth of a first child is therefore considering the possibility of describing *specific patterns* of change at this time. At the broadest level therefore I would say that I am here concerned with a view of the person as able to change in a positive sense and I would like to show that it is possible to measure empirically the processes involved in such a change. Such a study is relatively unusual in that it is concerned with *positive* changes. Psychological studies concerned with change are most often concerned with negative changes (psychological disturbances, traumatic events and so forth.)

The theoretical framework involved is a psychodynamic one (which means it is concerned with processes as opposed to static attributes of the mind) and the links with psychoanalytic theory must be spelled out. As Guntrip points out (1971), psychoanalytic theory has some contradictory features. 'Freud was trying to ride two horses at once, that of mechanistic theory with his economic and topographical points of view, and that of personal theory in his dynamic point of view worked out on the basis of psychogenic processes in the medium of family relationships'. That is to say that on the one hand he described mental phenomena in terms of their

---

[1] I will stick to the unsatisfactory convention of using the masculine gender to cover both masculine and feminine designation.

location within the psychic apparatus – id, ego, superego (topo-graphical) and of the distribution of energy within the psychic apparatus (economic), while on the other hand he attempted an understanding of a person's development within the context of his family relationships.

Since psychoanalytic theory has such contradictory features it is appropriate to state which aspects have deliberately not been used. No attempt is made at causal explanations in terms of instincts or psychosexual development. This sort of explanation destroys the person as a complex and unique agent. No attempt will be made either at causal explanations in terms of childhood events. It may not be possible to recapture and do justice to the complexity of the past. While research can probably never capture the full richness of a personal experience, it is better to approach it through the direct study of experience as it is lived than by reducing it to a few historical antecedents and a mechanistic model of man.

Notions of interaction, concomitant events and process will generally replace notions of causality. My emphasis on development and growth is closer to that of the ego psychologists such as Erikson than it is to Freud's view. For Erikson 'the complexes and conflicts unearthed by psychoanalysis in its first breakthrough to human nature are recognized as existing; they do threaten to dominate the development and accidental crisis of life. But the freshness and wholeness of experience and the opportunities arising with a resolved crisis can, in an ongoing life, transcend trauma and defence' (Erikson, 1968). To always look for causes reduces the individuality of the ex-perience and does not do justice to the creative aspect of the present.

Kelly developed a theory in an attempt to step away from the deterministic model which psychology has inherited from the physi-cal sciences in the eighteenth century. This break enabled him to explore such areas as intentionality, meaning and experience. He called his theory Personal Construct Theory, emphasizing the im-portance of the way each person construes the environment. To some extent Kelly starts where psychoanalytic theory stops. Kelly believes that we are responsible for our constructions. Constructs are imposed upon events, not abstracted from them. 'A person's processes are psychologically channelized by the ways in which he anticipates events' (1955). What is important is how the person anticipates events; the ordinary man, he says, is a scientist – a scientist who has hypotheses and makes predictions about events, and modifies them when they turn out to be false. I would add that the scientist and the ordinary man can be extraordinarily recalcitrant to discard hypotheses which have proved false – this is what accounts for prejudices and stereotypes ('women are hysterical') and for neurotic conflicts ('masculinity and unemotionality go together; I am a man and I must choose between being masculine and unemotional or not masculine and emotional'). For some people, no amount of disproving will change their belief that women are hysterical or that masculinity precludes feelings. Kelly rejects explanations in terms of childhood events and past circumstances. He looks at *how* a person anticipates events not *why* he anticipates them in such a way. The psychogenetic part of psychoanalytic theory, and personal construct theory therefore focus on two different questions, why and how. In this book I will be concerned with Kellian notions and problems: the person as actor, as involved in a continual process of reappraisal and change, of reorganization and adaptation. This interest dictated my use of the method Kelly developed (Repertory Grid Technique) and which I will describe later. I do not feel it necessary however, as Kelly did, thereby to reject psychoanalytic notions; the two approaches are complementary and compatible.

Important concepts which pertain to the study of the person-as-changing and which are useful to consider in the context of pregnancy and the birth of a child are those of 'crisis' and 'developmental stage'. With the birth of her first child, the woman is confronted with an objective, important and irreversible event. In this sense my research relates to studies of crisis situations if we retain from 'crisis' the connotations of urgency and irrevocability. Even more appropriate though than crisis in the context of pregnancy and birth is the notion of developmental stage. This notion is used by such different authors as Erikson and Piaget and implies the ideas of progression and total structure. Human growth is seen 'from the point of view of the conflicts, inner and outer, which the vital personality weathers, re-emerging from each crisis with an increased sense of inner unity, with an increase in good judgement, and an increase in the capacity "to do well" according to (the person's) own standards and the standards of those who are significant to him' (Erikson, 1968). There is a continual interchange between the individual and his environment or, to use Piaget's terminology, a continual process of 'assimilation' (that is to say an incorporation of the outside world into the person's own activity – as when the child uses a stick to represent the horse he gallops off on) and 'accommodation' (a regulation in function of the outside world – as when the child imitates somebody else) which results in an ever increasing adaptation of the individual. New events must be integrated in the light of the present. This process of adaptation is similar to the one occurring at a biological level when, for example, the organism absorbs substances and transforms them in relation to its present state. Such a process of adaptation both at a biological level and at a psychological one, is indispensable to life itself. Developmental stages, that is, passages from one level or form of organization to another, have been described in childhood and are inherently related to biological maturation – for instance the capacity to symbolize (in particular the advent of language) if we think of Piaget, or the upsurge of instinctual urges at puberty if we think of Erikson. The birth of a first child seems to be such a biosocial event, requiring cognitive, emotional and social reappraisal and restructuring encompassing both external events and internal ones which have been mobilized. It seems justified to look upon it as a turning point, possibly leading to a new developmental stage.

It is necessary to point out that if, as I suggest, the birth of a first child can provide the setting for the passage from one stage to another in a woman, such a notion of developmental stage is slightly different from the way it is used by Piaget or by Erikson when he talks about puberty. Indeed, except in a small number of cases where there is a serious biological or psychological disturbance, every person goes through, for example, the acquisition of language or pubertal changes. On the other hand not every woman has a child, either for reasons of personal choice, or because she does not get involved in a relationship, or for reasons of sterility. It would be a grave error automatically to term such a woman abnormal or immature. Conversely it would be wrong to say that every woman who bears a child goes through a stage of development.

What I am really trying to stress when I talk about developmental stage is on the one hand its link with other bio-social events and on the other the fact that such an event can be used by a woman towards a positive change, a greater understanding of herself, a reappraisal of relationships. Other events in the life of a person may be equally important in promoting positive change (marriage, deaths, separations, religion, new *Weltanschauung*); the difference with the birth of a first child is the biological aspect.

However, a disadvantage of the term developmental stage is that it becomes too easily oversimplified and turned into the idea that all women with children are 'more developed' or 'mature' than women without children. Maybe the idea of 'growth' is a better and safer one to describe the positive changes which might occur with the birth of a first child; it does not imply an immutable fixed stage which some women only can reach. 'Growth' is relative for each person, can imply different things and can only be understood in the context of each personal experience – rather than as an immutable and universal blueprint. The only thing which is sacrificed with the use of this term is the idea of an important event and turning point promoting a rapid and extensive change.

These considerations lead on to the second perspective of my research, the area of mental health. My concern is with a notion of 'positive mental health' – that is, of mental health as more than just the absence of disease (Jahoda, 1958). 'To oversimplify the matter somewhat, it is as if Freud supplied us the sick half of psychology and we must fill it out with the healthy half' (Maslow, 1969). My own work attempts to capture the processes involved in a healthy adjustment to the birth of a first child. The criteria of maladjustment which I have used are strict in order to delimit a 'very healthy group'. One of the aims of my research is to try and show that process rather than homeostatics characterizes these women, in other words that something more than an absence of symptoms takes place. Here again we face a difficult and tricky word: adjustment. Adjustment often refers to adjustment to the particular social situation at the expense of the person's potential. This is how it is attacked for example on the cover of a recent publication, *The Radical Therapist* which reads: 'therapy means change not adjustment'. I agree entirely with this. Similarly I am concerned with change in the present research. When I talk about women who are well adjusted to the birth of their child, I am referring to a total situation where the woman is at peace with herself-in-the-environment. This does not automatically imply either that she must conform to the environment or that she must give up her individual creativity or that she must fight her social environment. In some cases it is true, the woman who is at peace with herself does conform with the environment either because her needs coincide with the social role she is required to play or because this is, at this time in her life, the only way she knows how to be at peace with herself (i.e. because the social role is so internalized that she cannot step back from it and fight it). I will use 'well adjusted' in the first instance to include both real fulfilment (which is true health) and a pseudo-adjustment in the sense of satisfaction with conformity. Personal and social are so intimately linked that it is probably never possible to fully distinguish the two. I will attempt some distinction later.

I would like to stress that, just as growth can mean different things in each person's case, it differs in terms of timing and speed. Whereas one woman may experience most difficulties just after the birth of her child, another may not resolve her conflicts for many months. I cannot emphasize this enough since, it might be thought that 'once healthy always healthy' or 'once unhealthy always unhealthy'. This is definitely not my view; I think on the contrary that people go through periods of greater or lesser conflicts and periods of better or worse ability to cope with conflict. A number of times I have mentioned to medical people that I was doing research on changes in women with the birth of a first child; they immediately raise their shoulders in despair and say: 'oh! the "postpartum blues" you mean – it's about time we knew what it's all about'. This to me typifies the difficulty people have in accepting the total person with his or her moods and mood swings, obviously greater in a new and important situation without needing to classify it and look upon it as an illness. In fact, in some cases, being able to experience, anticipate and express conflict may lead to a greater ability to cope rather than 'live out' these conflicts. As Reva Rubin (1967) points out, it may be necessary for a certain amount of 'grief work' for the former self to take place during pregnancy if the new state is to be enjoyed. This notion that awareness and expression of conflict and anticipatory anxiety are generally a sign of psychological health has been expressed by different authors (Janis, 1968; Winnicott, 1971a). It is in keeping with a view of the person I presented earlier as able to have a realistic appraisal of and integrate the different aspects of himself and the environment.

Finally, the third perspective of this book relates to the understanding of femininity. Within the last few decades, traditional views of femininity have been repeatedly questioned. Anthropologists have made us particularly wary of what were once considered to be inherent attributes of femininity. Social psychologists have shown us the extent to which stereotypes influence differential behaviour of mothers towards their male and female children.

The attack against traditional concepts of femininity is aimed not just at popular myths and images but also, with justification, at psychological theories. Freud, in particular, not only described feelings of inferiority in women for not possessing a penis but also implicitly implied their inferiority by not describing any positive experience they might possess instead. This is epitomized in his reducing the pleasure of having a baby to that of a symbolic penis. In this sense, woman is the same as man but minus something. The boy's development is the prototype of male and female development and no attention is given to the girl's specific experience. Difference in a positive sense receives no consideration. Stern (1966) pointed out that 'the desire to receive, to hold and to nourish is as primary and irreducible as the phallic one', which is not to say that woman is purely receptivity. As Erikson put it, 'the existence of a productive inner bodily space safely set in the centre of female form and carriage has, I would think, greater actuality than has the missing external organ'. Many feminists decry this idea of 'inner space' as chauvinist; I think it can be chauvinist: firstly in the way it is presented – generally by men and in an idealized way which smells suspiciously of the chivalry covering up the denigration (the well known phenomenon of falling over backwards); secondly in the assumptions sometimes expressed – put in a blunt non-disguised fashion by Dr Horatio Storer in 1871 'woman was what she is in health, in character, in her charms, alike of body mind and soul because of her womb alone'[1]; finally in the implications sometimes derived – women are made to have children, women should have children, women should devote their life to having children, women who do not are not real women. None of these implications is necessary. I think it is important to consider the meaning of this inner space to women. I will come back to this later.

Another cultural myth which Freud has helped to strengthen is that of female passivity. 'Along with the abandonment of clitorical masturbation a certain amount of activity is renounced. Passivity now has the upper hand, and the girl's turning to her father is accomplished principally with the help of passive instinctual impulses. You can see that a wave of development like this, which

---

[1] Quoted by Ben Barker-Benfield (1972), 'The spermatic economy: a nineteenth century view of sexuality', *Feminist Studies*, Vol. I.

clears the phallic activity out of the way, smoothes the ground for femininity' (1933). So entrenched in occidental thinking is this notion, that it has even been adopted by many women psychologists. Esther Harding, a Jungian analyst, writes about woman's 'fundamental instincts of modesty, passivity and reserve . . . it is the woman's nature to hold herself in the background, to maintain a passive attitude and, psychologically speaking, to veil herself and her reactions and to seek her goal only by a devious and largely unconscious route' (1933).

A recent study of para-natal emotional adjustment (1970) illustrates the extent to which traditional ideas of femininity still dictate interpretations of the data. As part of a large investigation Nilsson administered a Masculinity–Femininity scale to 165 pregnant women. This scale consisted of ten adjectives expected to indicate 'masculinity' (e.g. strong, self-confident) and ten adjectives expected to indicate 'femininity' (e.g. gentle, emotional, dependent). Each woman chose the five adjectives that best described herself and the five adjectives that least described herself. The author admits that this scale has been shown to possess only a weak capacity for differentiating between men and women with a relatively high level of education but feels that 'nevertheless, it should be possible to regard the women's choices of "masculine" and "feminine" traits in the test as expressing personality characteristics that are of importance in adjustment to childbirth'. He found that women who assessed themselves as more "masculine" than others reported psychiatric symptoms during pregnancy to a lesser extent. They also reported psychiatric symptoms during puberty to a lesser extent than others, fewer neurotic symptoms and also reported dysmenorrhea (painful menstruation) less often. These women more often said at the interview that they resembled their fathers and less often stated that the husband was the dominant partner. Motherhood was less often their primary aim.

Rather than question the Masculinity–Femininity test he used and wonder if the women who see themselves as most gentle, emotional, dependent and so on rather than strong, self-confident and so forth, are more feminine in more than just a purely cultural, possibly dysfunctional way, the author suggests that the 'masculine' woman more often wishes to appear 'healthy' and therefore more often denies neurotic symptoms, dysmenorrhea and psychiatric symptoms during puberty and pregnancy. The assumption being, of course, that the women who are strong and self-confident are more masculine and therefore less healthy.

However, the rebellion against the 'feminine mystique' and this equation of femininity with passivity, masochism and inferiority has often led to the confusion of equality with sameness. Simone de Beauvoir (1949) asserts that the notion of femininity is an invention by men to serve their interests and that there is no feminine nature: 'On ne nait pas femme, on le devient'.[1] In her eagerness to destroy the myth of female inferiority, Simone de Beauvoir has rejected the possibility of any positive differences in female and male modes of experiencing. Woman is not purely biology, she tells us, and therefore it is possible for her to go beyond this and be equal to man in a man's world. The fallacy in her thinking lies in seeing man's modes of experiencing and behaving and his biology as superior and thus having to deny the importance of this difference in order to proclaim equality. This fallacy is similar to that pointed out by Lévi-Strauss in the study of cultures: there are inferior cultures only if we apply notions of inferiority and superiority developed in our society. Indeed, woman is not purely biology; yet it seems to me that the only possible starting point if we are to understand femininity is at the biological level. Femininity is the 'nature of the female sex'; the female sex is the one 'that bears young or produces eggs' (*Webster's Dictionary*). We must start by looking at this childbearing aspect if we are to define femininity. Some of the confusion which has led a large number of feminists to reject the biological level arises from the widespread assumption that any behaviour or attitude must be male or female. It seems on the contrary that it may be possible to define large areas where femininity and masculinity are not applicable. More than this even it seems to me that we might find many attitudes and behaviour where both masculinity and femininity are applicable if these attitudes are required both to beget and to bear young. In this sense we could consider two separate dimensions, that of femininity and that of masculinity rather than masculinity and femininity being at opposite poles of one dimension. This book is only concerned with the femininity dimension and the basic postulate is that femininity refers to those qualities which make for a good adjustment to the biological female reproductive role. Further research would be needed to delimit the areas to which the terms femininity and masculinity can apply. It may be that the terms are applicable to a number of other areas. For instance, there may be specifically masculine and feminine ways of experiencing time and space, relating to male and female

[1] One is not born woman, one becomes it.

biology and physiology. The reason why feminists are often reluctant to admit or explore such a possibility seems to me related to three things: the inferior status which has generally been ascribed to what is feminine, the quasi-moral value of ascribing to female attitudes and behaviour if one is a woman, the danger that a biological approach can be used in a repressive and reactionary way when learning and personal choice and freedom are disregarded. Understanding biological make-up is too often equated with having to conform to such a make-up: in this specific case it might lead to assertions such as that a woman's primary aim should be motherhood.

My research is an attempt to understand femininity in its biological context, to understand which are the qualities required for a woman to bear a child, and to put to the test some psychoanalytic ideas concerning motherhood. Very little work has been done along these lines. In a recent book, Kline (1972) reviews the research which has been carried out to test different aspects of Freudian theory. In the index of this four-hundred-page book, only two references are given under the heading 'femininity'. They refer to two studies carried out by Hall on dreams. Hall relates the dream of being attacked, more frequent in women, as representing being castrated and femininity is linked to the passivity of the dreamer being attacked. Kline suggests that 'the links between femininity and the dream content are not obvious but rather a tribute to the skill of Hall in seeing relationships and educing correlates'.

These three perspectives I have just outlined – a conception of the person as able to change and develop throughout life, a conception of the healthy individual as one who is able to mature through the integration of positive as well as negative elements within himself and able to be at peace with himself-in-the-environment, a conception of femininity as those characteristics which are specifically necessary for a healthy adjustment to childbearing – converge in the study of the birth of a first child as a process of growth.

*. . . Oh, the black rage that comes over me sometimes, especially at
night. The nerve of this creature, the impudence! Placidly leaching food
from my body without even an invitation. Who invited it to this feast?
Don't they know when they're not wanted? Surely the rush of
adrenalin through my blood must be transmitted to it, too; if there were
only enough, might it not kill it? The only possible way in which anger
might kill . . .*

*. . . Responsibility begins even before birth; I may not destroy or
humble my body by neglect because now it is someone else's body too. . . .*
Abigail Lewis

Chapter 2
Points of view

And when our baby stirs and struggles to be born
It compels humility; what we began
Is now its own. Anne Riddler

Strictly speaking there are no such things as pure facts. All facts are
selected from a universal context by the activity of our consciousness, and
hence they are always interpreted facts. This does not mean that we cannot
grasp the reality of the world; it simply means that we merely grasp
certain aspects depending on the point of view we adopt. A. Giorgi, 1970

Let us describe the expectant mother as one who is just as expectant
in her cerebrum as she is in her uterus. F. W. Goodrich, 1961

There exists a vast literature connected with pregnancy and childbirth. A very large proportion of it consists of psychiatric studies per-
taining to incidence and nosological characteristics of pathological
reactions, that is to the description, classification and frequency of the
difficulties encountered in connection with childbearing. Occasionally they aim to test a specific hypothesis concerning the etiology
(cause) of a difficulty. They are generally large-scale studies. For example, Tetlow (1955) was interested in the cause of psychoses
occurring around the birth of a child. His investigation consisted of
sixty-seven women admitted consecutively to hospital for psychoses
complicating childbirth. A control group consisted of fifty healthy
women giving birth during the same period. Another control series
included fifty women of comparable age admitted to the same
hospital for psychosis not related to childbearing. Patients as well as
their relatives were interviewed. The information collected referred
to such things as psychiatric problems in other family members
and neurotic traits in childhood of parent (e.g. nail biting, night
terrors, stammering). Tetlow concluded from his study that

personality predisposition (in terms of family history of psychosis, neurosis or minor neurotic symptoms, and in terms of personal history of psychosis, neurosis or abnormality of personality) exists in both psychosis related to childbirth and psychosis not related to childbearing. However, it may be that the personality problem in the women who develop a psychosis around childbearing 'lies in the reproductive function, particularly where this has related to the setting up of a home and the rearing of children in the normal fashion'. In support of this he gives the fact that there were twelve 'illicit' (unmarried women or births resulting from an extra-marital relationship) pregnancies in the group of women who suffered from psychosis around childbearing, as opposed to one in each of the other two groups.

A smaller proportion of studies are psychoanalytic studies. These are based on a limited number of cases and are concerned with childbearing as an aspect of female sexuality. Therese Benedek has been interested in all aspects of the psychology of women, and in particular the psychology of pregnancy, through her experience as a psychoanalyst. She describes the different feeling states during pregnancy accompanying the hormonal changes and the psychological difficulties which may interfere with a healthy adjustment.

Aside from these medical and psychoanalytic studies, there are a number of more specifically psychological studies employing a stricter methodology and concerned with personality variables. They are difficult to compare with each other in view of the important methodological differences, such as the choice of subjects (with respect to parity,[1] social class, marital status), time of interview, choice of methods of investigation. Sometimes the procedures are dubious. One study, for instance (Blau *et al.*, 1963), on mothers of premature babies, interviewed women one to three days after the birth of the child. Interviews and test results compared these women with women whose babies were not premature. The authors concluded that the mother of a premature baby tends to be 'uncertain about her feminine identification and development. She tends to have unresolved conflicts about her heterosexual and maternal status in reaction to an outstanding mother figure and a less conspicuous vague father image; and she seems to be in need of a more outside emotional support during pregnancy.' They also describe how she tends to be more negative towards the pregnancy and

[1] Whether the woman is having her first or subsequent children.

hostile to the foetus. She is more apprehensive towards labour and delivery.

To infer prenatal attitudes from an interview postpartum[1] seems rather hazardous. Attitudes have been shown to change significantly after delivery (Zemlick and Watson, 1953). In this particular case it seems most likely that the prematurity would have had a profound effect on the woman's feelings about herself, the pregnancy and the child.

A retrospective study, that is a study which infers a pre-event state from the state after the event, is always hazardous. When the event is as influential a one as childbirth, then it seems useless. Even the so-called stable IQ has been shown by Davids and DeVault (1961) to change after the birth of a child. Women who had recently experienced difficult deliveries or given birth to abnormal children had significantly lower IQ performances than did women who had undergone a normal childbirth (though both groups had similar IQs during pregnancy) – which is, by the way, a nice example of how emotional factors influence intellectual performance.

Methods of investigation range from interviews and questionnaires (including specially constructed scales) to personality and projective tests (tests which look at a person's personal interpretation or elaboration of an ambiguous picture, sentence, ink blot, etc.). Obviously the findings are dependent on the methods used, and the choice of methods is dependent on the researcher's approach, which in turn reflects values. Therefore in reviewing the literature, the distinction between medical, psychiatric, psychoanalytic and psychological studies will be subordinated to the particular stance taken by the investigators. I find it useful and important to distinguish two sorts of studies: those which look at pregnancy and the birth of a first child as a hurdle to be overcome, with health being seen as a return to a prepregnancy state, and those which, like my own, look at pregnancy and the birth of a child as a process in which specifically feminine elements are experienced and integrated into the personality.

I will start by using this distinction between 'hurdle' and 'development'. For the sake of clarity I will then consider specific disturbances although the studies involved would each, by their explicit or more often implicit orientation, fall into one of the two categories mentioned above. Most of them in fact belong to the hurdle

[1] Postpartum: after the birth of the baby.

orientation and view health in a static way and as simply the absence of symptoms. This separate section on disturbances will enable a clearer understanding of my own methods described later on.

Hurdle versus development

(a) PREGNANCY AS HURDLE

Many studies view pregnancy as a hurdle to be overcome. Pregnancy is said to be accompanied by transient changes which can lead to disorganization and pathological reactions in 'weak and neurotic personalities'. As the other side of the coin, a normal, healthy outcome consists of a return to the previous (prepregnancy) equilibrium. In this sort of approach pregnancy is implicitly thought of as some sort of illness inflicted on the woman, from which she may or may not recover. Not only is pregnancy some sort of illness but moreover would belong to what Lomas (1973) has called 'mechanical' illnesses. 'Traditional medicine', he writes, 'restricts the concept of illness to those forms of it which seize upon the person and impose their own pattern upon his life (I shall term these "mechanical" as opposed to "meaningful" illnesses)'. Interestingly, in this approach, the child is almost incidental since it is purely something physical happening to the woman and since meaning is not considered.

In fact there seems to be no adequate word which describes the whole experience of pregnancy, childbirth and mothering as a total process – this says something about the prevalence of the 'hurdle' assumption in our culture. An example of the 'hurdle' approach is a study done by Chapple and Furneaux (1964). They administered a personality questionnaire (Maudsley Personality Inventory) to forty-two primiparous pregnant women twice during pregnancy and twice after the birth. The Maudsley Personality Inventory yields two scores: one score on the neuroticism scale and one score on the extraversion–introversion scale. Chapple and Furneaux found that stable women (women who scored low on neuroticism) did not change their extraversion score much, whereas neurotic women (women who scored high on neuroticism) tended to become more introverted as pregnancy progressed but reverted to their previous scores in the postpartum period. Looking at it differently, they distinguished women on the extraversion scale and found that as pregnancy progresses, the more introverted women became more neurotic, and the more extroverted women became less neurotic;

both groups returned to previous scores after the birth. The authors give as an explanation the notion that pregnancy acts as a 'non-specific stress' to which the response varies according to the initial personality of the patient. This is indeed the notion of a temporary non-meaningful disruption.

Using a different neuroticism questionnaire (Cattell Neuroticism Scale Questionnaire), Jarrahi-Zadek et al. (1969) found that of the eighty-six pregnant women they tested 20% had scores symptomatic of psychiatric disturbance during pregnancy (last trimester) and 15% had such scores on the third day after the birth. This was only the case for 4% of the women in a non-pregnant control group. Kear-Colwell (1965) found that 33% of the one hundred women they tested on the Neuroticism Scale Questionnaire had scores indicative of disturbance in the first week postpartum as opposed to 4% of non-pregnant women. The increased level of neuroticism was not related to age, social class, type of delivery, length of labour. The author concludes that 'the increased level of neuroticism is a general feature of childbirth rather than a feature governed by particular aspects of the experience'. A number of other authors have described increased scores indicative of neuroticism in pregnant women (Hook and Marks, 1962; Treadway et al., 1969).

These studies confirm the notion of emotional upheaval but I would strongly question talking about 'increased neuroticism' when considering a situation of normal upheaval (I will come back to this question in a later section). These studies are not very far-reaching or illuminating in their findings and this, I would suggest, is mainly due to the fact that they use standard questionnaires (constructed to discriminate psychiatric patients from non-patients) and rely on group means. It is of interest that Jarrahi-Zadek (1969) found a greater spread in scores, in the above-quoted study, for the pregnant group than the non-pregnant group but he does not go on to find out more about those women who obtained higher scores versus those who obtained lower scores.

Some authors attempted to differentiate women in terms of their adjustment in order to find correlates to pathological reactions. Using personality questionnaires (MMPI, MPI) they found that women in the abnormal group (defined in terms of prenatal or postnatal difficulties) tended to obtain abnormal scores during pregnancy (McDonald, 1968; Ringrose, 1961; Coppen, 1958a) or postpartum (Pitt, 1968). This does not tell us much more than the fact that women

B

who present with difficulties appear more disturbed on a questionnaire.

Other authors have attempted to relate complications in pregnancy to psychiatric history and to stressful events. Seager (1960), for instance, found that women suffering from emotional illness in the puerperium[1] showed a higher incidence of previous psychiatric illness, morbid family history and predisposing personality traits (assessed by the patient's and relatives' descriptions). Mothers of premature babies, according to Gunter (1963) present significantly more psychosomatic and neuropsychiatric symptoms and recall more stress situations (stress situations refer to such things as death within the immediate family, desertion by husband or a parent, economic need, physical disabilities, etc.). Since here again the mothers were studied after the birth of their child, one wonders if most of the difference is not accounted for by the women's reaction to having a premature child. For example as Gunter says, 'it would seem probable that, if a subject felt adequate to deal with the problems in her life situation, she might not define (economic needs) as problems to the investigator, but if she felt inadequate to solve a particular problem, she might refer to it frequently in the life history and pregnancy charts' (most of the subjects were derived from the lower-income group). I would conclude from this that the stresses recalled are intimately linked to the experience of having given birth to a premature child rather than conclude something about the 'psychopathology and stress in the life experience of mothers of premature infants', which is the title of Gunter's paper.

Anxiety is the most general concept that has been used to describe the psychological condition of women with obstetric complications. Davids and DeVault (1962) administered the Manifest Anxiety Scale (MAS) which is a true–false questionnaire referring to physical and emotional feelings commonly believed to be indicative of manifest anxiety, to a group of women, during pregnancy and in the postpartum period. They found that the women who were later to have abnormal delivery-room records (labour and delivery but also such complications as 'cord around the neck' or 'congenital hip dislocation') had higher manifest anxiety scores during pregnancy than the women who later had normal delivery-room records. There was no difference in anxiety following delivery. Similar results were obtained by McDonald (1968) who compared women who experienced normal pregnancies, labours and deliveries with women who underwent

[1] Puerperium: six weeks after childbirth.

a heterogeneous variety of clinical complications (such as third trimester bleeding or prolonged labour). The latter had higher scores than the former on the Manifest Anxiety Scale as well as on another anxiety scale (IPAT). Brown (1964) also used the Manifest Anxiety Scale during pregnancy but he did not find that the level of expressed anxiety related to the length of labour though it did relate to bodily symptoms during pregnancy. The length of labour is a narrower criterion than the ones chosen by the two previously quoted authors which may account for the discrepancy in results.

A number of authors introduce the idea of suppression or repression of emotions. Cramond (1954), for example, found no relation between uterine dysfunction (difficult delivery) and anxiety assessed postpartum but felt that the dysfunctional group tended to suppress or repress emotions. By the way, here again we have an example of an investigation conducted after the event (difficult labour) which cannot but influence results. Cramond infers suppression or repression of emotions in the dysfunctional group from their greater tendency to suffer from peptic ulcers or symptoms suggesting this condition coupled with little overt anxiety and a pleasant cooperative manner concealing a reserved attitude. This tendency to inhibit the expression of fears in women suffering from prolonged labour has been described by several other authors (Jeffcoate, 1955; Scott and Thompson, 1956; Watson, 1959). Zemlick and Watson (1953) found that although anxiety (measured by a projective test) did not relate to time in labour, it did relate to adjustment in labour and delivery based on the obstetrician and the senior author's observations. This relationship they felt refers to 'a phenomenon observed by many clinicians, that anxiety produces tension in pregnancy and this tension carries over into the delivery room'. Like in so many of these studies the sample is very small (15 women). Also the measure of anxiety is a different one (a projective test rather than a questionnaire). These differences make comparisons very difficult.

A problem highlighted by these studies is the problem of distinguishing between someone who is not anxious, someone who represses his anxiety (which means that unconsciously he is anxious), and someone who consciously withholds fears from the interviewer. Even if we accept the notion of unconscious anxiety, we cannot call upon this explanation every time it is convenient. The use of questionnaires makes particularly difficult the distinction between conscious and unconscious response. In any case the use of standard questionnaires seems rather dubious when specific problems related to a 'normal' event such as pregnancy are being considered. Kogan *et al.* (1968) pointed out that personality questionnaires are insensitive to subtle changes in specific groups because the scales were not constructed on these specific groups. In his study of personality changes in unwed mothers following parturition, using the Interpersonal Check List (where the person is asked to check the descriptive terms which apply to him or her and various other people), Kogan did not find any significant changes when the standard scales were analysed. However when the scale structure was abandoned and items were regrouped by factor analysis it was possible to identify significant changes. The women were shown to see themselves as becoming more self-reliant, warmer and less indulgent following parturition. This points to the danger of using preconstructed questionnaires and scales.

Thus, the 'hurdle' approach considers pregnancy as an event capable of producing pathological reactions, probably in anxious and neurotic women, or of allowing the maintenance of a status quo in more adjusted women. By the very nature of the tools used (MMPI, MPI, NSQ) the results can only point to a notion of pregnancy as a hurdle; these tests are designed to assess fairly stable attributes of personality and are insensitive to change. The theory on which they are based would not predict changes in neuroticism after delivery. By using tests that focus on the stable characteristics of the personality they eliminate the possibility of finding any change. In any case, is neuroticism what we are really interested in and is it helpful to call neurotic those women who experience particular difficulties at the time of having a child? Such labels are hardly conducive to an understanding of what a woman is experiencing at this time, what having a child means to her and how this will affect her future.

(b) PREGNANCY AS DEVELOPMENT

Other studies, more in line with the framework I adopt myself, view pregnancy as a developmental phase. Development, as is pointed out by Therese Benedek (1959), refers to the interaction between maturational processes and environmental influences which lead to a higher structuralization – 'Motherhood plays a significant role in the woman's personality. Physiologically it completes maturation; psychologically it channelizes motherliness'.

Like puberty, pregnancy is a biosocial event, leading to a new level of organization and equilibrium. Greta Bibring (1961) believes that all first pregnancies include an element of crisis as an indispensable factor leading from the condition of childlessness to the significantly different one of parenthood. 'Crisis has to be understood here not as a pathology but in its true general sense as a decisive stage in the course of events – a turning point that brings with it unsettling and dislodging of habitual solutions' which have become inappropriate.

However, it is important to emphasize, as Loesch and Greenberg (1962) have done, that pregnancy is not necessarily developmental – 'Certain processes and internal events must be mobilized if it is to function as a developmental period.' In this way, their unmarried subjects who had their babies adopted showed little evidence of psychological changes. This is a good example of how the meaning of the experience for a particular person must be considered. Greenberg and Loesch as well as Greta Bibring and Reva Rubin who have both studied this period fairly extensively, feel that the main development occurs *after* the birth of the baby, when the actual experience of motherhood takes place. This kind of consideration changes the emphasis from the purely intrapersonal characteristics (such as neuroticism) considered by the 'hurdle' authors to an inclusion of inter-personal characteristics (such as mother–baby relationship). The French psychoanalyst Racamier (1967) suggests the use of two different words, *maternité* referring to the biological event, *maternalité* referring to the psychological and emotional development which takes place when the event is integrated. In this sense *maternité* would be the only word applicable to Loesch and Greenberg's women who had their child adopted. 'L'expérience maternelle peut se considérer comme une véritable phase du développement de la personnalité féminine – la maternalité – presentant comme toute phase du développement un double aspect de crise et d'intégration des pulsions, du moi et de l'identité personnelle ou du self' (Racamier).[1]

Let us turn to the specific areas where crisis and adjustment are likely to occur. These are obviously not independent and I will distinguish them only for the sake of convenience.

First the reassessment of relationships. This has been emphasized by

[1] The experience of motherhood can be considered to be a developmental phase in the female personality – *la maternalité* – which presents like all developmental phases a double aspect of crisis and integration of drives, the ego and the self.

psychoanalysts. They mention, above all, the importance of the woman's relationship to her own mother. From dependent she becomes co-equal partner. Early experiences of satisfaction and frustration, of love and hate, have led to good and bad mother images which now colour the woman's representation of herself as a mother or mother-to-be. 'The woman's identification with her own mother motivates her attitude towards motherhood and determines her behaviour towards her children' (Benedek, 1949). In the case of successful maturation, there is a useful identification with the mother as a prototype of the parental figure (Bibring, 1959). Racamier contends that, in the cases of depression, an identification with the good mother image is impossible or problematic.

The relationship to the husband will also be modified. His own reactions to becoming a father will be important in this respect. The family unit shifts from a dyadic one to a triadic one and difficulties may occur when the system is too rigid as when, for instance, one of the partners refuses to allow a third person into the relationship (Lomas, 1959). For the woman it is a question of being both wife and mother, for the man of being both husband and father.

The second area involves the acceptance by the woman of her female biological role. Rheingold (1964) talks about the birth of a baby being a 'degree in femininity'. The physiological experience of femininity should be accompanied by a greater sense of psychological femininity. 'Seule la maternité, c'est-à-dire l'enfant, donne à la femme la pleine conscience de la valeur et de l'accomplissement de sa féminité' (Racamier).[1] In passing it is perhaps worth noting the idealized way in which maternity is described, in particular by male authors. In more realistic terms it is important to consider that a woman's feelings about her body are important at this time. A woman who denies or rejects her body cannot be a nurturant mother. William Menninger (1943) attributes physical symptoms during pregnancy to a rejection of the feminine role – 'The individual functions as a total unit, not as two separate entities (physiological femininity and psychological masculinity) and . . . a failure of integration will manifest itself in symptoms.' In fact it seems that physiological symptomatology during pregnancy such as nausea and vomiting is more likely related to conflict over the pregnancy rather than simple rejection. Chertock et al. (1963) found a relationship

[1] Only maternity, that is the child, gives the woman the full awareness of the value and accomplishment of her femininity.

between vomiting and ambivalence of attitude on the part of the mother towards the child, but no relationship with open rejection – in support of this they mention that in France unmarried mothers rarely vomit. As Jean Hanford (1968) points out, no matter how much a woman desires a child there will be some negative aspects to be faced.

Thirdly, childbirth involves a change of status. In some cultures the first childbirth results in a change of name for the mother. Motherhood marks the entry into a new and unfamiliar role with its unfamiliar tasks and expectations. Becoming part of the 'Mother' category is a shift to a counterpositional role, that is, in the daughter–mother complementary roles there is a shift from the former to the latter. This means taking care of, instead of being taken care of. This new role is irrevocable and all-embracing. The woman will remain a 'mother' for ever with all that the word implies. It is what J. Perlman (1968) has called a 'vital role' to distinguish it from transitory roles which can be abandoned. Vital roles are both time-extensive and emotion-extensive. In our society the mother role is often defined narrowly, which may increase the conflict at the time of taking on the new role. I will come back to this later. The husband–wife relationship is also modified by the advent of these new roles (mother and father). The male–female differentiation and the division of labour become more evident. The expectations of each partner may be congruent or may lead to conflict.

From the point of view of roles, the shift in the woman's self-perception probably takes place mainly *after* the birth of the baby when the woman is actually confronted with the role-partner and when others' perception of her and their expectations become more definite. Melges (1968) studied women who were suffering from postpartum emotional disturbances. He found that they were often subjected to conflicting messages from the environment on how to take care of the infant. Mother, sister, husband were all offering different advice. The new mother felt reluctant to take any advice or give any hint of inadequacy for she felt that this would reflect on her worth and femininity. The lack of feed-back from the infant was something which these women also found difficulty in coping with. Mothering of a non-communicative infant seemed to hinder their self-definition. For 82% of their large sample (one hundred women) the onset of the illness was within the first month, which is when the infant is most uncommunicative. The most frequent onset was four days after the birth which coincides with the time most of the women were discharged from hospital and therefore faced with responsibilities. Finally the husbands of these women remained generally uninvolved. Particular difficulty was experienced when there was a lack of model, the woman's own mother being felt to be rejecting – 'Uncertain in their roles as mothers and yet without a positive maternal model, these women felt lost and confused'. Reva Rubin (1967) looked at the processes involved in the attainment of the maternal role. She studied in depth (twelve interviews during pregnancy and eleven within the first month postpartum) five primiparous[1] women and four multiparous[2] women. She described the following operations involved in taking on the new role: 'mimicry', the imitation of behavioural manifestations of the role; for example, women becoming mothers for the first time tended to put on maternity clothes several months before the functional properties of the clothes were relevant. Taboos and the magical properties of certain foods were based wholly on the authority of the models (friends, relatives). 'Role play', the acting out of 'what a person in this situation does', a trying out of the behaviour: the women becoming mothers for the first time searched the environment for a child to role play with; they would for example offer to baby sit. 'Fantasy' refers to the daydreams and dreams about the new role: fantasies swayed between being romantic, idyllic and being gargoyle type fantasies. 'Introjection-Projection-Rejection', a similar process to 'mimicry' except that it is more discriminatory: the person searches the environment for a model which is then matched for 'fit' with the behaviour or event experienced; it then either reinforces the experience or is rejected. 'Identity', the end point, when the person feels a sense of comfort in their role. Finally 'Grief work', the process by which the former identity is relinquished: it involves the review of attachments and associated events of a former self. In the case of primiparous women, the acquisition of a new identity and the grief work did not fully take place until after delivery when the role partner (the child) is present. This confirms the view often put forth that maximum change takes place after delivery (by the way if you remember this is something completely ignored by the 'hurdle' authors since for them normality refers to the return to a prepregnancy state in

---

[1] Primipara: a woman having her first child. (The adjective is primiparous).

[2] Multipara: a woman having her second or subsequent child. (The adjective is multiparous).

the postpartum period). Another reason for expecting maximum
change after delivery is the fact that the pregnant primipara generally
receives a great deal of attention and solicitude. During the last
trimester she is particularly dependent on her environment. With
the birth of the baby she is suddenly thrown into the responsible,
care-taking position. She is no longer dependent but is depended
upon.

It is important, however, to remember, when one is thinking about
roles, that the process is a two-way one: the interpretation of the role
by the self, its appraisal and reappraisal is as important as the modification of the self to fit the role. With the birth of a first child, the
woman may have to modify her stereotyped idea of the mother role
often tainted by the Christian image of the all-sacrificing Perfect
Mother. Indeed the role of mother in our culture is often narrowly
defined. In terms of emotions, a mother must only have and express
positive feelings for her children. She must be sacrificing at the expense of her own needs, and enjoy this – i.e., be masochistic (which is
quite different from the 'mutual concern' described by Enid Balint,
1972). In terms of occupation, a mother must only be concerned with
her child at the exclusion of a career. In fact many women find themselves to be in conflict with the mother role. Richard and Katherine
Gordon (1967) administered a questionnaire to 335 women and found
that two factors were associated with postpartum emotional difficulties: a 'personal insecurity factor' relating to past experiences and a
'role conflict factor'. They found that, though both were important,
present-day role conflict was more important than personal insecurity
related to past experience in producing continuing difficulties.

In other words the mother role is a very prescriptive and narrow
one. Many women will find themselves in conflict with it, if they
attempt to conform to the role in its rigidly defined form.

Another role worth mentioning is the pregnancy role. The
symptomatology present during pregnancy is partly determined by
cultural expectations. Margaret Mead (1950) found that in some cultures morning sickness in pregnancy is completely ignored while in
other cultures it is expected of every woman so that the woman who
displays no nausea is the exception; in still other cultures it is thought
to occur for first pregnancies only. 'Where it (morning sickness) is
culturally stylized as appropriate for any period of pregnancy or
order of pregnancy (such as first pregnancy only), a large majority
of women will show this behaviour; where it is not, only a very few

will. Convulsive vomiting is a capacity of every human organism, which can be elaborated, neglected, or to a large degree disallowed.'

There is also a variation in the extent to which pregnancy is thought of as some sort of illness or as a normal state. This also will affect behaviour and symptomatology. Rosengren (1961b) showed that women who regarded pregnancy as an illness tended to have significantly longer labours. Women whose views of pregnancy were in conflict with their doctors' views of pregnancy (either one of them seeing it as an illness, the other as a normal state) were even more likely to have longer labours than those whose views were not in conflict with their doctors' views. This notion of pregnancy as illness versus pregnancy as normal state parallels the implicit value I have noted in the hurdle versus development authors.

To summarize, the developmental approach deals with pregnancy as a turning point, leading to a reorganization of relationships and a change in role and status. As can be seen from the literature quoted, these ideas have often been put forward by psychoanalysts, generally based on their clinical experience of analytic patients rather than on planned studies. The notion of role and identity though has led to some social psychological studies (Reva Rubin, Gordon and Gordon). This approach is also different in terms of more general values: it is concerned with the person as a whole (where physical and psychological are intimately related), with meanings (the meaning of the pregnancy and the child for a particular woman) and with relationships (most change is described after the birth when there is a relationship between mother and baby).

Disturbances

> *Several months later. Began to feel heavy, and tremors inside of my womb.*
> *My breasts are full of milk.*
> *It does not belong in my life, for I have too many people to take*
> *care of. I have, already, too many children. . . .*
> *He kicked and stirred.*
> *So full of energy, my child. How much better it would be if you*
> *had stayed away from earth, in obscurity and unconsciousness, in the*
> *paradise of non-being. My little one, not born yet, you are the future.*
> *I would prefer to live with men, in the present, not with a future*
> *extension of myself into the future.*
> *I feel your small feet kicking against my womb. It is very dark in the*
> *room we are sitting in, just as dark as it must be for you inside me,*
> *but it must be sweeter for you to be lying in the warmth than it is for me*
> *to be seeking, in this dark room, the joy of not knowing, not feeling, not*
> *seeing, the joy of lying still and quiet in utter warmth and darkness. All*
> *of us forever seeking again this warmth and this darkness, this being*
> *alive without pain, this being alive without anxiety and fear or*
> *aloneness.*
> *You are impatient to live, you kick with your small feet, my little*
> *one not born yet. You ought to die in warmth and darkness. You ought*
> *to die because in the world there are no real fathers, not in heaven or*
> *on earth.*
> *The German doctor has been here. While he examines me, we talk*
> *about the persecution of the Jews in Berlin.*
> *Life is full of terror and wonder.*
> *You were not built for maternity. Anais Nin[1]*

A large proportion of the literature is concerned with disturbances during pregnancy and the puerperium.[2] These studies have sprung out of a desire, on the one hand to help patients suffering from such illnesses, on the other hand to understand normal pregnancy. As I said earlier I am considering these in a separate section for the sake of clarity – they could all be classified in terms of the developmental/hurdle distinction I made (most often belonging to the hurdle category). Indeed the studies I did mention earlier were generally also concerned with disturbances.

[1] Her child died in the womb.

[2] Puerperium: the six weeks after childbirth when the mother's body is returning to its prepregnancy state.

These studies belong to the general area of psychosomatic research. Progress in this field has been made with the work done on the autonomous nervous system, the endocrine glands, and the cerebral cortex; though many problems still remain with regard to specificity and mechanisms.

Alexander (1943) distinguishes three types of condition in which emotional factors play a fundamental part. Hysterical conversion symptoms are expressed by the voluntary neuromusculature or sensory perceptive systems whose original function is to relieve emotional tension. The symptoms express at the same time both the repressed emotion and its rejection. For example anger which cannot find expression through yelling, shouting or hitting might lead to hysterical aphasia (inability to speak) or paralysis. Vegetative neurosis is not like the hysterical conversion symptom an attempt to relieve an emotional tension in a symbolic way but is the physiological accompaniment of emotional states. For example the state of rage is accompanied by various physiological processes meant to enable the organism to adjust to the task of fighting. The elevated blood pressure does not appear in the place of the emotion but simply accompanies the emotion of rage. The hypertensive patient's pathology consists in the fact that he is under a constant or frequent but unexpressed emotional tension. A vegetative neurosis consists of a dysfunction of a vegetative organ which is not, like the hysterical conversion symptom under the control of the voluntary neuromuscular system. Psychogenic organic disease (such as peptic ulcer) are often the end result of a vegetative neurosis.

Psychophysiological disorders range from minor physiological disorders to structural changes. As Menninger points out (1939), the somatic expression of emotions which are at first only functional responses, in time modify structure. The concept of resistance can be a useful one when considering the person as a unit. 'Even in the common infections it is clear that the cause of a patient developing, say, meningococcol meningitis, often has as much to do with the patient's resistance as it does with the meningococcus' (Alec Coppen, 1958). Resistance can relate to such things as personality or constitution or previous stress.

One of the main controversial and unresolved problems is the problem of specificity. Some authors (Dunbar, 1946) tried to correlate disorders with specific personality profiles. Others related disturbances in specific vegetative functions to particular emotional states (Alexander, 1943). Others yet found that individuals show maximal activation in the same physiological function, whatever the stress (Lacey *et al.*, 1953). (For example, one person will always react to stress with a digestive disorder.)

In the literature relating to psychogenic obstetric complications we come across these same problems and approaches. Is a particular obstetric complication related to a particular type of emotion or conflict, is it related to a particular personality type, is it connected to a person's 'weak spot'? Most studies have concentrated on one disturbance and I will review the findings concerned with specific pathological reactions under five headings. I will then look at the possibility of a unified theory which would account for the various forms of disturbances.

I. TOXAEMIAS OF PREGNANCY: ECLAMPSIA AND PRE-
ECLAMPSIA

Toxaemias complicate 6 to 7% of all gestations and their cause is an important unsolved problem. Eclampsia is the severe form and is characterized by convulsions and coma associated with hypertension, oedema (swollen state of the tissues) or proteinuria (protein in the urine). Toxaemia is rare or absent in many non-Western areas, and these societies suffer from the condition only after contact with Westernized societies. Soichet (1959) describes the communities where pre-eclampsia is rare or absent as communities giving women a particularly important place. Pregnancy and delivery are joyful events and the infertile woman is considered inferior in these regions; whereas in our civilization emotions concerning pregnancy are conflicting. He suggests that a woman who develops toxaemia feels ambivalent towards pregnancy. She wants the pregnancy to prove that she is a woman and is filled with guilt upon the slightest infringement on her fantasies and ideals. Toxaemia, he suggests, would be a defence against a feeling of inner defect and a somatic solution to conflict, just as schizophrenia is a mental solution to conflict; indeed toxaemia is extremely rare in currently schizophrenic patients. Wiedorn (1954), in line with this, found that the incidence of toxaemia is much higher in patients who had had a schizophrenic illness prior to pregnancy or who developed such an illness later on; he also considers toxaemia to represent a 'psychotic equivalence on a physiological level of response of the organism' to stress.

In his study of fifty toxaemic and fifty control patients, using interviews and questionnaires, Alec Coppen (1958a) found that the first group presented difficulties at every stage of the feminine development: menarch (they had often resented the onset of menstruation), sexual intercourse (which they more often did not enjoy or found aversive), attitude to pregnancy (the pregnancy was less often planned and the very fact of being pregnant was often a considerable emotional disturbance in itself). They reported more events during pregnancy which they experienced as disturbing (illness or death of a friend or relative, financial worries, premarital conception or illegitimacy associated with guilt and family condemnation, etc.). The fact that the women were interviewed after the onset of the toxaemia make these findings less reliable – though the author reports that one of the non-toxaemic controls who later developed a toxaemic condition, had ratings more like the toxaemic group than the non-toxaemic group. Alec Coppen also found that the toxaemic women tended to have a more masculine body build and suggests that their psychological difficulties in adjusting to the feminine role relates to their atypically feminine body build. Personality factors and atypical physique would lower the threshold which may be further diminished by environmental stress. Once the threshold is lowered beyond a certain point, signs of toxaemia would appear. But what actually produces the disease is unknown.

It should also be noted that there is a considerable literature on the psychosomatic aspects of hypertension, one of the main signs of toxaemia. Inhibited aggressive impulses which appear in connection with anciety have a specific influence upon the fluctuations of blood pressure (Alexander, 1939). Cannon has shown experimentally in animals that elevation of the blood pressure is characteristic of the emotional state of fear and rage. Another sign of toxaemia, excessive weight gain, can be related to overeating in the anxious, insecure patient (Walser and Detroit Michel, 1948).

2. PREMATURITY

As far as I am concerned—there is no other name than death for that slow devouring growth of the baby that eats the flesh, the strength and the intelligence of the woman who carries it as a cancer might eat her life Françoise Mallet-Joris

Prematurity affects, according to Blau (1963), about 7·4% of births in the U.S.A., over 50% of which occur with no obstetrical or other medical organic causes. Prematurity is defined as a birth weight of 2,500 gms or less (World Health Assembly, 1950).

Karen Horney (1933) differentiated mothers of premature infants from mothers with full-term infants as having more negative feelings towards pregnancy and the foetus and showing uncertainty about their feminine identification and maternal status. Unfortunately, like many studies referred to in this section on disturbances, this was not a prospective study, that is they were interviewed *after* the premature birth (3 to 4 days); it is quite likely that their uncertainty reflected in part their feelings about having a premature child, and the difficulty encountered by young mothers if their newborn is removed from them to be placed in an incubator.

In fact all the studies of prematurity which I have come across (I mentioned one by Blau and one by Gunter earlier on) are retrospective. This obviously relates to the small occurrence of such a condition. The sample of women studied would need to be very large if a sufficiently large number of women who later had premature babies for no organic reason were to be collected (a sample of 400 might yield roughly fifteen). Of course the retrospective nature of the studies only affects certain findings. For example Laurie Gunter found that mothers of premature babies more often showed feelings of fear, inadequacy, nervousness and anxiety. This is likely to be influenced by the recent premature birth. The same goes with the finding that these mothers were more dependent or helpless. What could make one feel more helpless than the birth of a premature child? On the other hand, her finding that 'mothers of premature infants had been neglected or deserted by their mothers more frequently than mothers of normal infants' is more ambiguous. 'Desertion' would not be affected by the prematurity while 'neglect' would be a subjective statement and therefore influenced by the woman's present feelings. Gunter also reports that a larger number of the mothers in the premature sample were separated from their husbands at the time of the birth – this time an objective fact.

There are other problems connected with many of the studies reported in this section. Gunter herself mentions, in relation to her own study, the smallness of the sample (twenty mothers of premature infants and twenty controls) and the special population used: in her case as in many, black women (with all the differences associated with being a minority group).

3. UTERINE DYSFUNCTION

In sorrow thou shalt bring forth children. Genesis, 3

I have seen the white clean chamber with its instruments
It is a place of shrieks, It is not happy
This is where you will come when you are ready
The night lights are flat red moons.
They are dull with blood
I am not ready for anything to happen.
I should have murdered this, that murders me. Sylvia Plath

Douglas Baird (1952) defined normal labour as one in which the vertex (head) presents and is completed in 24 hours or less by spontaneous delivery without injury or undue discomfort to the mother. Examining the literature, once again there seems to be agreement as to the role of social and psychological factors on uterine functioning through the sympathetic nervous system, although there is a divergence of opinion concerning their exact nature and importance.

On a broad level, cultural expectations modulate the experience of childbearing, and the woman's behaviour in childbirth. Margaret Mead describes how 'women may be expected to groan or shriek in a manner designed to make all young female spectators indisposed towards birth and definitely predisposed to shriek when their own "time" comes. Or women may learn that a woman in labour should behave with quiet decorum, paying attention to the business in hand, and certainly not dissipating her strength or disgracing her family with a lot of loud-mouthed yelling. So child-birth may be experienced according to the phrasing given it by the culture, as an experience that is dangerous and painful, interesting and engrossing, matter-of-fact and mildly hazardous, or accompanied by enormous supernatural hazards'.

Reva Rubin talks about how the pregnant woman expects that her experience will be just like her mother's. If her mother had a long labour, a dry labour, a big baby, etc., this is what she expects to have. Psychological characteristics have also been invoked. Patients suffering from uterine dysfunctions have been described as suppressing or repressing their emotions (Cramond, 1954; Watson, 1959; Jeffcoate, 1955), as more anxious (Davids et al., 1961; Zuckerman, 1963), as more rejecting of pregnancy (Hetzel, Bruer and Poidevin, 1961). Two different studies used the masculinity–femininity scale of a personality questionnaire (MMPI). Irving Fox (1964) reports a relationship between the masculinity score and the length of labour; Zuckerman et al. (1963) however finds no relationship between masculinity on this test and difficulty in childbirth.

The physiological mechanism involved in uterine dysfunction, according to Mary Crawford (1968), is a secretion of epinephrine into the blood stream as a result of anxiety; this in turn restricts the blood supply to, and inhibits the contractions of, the uterus. She hypothesized and confirmed that women who reported more than average symptoms of muscle tension during pregnancy and showed signs of anxiety at the beginning of labour (expressed fear, high pulse rate, etc.) developed physiological disturbances related to uterine dysfunction, or their infants developed physiological disturbances related to hypoxia (lack of oxygen).

As with studies related to other disturbances, the method of enquiry may account for differing results. For instance, some authors have tried to relate attitudes to pregnancy with difficulty in childbirth. Using a very simple questionnaire (with questions such as 'was this a planned pregnancy?' 'Did you want to have a baby at the time you became pregnant?'), Winokur and Werboff (1956) found no relationship between planning of pregnancy and desire to have a baby on the one hand, and length of labour. Engström et al. (1964) on the other hand did find a relationship between negative attitudes during pregnancy and difficulty during labour; however the negative attitudes during pregnancy were assessed through an interview rather than a questionnaire and covered not only negative attitude to the pregnancy but also such things as housing problems and anxiety for the child. The whole question of comparison between studies becomes even more complicated if we consider the different ways in which a difficult delivery is assessed and whether it is assessed by the obstetrician, by an observer or simply assessed from the notes. For example Winokur and Werboff used a measure called 'tolerance of labour'. A rating was given by the attending obstetrician and defined as follows: 'A woman was rated as being more tolerant if she gave few or no statements about being afraid; was anxious to get on with the labour; seldom asked for relief; made few or no outcries;

was cooperative in "pushing down". A woman was rated as less tolerant if she gave frequent verbal outcries; showed apprehension on entering the labour room; gave frequent expressions of fear; asked for relief of pain often and earlier than usual in labour; if her sedation was less prolonged than usual in its effect; and if she was uncooperative in "pushing down". Five obstetricians were involved in the rating of 124 women.

In Engström *et al.*'s study the obstetrician present at delivery registered the 'emotional reactions during delivery'. The following items were registered: Tension and worry on entering hospital, remarkably painful first stage, emotional instability during first stage, remarkably painful second stage, emotional instability during second stage, remarkably painful delivery, emotional instability during delivery, general anaesthesia during delivery, negative reaction immediately after delivery. If we consider the vagueness of such criteria as 'emotional instability during first stage' and the differences in criteria between the studies, it is no wonder that a consensus in result is difficult. Even such seemingly simple measures as length of labour are not so straightforward and reliable since it depends on when one starts timing the beginning of labour.

4. POSTPARTUM EMOTIONAL ILLNESSES

Il est né, j'ai perdu mon jeune bien aimé.
Maintenant il est né, je suis seule, je sens
S'epouvanter en moi le vide de mon sang . . . Cécile Sauvage

And then, what possible relation
Exists between the darling of one moment
And the crimson barbarous brat of another instant. Anne Ridler

Since antiquity the problem of psychosis developing in the postpartum period has attracted attention. Hippocrates, for instance, thought that this disturbance was caused by the stoppage of the normal secretion of milk which was then directed to the brain instead of to the breast. He considered that the bleeding of a nipple of a woman recently delivered of a baby was an ominous sign. According to Zilboorg similar views were still held in the eighteenth and nineteenth century when Levret for example observed particles of milk in the brain of a woman who died while suffering from a postpartum psychosis. Another theory propounded in the seventeenth century was that puerperal mental disorders are caused by vapours arising from the uterus to the brain.

It is now felt that postpartum mental illness is not a distinct clinical entity but a mental illness which is similar to one at any other time; symptoms, course and prognosis are felt to be similar to non-postpartal mental illness. The psychological content is however linked with maternity: feelings of inadequacy, inability to care for the baby, fear of damaging the baby, etc. During the last century a vast number of studies have been published, mainly medical and psychiatric studies giving statistical information and description of the illnesses. There is little agreement as to the total incidence of postpartum illnesses, incidence of the different diagnoses which have been given (schizophrenia, manic-depression, psychoneurosis), incidence within social class and parity group (first pregnancy, subsequent pregnancies) least of all aetiology. For example, estimates of the percentage of total mental hospital admissions of females for postpartum mental illness range from 0·2 to 18% (Vislie, 1956; Ostwald and Regan, 1957). Estimates of the incidence varies from 1 in every 300 to 1 in every 1,000 deliveries (see Gozali and Demorest). Part of this lack of agreement is due to unclarity in definitions and explanations of nomenclature. A good example of this is the definition of 'postpartum'. The obstetrician often refers by that term to the 6 weeks following delivery. Some authors favour retaining this lapse of time to define postpartum mental illnesses but others favour extending it. Paffenberger (1964) extends it to 6 months, McNair (1952) to one year and Foundur et al. (1957) gives no particular time. Some authors also include disturbances which occur *before* childbirth (Martin, 1958).

As with most mental disturbances, purely physical causes have been suggested. These have been mainly endocrine. The peripartum[1] period being one in which there are great fluctuations in hormonal blood levels (Hamilton, 1962).

In favour of psychological explanations are the reports of 'postpartum equivalent reactions' after the *adoption* of a child (Victoroff reports three such cases, Tetlow reports six, Melges reports three). Similar reactions have also been described in men whose wives

[1] The time before and after childbirth.

have recently delivered. Psychodynamic explanations can be divided into those which emphasize intrapersonal problems and those which look at the interpersonal conflicts. In the *intra*personal approach, explanations have been given in terms of Freudian notions of psycho-sexual development. Zilboorg (1929) considers women who succumb to postpartum psychosis to 'show a predominance of schizoid characteristics and from the point of view of libido development they appear to have carried over into adult life anal libidinous attitudes and to have never reached the so-called vaginal stage of development'. Yet another intrapersonal problem is that of masculinity–femininity. Zilboorg goes on: 'they seem to have been arrested in their growth in what Freud terms the phallic stage; hence they are all chronic masturbators and sexually frigid; they are potentially homosexual, their homosexuality, as a rule, not coming to the fore except in the psychosis. It was found that they had not outlived the Oedipus phase of their psychological growth and that their unconscious clinging to the Oedipus situation was intimately interwoven with the uncon-scious desire to belong to the male rather than the female species; hence they appear in part to identify themselves with their fathers and in part to harbour a revengeful feeling because they are not male.' Lomas (1967) also found that frigidity was often a precursor of post-partum illness. He considers frigidity to refer to the total attitude of a woman towards the man, an attitude of fear, hate, envy and rejection. This kind of woman, who cannot love, will be placed in a situation of great stress when she has, as when her baby is born, 'a clear, even desperate, demand made on her to provide something that she is incapable of providing'. Lomas (1960) stresses that women suffering from postpartum illnesses can also present problems of feminine identity. 'The classical psycho-analytic view that childbirth is equated in the woman's mind with castration . . . does injustice to the positive aspects of this climax of feminine biological achieve-ment . . .' 'That a puerperal mother will both fear envy and be envied is a logical consequence of Melanie Klein's belief that one of a child's most important feelings is envy of his mother's creative capacity.' The woman will fear her mother's envy either because her mother indeed is envious or because she thinks her mother is envious of her in the same way as she was envious of her mother. Anne Hayman (1962), in her study of sixteen women suffering from puerperal break-down, felt that problems of masculine identification (the baby rep-resenting a phallus) were more significant in the less disturbed women while problems of feminine identity were more important in the cases of psychotic depressions.

Guilt is an important aspect of puerperal breakdowns. Lomas refers to guilt when the baby symbolizes a greedily stolen quality from the parent. Zilboorg (1931) and Karen Horney (1933) refer to guilt in connection with hostility impulses against the child. Victoroff (1952) believes that, 'At the central core of the parapartum psychoses, regardless of the numerous causative factors, is the urge to annihilate the child'.

A number of authors point out a lack of maternal identification in patients suffering from postpartum mental disturbances (Ostwald and Regan, 1957; Edith Anderson, 1963; Wenner, 1969). In the intrapersonal perspective, one can also mention role conflict. Rita Stein (1968) studied a group of ten women who encountered their first 'break with reality' during pregnancy (antepartum group) and ten women who encountered their first 'break with reality' after the birth (postpartum group). She found that both groups feared a change of status with maternity. The pregnant women who became ill were educationally and occupationally more independent and more outgoing than those with postpartum psychoses. They found their marital roles unsatisfactory and were in conflict with their husbands' expectations. 'They did not desire maternity and feared their change of role and status in already existing difficult marital adjustments. They had more difficult female identifications to realize'. The women with postpartum illnesses 'were glad to be pregnant and it was only when they were face to face with the baby that they were confronted with a realization of their change of role and status . . . Confusion in female identification differentiates this woman from the lack of maternal identification spelling out the role of the disturbed pregnant woman.'

These different areas of difficulty are obviously not separate. None of them can be considered 'the cause' of the postpartum illness. As with any psychological or psychosomatic difficulty it is futile and misleading to look for a determining factor or factors. All that can be done is to point out the features which seem to be prominent in women suffering from such an illness. Most of these studies mention the woman's inadequate relationship with her parents. 'All of the women had disturbances in their early home life and in their parental relationships, so that identification with either parent was not consummated to their satisfaction' (Rita Stein). But is it not so, that many women with unsatisfactory parental relationships do not develop postpartum mental illnesses? And is it not also the case, as mentioned in relation to other disturbances, that the woman in such a crisis is bound to distort her past? Is it not also possible that some of the conflicts encountered by these women are present, though to a lesser degree, in all puerperal women? Sylvia Markham (1961) gives support to this idea. She concluded from her comparative study of psychotic and non-psychotic puerperal women that what differed was not the kind of conflict experienced but the way in which this conflict was resolved. The non-psychotic puerperal women, just like the psychotic ones, expressed 'oral dependency', 'hostility to a mother figure', 'castration feelings', depression. However none of the normal mothers manifested the parasitic, clinging relationship noted in the psychotic mothers and were able to transfer their libido from their mothers to their children. 'The conflicts differed little in the two groups. However where the hospitalized group perceived their children as a drain on their emotional resources and as rivals for oral supplies, the control mothers were able to use their children to solidify their defensive structure and to further their emotional growth.' The women in the psychotic group manifested severe confusion in identification in which self, mother and child became indistinguishable at times. Other people have described similar manifestations in disturbed and non-disturbed women. A tendency towards regressive behaviour accompanying feelings of depression and depletion is an almost universal finding in puerperal women (Atrachan, 1965).

A number of authors have stressed *inter*personal aspects relating to postpartum illnesses. Kline (1955) mentions the woman's competition with the baby for the love of her husband. Lomas (1967) describes a kind of marital relationship where there is no place for the child. When the wife treats her husband as a baby or when the husband acts as a mother to the wife, 'there could be no room for a real baby, and one possible consequence of his appearance is puerperal breakdown'. In this sense the puerperal breakdown is best conceived as 'the most spectacular manifestation of a family catastrophe'. Susan Beach et al. (1955) in a study of eight cases of postpartum psychosis found that the husbands tended to be 'overprotective' of their wives and tended to deny 'the adequacy of their wives to function as adult women in periods of minor distress'. These men tended to compete with their wives in the female role, furthering their wives' feelings of inadequacy as women. The authors conclude: 'women who tend to destroy the masculinity of men are sometimes described as "castrating females". We suggest that there is a male counterpart to this classification, and that the husbands of women with post-partum psychoses fall into this group.'

Finally the mother–baby relationship may be a problematical one. Melges (1968) pointed out the difficulties some women find in their relationship with the baby from whom they get little feedback; their feelings of inadequacy and helplessness are made worse by the baby's poor communication skills.

Rosberg and Karon (1959) describe the analysis of a woman suffering from a postpartum psychosis. Their article, written up as 'a direct analytic contribution to the understanding of postpartum psychoses', touches on some of the points mentioned earlier. It gives the flavour of such an illness. The patient is a woman in her thirties. 'The reason for her illness, she said, was that "my husband made me pregnant". Pregnancy she referred to, as "going through the mill". "The mill is responsible for my illness." At other times she would deny any relationship between intercourse, pregnancy and children; she would then say that children came by an arrangement "with the state" . . . As the analysis progressed, it became clear that her husband had, in many ways, replaced her mother in her emotional life. Their relationship to her might best be described as dominating dependence whereby the mother, and later the husband, dominated her so that she would gratify their own dependency needs. Her mother had forced the patient to assume the mothering role to the patient's own siblings, and finally to the mother herself, on innumerable occasions. The transfer of this attitude to the husband is exemplified by the patient's description of the role of the ideal wife: "A good wife calls her husband at his place of business at least six times a day to make sure that things are going well and that she's available in case anything comes up. Also she tells him what to eat, and how much to eat, and also when to change his underwear and his outside apparel. If she doesn't do this, she can't be considered a good wife" . . . "Being through the mill", her expression for pregnancy, referred to the "mill" where flour was made; flour was white like semen and milk. Pregnancy, she said, was being "filled up with semen and blood and milk". The swelling had the significance of becoming "more and more full". "It's the one time I was completely full." In other words, a pregnancy represented the final solution to the oral problems of her life. These may be summarized as having to give (be a mother) instead of receiving (mothered) which is the need of every child. The husband (who replaced the mother) was at last giving, instead of taking, during intercourse. But he could never give enough. When, however, she had actually been pregnant, this signified, on the level of fantasy, that she was getting "fuller and fuller" of milk. The satisfaction she longed for was at hand; but just when she was satisfied, the child would be born, and she would be empty again. During the period of her psychosis in which she had gained the excess weight (55 lb more than her normal weight), she had eaten prodigiously and was so fat "that I couldn't move". She said she had been trying to fill the emptiness, but she had never been satisfied.'

I have been talking up till now mainly of postpartum psychosis the incidence of which is, let us say, one to three per 1,000. It is an extreme reaction. At the other end of the spectrum, mild reactions are characterized by crying and slight depression. These 'postpartum blues', as they have been called, are thought to affect most women (up to 80%). According to Yalom et al. (1968) the most characteristic sign is crying, other signs being irritability and hypersensitivity to what is interpreted as rejection. The crying is not necessarily associated with feelings of depression, sadness or hopelessness. In their study of thirty-nine puerperal women, they found that postpartum depression was associated with various endocrine related factors. Women with an early menarch,[1] greater menstrual difficulties, prolonged menstrual flow are more likely to become depressed postpartum. The authors feel that this might relate to studies showing that early-maturing girls encounter many problems stemming from early development of sexual characteristics. These women might find it more difficult to accept the feminine role. On the other hand it could be that the rapid shifts in hormone level occurring in the puerperium accentuate the metabolic abnormalities in these women. 'There is evidence to suggest that progesterone is a central nervous system depressant and excessively high levels, unusually steep gradients, abnormal progesterone metabolites, or an abnormal oestrogen–progesterone ratio may produce a depressed mood state'. This is a nice example of how closely linked psychological and biological phenomena are. As Yalom et al. put it: 'In females, the study of stress in the life cycle demands attention to endocrine–behavioral interaction, since some of the

[1] Menarch: onset of menstruation.

times of greatest life stress (i.e. menarch, pregnancy, menopause)[1] occur simultaneously with marked fluctuations in the level of circulating hormones'.

Eight months postpartum twenty-two of the women they studied were available for follow up. Only one of them had required psychiatric treatment (a woman who had had psychiatric treatment in the past). The authors conclude that 'the postpartum blues syndrome is apparently self-limited and relatively benign'. As most studies, they found that postpartum depression was more likely to occur with first pregnancies. Depending on the theoretical approach endorsed, as touched on earlier, the two extremes – postpartum psychoses and postpartum blues – will be thought of as gradings on a continuum (psychoanalytic notion) or as separate entities.

Brice Pitt (1968) set out to study what lies between the severe puerperal depression and the weepiness of the blues. As I will myself be concerned with this intermediary state, I will relate his findings in detail. Pitt's criteria for the presence of puerperal depression were that: women should describe depressive symptoms (Hamilton depression scale), these symptoms should have developed since delivery; these symptoms should be unusual in their experience and, to some extent, disabling; these symptoms should have persisted for more than two weeks.

10·8% of the 305 women in his sample were diagnosed as suffering from puerperal depression. The depression was to be distinguished from the 'blues' by its longer duration. Pitt devised a questionnaire to measure maternal anxiety and depression before and after childbirth. There was a general highly significant tendency for questionnaire scores to drop by three points after delivery – that is, on the whole women tended to be less depressed and anxious postpartum than they had been during pregnancy. Those women whose scores increased considerably (more than six points), that is, who showed signs of being more depressed and anxious postpartum, were interviewed as potential depressives; a random selection of women whose scores increased only slightly, and of women whose scores were unchanged or diminished, were also interviewed.

The questionnaire's success in finding cases of puerperal depression, as defined above, was significant. The author talks of 'atypical depression' because of the prominence of neurotic symptoms (anxiety, irritability, phobias) overshadowing the depression, and because some

1 Menopause: the cessation of menstruation.

of the symptoms are opposite to those of classical depressive states (for example, worsening at the end of the day, early insomnia). Pitt found no significant relationship between depression as defined by his questionnaire and complicated delivery, previous psychiatric history, unplanned pregnancy, endocrine factors, anxiety in pregnancy, social class or breast feeding. He did find differences on a personality questionnaire: the depressives were more neurotic and less extroverted than the non-depressed puerperal women. But as he himself points out, these neuroticism and extroversion scores may be reflecting the depressed state rather than give any evidence of a personality disposition. Pitt's study belongs to the 'hurdle' rather than 'process' type study; it is however useful in that it defines and delineates a common form of postpartum reaction. One particular advantage of the questionnaire he devised is the fact that it considers changes in scores rather than absolute values. What is important is the difference in score between pregnancy and postpartum in the same woman rather than a comparison in scores of different women. In this sense it is more in keeping with the notion of process, even if his attempt to relate it to a personality questionnaire is not.

5. HEALTH OF THE BABY

You were the sum of all my inmost dreams:
You were the ache and longing in my heart;
And you were on the earth.
So all the night I lay
And stared into the dark,
Forgetting pain of birth,
Forgetting terror stark.
Until the break of day
I never stirred, it seems. Joan Kinmont

Studies indicate that foetal environment, including maternal emotions, can affect the foetal psychophysiologic apparatus (Sontag, 1941; Dunbar, 1946; Greenacre, 1944) through, for instance, endocrine output and oxygen supply. 'Having learned how powerful an influence the woman's unconscious pre-existing anxieties may exert on the physiologic phenomena of pregnancy, we must expect that the same dynamic forces still influence this part of the mother's body which we call the foetus' (Deutsch, 1949).

McDonald, in his previously quoted studies, included in his

'abnormal group', when considering the role of emotional factors in obstetric complications, developmental abnormalities observed in the infant at birth. These include such things as 'subnormal foetal Apgar Rating'[1] and 'foetal congenital defects'.

Behavioural characteristics of infants have also been linked to maternal prenatal influences. Infants of mothers experiencing prolonged periods of severe anxiety during late pregnancy have been observed by Sontag (1941) to be highly active and irritable, with severe food intolerance. Turner (1956) also pointed out a relationship between anxiety and fatigue during pregnancy, on the one hand, and difficulties such as increased restlessness and excessive crying and vomiting in the baby. Abramson et al. (1969) noted a relationship between emotional stress during pregnancy (assessed by an interview during pregnancy) and a low level of motor development at birth. The most frequent cause of the stress was the husband's unemployment or job insecurity (the women in this study were poor Indian women in South Africa); other causes were distress at being pregnant and illness in the family. There was no simple relationship of the baby's development with 'objective' conditions of poverty and diet. There was only such a relationship when the presence of stress was assessed on the basis of the woman's own report of her difficulties. By the time the baby was 13 weeks old there was no longer any difference between high- and low-stress groups. Ottinger and Simmons (1964) found a relationship between maternal anxiety during pregnancy (assessed by a questionnaire) and neonates' crying. The babies of the highly anxious mothers cried more; this difference was particularly significant before feeding. The authors feel that the difference is due to a prenatal and/or genetic phenomenon rather than a function of the differences in the mother's handling, since the difference in crying between babies of anxious and non-anxious mothers was more significant before feeding than after, and since significant group differences were found in the first four days of life.

With all these studies it is obviously difficult to disentangle genetic from prenatal psychological factors.

[1] Apgar Rating: numerical expression of the condition of a newborn infant 50 seconds after birth; it is the sum of points gained on assessment after birth of the heart rate, respiratory effort, muscle tone, reflex irritability and colour. The higher the rating, the healthier the baby.

6. DISTURBANCE OF THE MOTHER–CHILD RELATIONSHIP:

Mouth stretched into the ancient rictus,
The screaming baby – formidable
To the newly delivered mother. Too pure
an expression of something completely felt
Not to inspire fear; with no memory
To weaken or blur eyes snapping
A hatred no adult could muster
And which animals are exempt from.
Red devils, throbbing with such elemental power,
That the cringing woman
Must adore or kill him. Ruth Fainlight

Young stranger, who are younger still
Than ought on sea or land
What secrets of the stars were mine
Could I but understand. Eiluned Lewis

The condition which leads to the disturbance of the primary relationship
between mother and child keeps the infant in a state of tension. Whether
this is expressed in fitful sleep and crying and/or in feeding
difficulties, the behaviour of the infant reveals the disturbance of the
communication between infant and mother. Ruth Benedek

Even subtle disturbances in the mother–child relationship and problems in the mother, have been shown to have an effect on the infant. Cornell (1969) related colic in the infant to characteristics of the mother, such as her own eating problems in childhood, her neuroticism score and her negative self-rating of her physical condition during pregnancy. Feeding disturbances (Escalona, 1945; Ribble, 1941; Anna Freud, 1947) excessive crying and sleep disturbances (Turner, 1956; Benedek, 1949) have been linked to a disturbed mother–child relationship. Sybille Escalona found in her study of young children of women in a Reformatory that a child's eating behaviour was very sensitive to upsets such as the departure of a person the child was attached to (other than the mother) and even to the emotional atmosphere prevailing in the institution at large. For instance the incidence of mealtime tantrums, refusal of food, vomiting, was always higher on parole days (day on which the State Board of Parole visited to decide who was to be released on parole) even though the routine was the same. She concludes that 'when infants and young children are brought into close contact with an adult, they perceive the emotional state of the adult and respond to it in a consistent manner'.

Many studies concerned with the mother–child relationship have centred around breast-feeding, both from the point of view of the choice or ability to breast-feed and from the point of view of its influence on the child's future development.

Both desire and capacity to breast-feed have been shown to be related to psychological and sociological variables. Bernheim and Charcot demonstrated that the flow of milk could be stopped or increased by hypnosis. Freud (1933) also mentions enabling a woman to breast-feed through the use of hypnosis and Helen Deutsch (1945) mentions the case of a woman who stopped producing milk every time her mother came to visit. She also reports that some women are unable to nurse successfully because of fearful fantasies of losing their individuality or of being swallowed up. The unconscious fear of being drained or devoured by the baby (which can inhibit breast-feeding) described by psychoanalysts relates to the woman's own baby wishes now projected onto the baby who thus becomes dangerous. Niles Newton (1963) reports that breast-feeding performance is closely related to what the mother says about her attitude towards breast-feeding. She interviewed pregnant women and found that 74% of those who said 'I am going to breast-feed' did so successfully as compared with 26% of those who did not want to but tried. These latter women were much more likely to report that the baby refused the breast, or that the baby had difficulty in sucking. There was also a significantly larger amount of milk given on a single day by the first group of women. Newton and Newton (1950) note three possible psychosomatic mechanisms influencing the course of lactation: 1. sucking stimulation: the woman who is doubtful about breast-feeding probably allows less sucking stimulation at each feed (this is supported by the fact that the negative attitude group used nipple shields more often, and the positive group had the highest incidence of fissures); 2. let-down reflex: pain, fear and emotion have been shown to inhibit the expulsion of milk; 3. regulation of blood flow: the precursors of milk are the blood stream, and blood flow is very sensitive to emotional stimulation through vasoconstriction and vasodilatation. Niles Newton also found that women who expressed positive feelings about breast-feeding felt that women's lot in life was as satisfying as men's and tended to think that childbirth was easy. They tended to have quicker labours.

Psychoanalysts have emphasized the notion of breast-feeding as an expression of the woman's feelings about being a mother. Racamier (1967) writes: 'Une femme qui refuse sa propre maternité et désire rester infantilement réceptive, ne peut allaiter normalement, car elle cherche beaucoup plus à boire elle-même qu'à donner à boire. Par ailleurs, la persistance de tendances aggressives dirigées contre la mère se venge des frustrations subies en les infligeant à son propre nourrisson.'[1] A woman's anxieties about herself as a mother may also reflect themselves in her fear that her milk is insufficient or not good enough leading her to switch to bottle feeding, or to her bad handling of the baby. 'A mother, doubtful of the quality of the milk she is offering to her baby, will handle the baby in a clumsy way and present her nipple so awkwardly that the baby may reject it' (Salzberger-Wittenberg, 1973).

It would be wrong to consider bottle-feeding as evidence of disturbance and, as Heinstein (1963) has pointed out, what is important for the development of the child is the total personal–social environment. Winnicott (1968) suggests that handling and holding are more important than the isolated fact of a breast-feeding experience. If a mother struggles to breast-feed, both mother and child may suffer.

Notions of interaction are particularly important in this area of the mother–child relationship. Recent work (Bowlby, 1969) has emphasized the importance of the infant's behaviour on the mother, thus balancing the one-sided view of the effect of the mother on the child. Indeed it is no longer thought that the child is a *tabula rasa*. One mother may be able to deal with a responsive, active child while getting depressed with a more placid unresponsive child, another woman on the contrary may feel overwhelmed by an active child while able to cope with a more placid one. One could thus imagine a situation where the mother's and the child's needs were increasingly frustrated and an increasingly inappropriate response produced in each partner, engendering a spiralling effect and a worsening relationship. Elsie Broussard and Miriam Hartner (1969) showed that the mother's view of her child is an important indicator. In a prospective study of 120 primiparae and neonates, they asked mothers to rate their infants on different scales when the babies were one month

[1] A woman who rejects her pregnancy and wishes to remain receptive cannot breast-feed normally for she wishes much more to be fed than to feed. Moreover she will take revenge on her child for the frustrations she herself experienced in relation to her mother.'

old. A 'risk rating' was given to those babies who were rated by mothers as being worse than the average baby on a number of scales (vomiting, difficulties with sleep, etc.). They found that those babies who had been given a risk rating when they were one month old, were much more likely to be thought to need psychiatric intervention at the age of four and a half (the assessment being made by an independent psychiatrist who had no knowledge of how the children had been rated as infants). The need for intervention did not relate to socio-economic status, age, prenatal or postpartum complications or to the sex of the child. So what was shown to be important here was the mother's view of her baby, influenced to varying degrees by how the baby actually was (the baby's behaviour reflecting partly, in turn, the mother's behaviour and view of the baby.)

Links

There are similarities, both positive and negative, in the studies reviewed. On the negative side is the fact that the literature is confused and often inconclusive. This is partly due to the number of disciplines involved – obstetrics, psychiatry, psychology, sociology, psychoanalysis – and the problem of comparing studies involving such different methodologies. Many of them are inadequate and lack rigour: few cases, use of questionnaires, comparison of normal and abnormal groups *after* the onset of the abnormality. Notions of causality are often used when in so complex an area it might be best to think in terms of interaction and multideterminants.

On the positive side of the similarity there are the themes which run through the subheadings. These relate to notions of conflict over pregnancy, difficult relationship with own mother, unsatisfactory feminine identification. The recurrence of these themes suggests the possible equivalence of the various disturbances. Indeed studies linking a specific disturbance to a specific personality type are inadequate or unsuccessful. Although many authors have found that obstetric patients are more psychologically maladjusted than 'normals', they have not found any reliable differences between the women suffering from differing difficulties, nor have they found any reliable patterns within groups. For example Ringrose (1961) showed that patients suffering from toxaemia presented abnormal personalities as measured by a personality test (MMPI) compared to non-toxaemic women, but the type of personality deviation was not constant; when the average scores were computed for the toxaemic women, they fell within the normal range (so that the deviations in scores were in either direction).

It therefore seems possible, and this is the conceptualization I will myself adopt, to consider the various complications as different possible alternative pathological reactions to the psychosociobiological stress of pregnancy and motherhood. The specificity, that is the form the disturbance takes, could be related to constitutional factors, developmental phases, physiological or psychological events – or more likely an interaction of all of these. The equivalence of symptoms has been put to empirical test by Vanden Bergh *et al.* (1966) in their study of habitual aborters. Habitual abortion is characterized by three consecutive spontaneous abortions (spontaneous termination of pregnancy before the twenty-second week of gestation). They decided to study the charts and to interview women who had received a Shirodkar operation. This operation is performed in cases where there is an apparent weakness of the musculature of the cervix[1]; this condition is often found in habitual aborters but also in other women. The operation consists of a suture placed around the cervix in order to prevent expulsion of the foetus before maturity. The authors hypothesize that in the case of habitual abortion, rather than postulate a congenital incompetence of the os, endocrinological changes, in part related to emotional stress, produce the premature dilation of the os. If this is so and 'if some patients who habitually abort are, in fact, solving emotional conflicts by unconsciously aborting their pregnancies through dilation of the cervical os, then with such a procedure as the Shirodkar operation, by which dilation is prevented and by which a habitual aborter is in a sense forced into motherhood, it could be expected that the severe underlying emotional conflicts would be precipitated and exacerbated postpartum'. They interviewed nine habitual aborters who had had a Shirodkar operation and nine women who had no history of habitual abortion but had undergone this operation because of an incompetent cervical os. They found that the incidence of postpartum psychosis was significantly greater in the habitual aborters than in the matched control group. Of the nine habitual aborters, five developed a postpartum psychosis (an incidence which is much higher than that in the general population) and three had psychotherapy during pregnancy. In the control group, one woman only developed a postpartum

[1] Cervix: the neck of the uterus which hangs down in the vagina.

psychosis and none had psychotherapy during pregnancy. These findings give some support to the authors' suggestion that the psychosis was an expression of the conflict which had been resolved by the abortions in the women thus 'forced' to have a baby. This calls to mind the study I quoted earlier (Soichet, 1959) showing that the incidence of toxaemia was lower in a group of women suffering from postpartum illnesses than in a group of 'normals' – as if here also there is an equivalence (this finding is repeated by Pitt, 1968).

Jean Hanford (1968) analyses the possible physiological mechanisms underlining such an equivalence of pathological reactions. Normal pregnancy is seen as a state of conflict (even when the pregnancy is desired), producing (like all states of emotional stress) a rise in levels of histamine and steroids in the blood. Conflict is greatest at the beginning of pregnancy and the levels of histamine and steroids are high at this time. There is then a drop as psychological defences are successfully instituted. A woman with severe conflicts over being pregnant, however, will not be able to resolve the conflict, or will do so only 'at great cost to herself emotionally and physiologically and to her child in utero'. In these cases, irregular patterning of levels of corticosteroids in the blood, indicative of difficulty in adjustment, will lead to such disturbances as spontaneous abortion, prematurity, foetal malfunctioning, etc.

This view is compatible with McDonald's (1963) who concludes, after reviewing the literature, that the best approach is perhaps to consider 'all complications as derivatives of a single common process'. He suggests that responding to stress with bodily defence might lead to dysfunctioning of the autonomic nervous system (the visceral component of the nervous system), the specificity being explained in terms of constitution and developmental history. Depending on a person's constitution and developmental history the dysfunctioning of the autonomic nervous system would affect a particular physiological component: the gastro-intestinal tract leading to hyperemesis (vomiting), smooth muscle leading to spontaneous abortion, prematurity or uterine dysfunction, the arterial system leading to toxaemia. But the common denominator would be an increase in anxiety during pregnancy, extreme in its duration and intensity in women with unresolved conflicts about pregnancy stemming from a variety of reasons. 'Mobilization of anxiety, the ANS (autonomic nervous system) activation which triggers a host of regulatory mechanisms,

c

may result from a multiplicity of unresolved conflicts about pregnancy. Adaptive failure at a particular point underlies the timing of complications. Specificity is accounted for by the interaction of constitutional differences and autonomic response specificity with a host of other physiological parameters.'

The five headings I set out earlier left out functional sterility[1] and spontaneous abortion as these have not been a focus in my own study. Obviously a unified theory of childbearing disturbances also includes these, and similar factors have been suggested for these difficulties to the ones I mentioned earlier.

According to Therese Benedek (1952) functional sterility is a somatic defence against the dangers inherent in the procreative function. She feels that the infertile woman has a stronger ego than the woman who gets pregnant and is then so overcome by anxiety that she becomes ill. In the case of the infertile woman, the conflicts regarding childbearing are repressed and she is free from anxiety. Marie Langer (1958) suggests that envy is an important factor in cases of psychogenic infertility. The woman's incapacity to identify with a fertile mother is a consequence of her envy of her mother when her envy and destructive impulses towards her mother were particularly strong and when adverse reality (accidents occurring to the mother) made her feel that she had destroyed her mother.

Different mechanisms will prevent pregnancy in such women; defloration phobia and vaginismus (spasmodic contractions of the vagina when the vagina or vulva is touched) prevent intercourse; expulsion of the semen prevents its passage through the cervical canal; spasm of the Fallopian tubes[2] prevents access to the ova; premature expulsion of the foetus prevents the birth of a live baby. Menninger (1939) mentions another possible physiological mechanism (postulated by Sellheim): an overactivation of the ovaries linked to emotional factors, resulting in a premature maturation of the follicles such that ova are discharged which are not yet ready for fertilization.

A complete account of the subject also includes motivation for motherhood; here again there is some evidence that the relationship of the woman to her own mother is important. As part of a larger

[1] Functional sterility is sterility without an organic reason.
[2] Fallopian tubes: the tubes branching out from either side of the uterus in which fertilization takes place.

study, Malmquist *et al.* (1969) looked at a sample of identical twins discordant for motherhood (that is one of the twins was a mother, the other not). There were eight pairs in which one member reported having been more favoured by mother, the other by father. In seven out of the eight pairs, the twin favoured by mother was herself a mother, the one favoured by father was childless. They do not say, however, if the childless twins were so out of design, that is whether the problem is one of motivation or of fertility.

As I have tried to emphasize, the values of the researcher are of prime importance in determining not only his assumptions but also what he will study, the way he still study it and the way he will conceptualize his findings. Although this is not always so, there is a tendency for those authors who look at pregnancy as a process to also tend to adopt a unified theory of disturbances and to think that mental health involves a different way of coping with conflicts rather than to assume qualitatively different types of conflict (although these different aspects are not often made explicit). It is my own position.

The symbols of the self arise in the depth of the body. C. G. Jung

Before closing this chapter, I would like to come back to the notion of femininity, touched upon in the first chapter. I will discuss this now in relation to the rest of this chapter and in relation to my own research. I will come back more extensively to the notion of femininity in a subsequent chapter.

Time and again, in the studies I quoted in this chapter, the notion has come up that women who are well adjusted to motherhood accept their femininity. However femininity is rarely defined, and few studies include any empirical material on this subject.

Studies of femininity have mainly used questionnaires (such as the MMPI) although authors agree that these only tap a cultural aspect of femininity (for example, they look at so-called feminine versus so-called masculine interests). Niles Newton (1955) suggests a distinction between cultural femininity and biological femininity. She argues that the female biological role is far from being as passive as society has often claimed it to be: 'The woman who is adequate in her female biological role must be active, productive, and capable of concerted effort. There is no harder physical exertion than normal childbirth. Developing and carrying a baby through pregnancy is an active process and breast-feeding a baby involves repeated active giving.' She herself used a traditional masculinity–femininity test (Terman's Masculinity–Femininity test) and found that the culturally feminine women defined by this test tended to dislike pregnancy and were extremely likely to wish to be men although they were quite satisfied with the woman's role in our society. In other words, these 'culturally feminine' women accepted our society's sex roles as appropriate norms, but, given a choice, they would have preferred to be men. I think one could interpret this in two ways: either it represents these women's acceptance and dislike of the role rather than a questioning of the appropriateness of the role; or it reflects the fact that part of the feminine role in our society involves feeling inferior and wanting to be a man.

Acceptance of the female biological role thus seems quite separate from that of the cultural role. Sarbin (1963) has pointed out the necessity of a female body-image as one of the components of female identity. Studying children's play constructions, Erikson (1968) found that boys and girls whom he had instructed to construct an exciting movie scene used space differently, in particular that girls emphasized the inner while boys emphasized the outer space. Girls' scenes tended to be a house interior, open or simply enclosed; people and animals tended to be mainly within such an interior and were mainly static; occasionally the interior was intruded by animals or dangerous men. Boys' scenes tended to be houses with elaborate walls or façades with protrusions (such as cannons); there were towers, there were entirely exterior scenes; more people were outside enclosures; there were more automotive objects and moving animals and also arrested movement (by a policeman for instance). There were many high structures; ruins were exclusively boys' constructions. 'It may come as a surprise to some and seem as a matter of course to others that here sexual differences in the organization of a play space seem to parallel the morphology of genital differentiation itself: in the male, an external organ, erectable and intrusive in character, serving the channelization of mobile sperm cells; in the female, internal organs, with vestibular access, leading to statically expectant ova.' With a similar line of thought in mind, Franck (1948) devised a Masculinity–Femininity test (FDCT) made up of a series of incomplete drawings which the subject is asked to complete any way he or she wishes to. She found that, just like Erikson's children, men and women completed the drawings differently both in terms of the content and of the form of the drawings. For example, men tended to expand and close drawings; women tended to elaborate within the stimulus area and leave it open. Women tended to draw objects moved by an external force as opposed to objects which were self-propelled. The final version of the test used those items which discriminated best between the sexes. A number of authors have validated the test, showing that it does discriminate between men and women, both in the USA and in Europe. No relationship was found between this test and measures derived from verbal masculinity-femininity tests, for instance tests based on 'masculine' and 'feminine' interests (Shepler, 1951; Lansky, 1960 and 1964; Nichols, 1962; Miller and Swanson, 1966). It has been suggested that the Franck Drawing Completion Test measures latent facets of Masculinity-Femininity, facets related to body image. Although all the studies have found a difference in score between men and women and a lack of relationship with verbal masculinity-femininity tests, they have on the whole been unable to relate these scores to anything else. For instance, Winer (1961) failed to show a relationship between the scores on Franck's Drawing Completion Test and a woman's expressed satisfaction with her own mother; Urbina (1970) failed to show a relationship with creativity. However two recent studies did find some relationship between scores on the Franck Drawing Completion Test and attitudes and values (Cottle et al., 1970; Bezdek and Strodtbeck, 1970).

With the idea of unconscious femininity and of body image in mind, I chose to use this test in my research. I will come back to discussing it in a later chapter.

. . . Wait, wait just a little while longer, I cry to my body, as one pleads for a last moment of consciousness before going under ether, for another moment of preparing before having a needle thrust into a vein. And, like a drowning man, my past suddenly becomes vivid – not the immediate past but the past before sex, the past of the hard little-girl body of six or seven, when you are all of a piece, like a statue carved with the fewest strokes from a block of wood, and you run with your legs stiff and outflung, your feet flat; before the body becomes graceful only through balance, and your growing hips slow your run to an awkward trot. I can see myself running around my grandmother's house and feel the gravel under my feet and feel the trees and the early crocuses growing all around me . . . And so I keep crying to myself to wait a little, to let me make sense of my own past before beginning someone else's present . . . Abigail Lewis

Chapter 3
What I want to study and how I go about it

I set out to test empirically the idea that the biological and psychological event of becoming a mother sets in motion interactive processes which can be adaptive or maladaptive. This view is held by authors who see pregnancy and the birth of a child as a process of development. I described their ideas in the last chapter; these mainly arose from clinical contact with a limited number of patients. The backbone of my research involves proving or disproving these intuitions. The more individual analysis and the additional findings form the meat of it. The basic hypothesis is that the healthy woman is the one who can modify her perception of herself and her relationship with members of her family in a way which is congruent with the new situation of having a child.

What then are these modifications which must take place? The area of primordial importance which came up time and again when I presented the 'pregnancy as development' authors, involves the woman's relationship with her own mother, at a time when she is herself becoming a mother. Psychoanalysts, in particular, stress the necessity of the woman's 'identification' with a 'good mother image'. The 'good mother image' refers to the image of a loving mother which the woman has retained from the positive nurturing she herself received in the past. Difficulties arise when she identifies with 'a bad mother image' – the image she retains from her negative experiences. Identification as it is used here refers to 'processes by which a person . . . borrows his identity from someone else' (Rycroft, 1968). The term 'borrows' is somewhat misleading in this case if we think of these images as being mental representations rather than external people.

Melanie Klein described the processes by which the external world is taken in as mental representation becoming part of the inner world of the child and the inner world colours the external world. These two processes (introjection and projection) interact from birth. The infant will therefore hold inside him or her a good as well as a bad mother image from the times he or she received or, more precisely, experienced good or bad mothering. According to different theories, the actual quality of the mothering (Winnicott) or the perception of the mothering modified by the child's impulses and emotions (Melanie Klein) are emphasized.

To come back to the woman who is having her first child, saying that she identifies with a good mother image means not only that she experienced good mothering, was able to recognize it as such and that such an experience was not outweighed by negative elements, but also that at *this particular point in time* she is able to call on this good experience. This is where a strict reliance on genetic explanations seems insufficient. Psychoanalytic theory pays insufficient attention to later events; the way in which, for instance, biological and psychological changes at puberty were experienced and the circumstances at this time must be important in moulding the girl's feelings about her body and her ability to be a good mother. The present social and psychological situation of the woman, in particular her relationship to her husband and the meaning of this particular pregnancy are also important. Psychoanalysis has been little concerned with phases in their own right, beyond childhood. Which is not to say that these phases are not coloured by previous one, but that later circumstances and relationships, biological changes, social situations are also important.

Another area of change involves the woman's feelings of satisfaction with herself as a mother when she takes on this new role. It is obviously linked to the previous point since identification with the image of a positively valued mother should lead a woman to a positive valuing of herself, while the identification with the image of a negatively valued mother should lead her to a negative valuing of herself. This also has roots in an interaction between the capacity for loving feelings for another person and a positive valuing of oneself.

Here too it may be necessary to take into account more than the past. The psychology of the healthy woman may include a spontaneous love of her baby which would give her confidence in herself as a mother. As Lomas points out, in refutation of the traditional psychoanalytic view, 'maternal love is based neither on defense mechanisms nor compromise adaptations such as narcissism and masochism but is a full engagement of the object, based, as is love in general, on a primary, spontaneous and realistic interest in the outer world'.

When considering how a person evaluates himself it is important to take into account another phenomenon which complicates matters. Psychoanalysts have described 'defence mechanisms'; these are ways in which the ego protects itself when there is a conflict, ways in which conflict is reduced when the anxiety would be too great. Denial, repression and reversal describe the avoidance of conflict by pushing out of consciousness the disturbing elements and, in the case of reversal, substituting their opposites. For instance, Ryle and I found in a recent study that psychiatric patients tend to express either less or more satisfaction with themselves than do non-patients. In cases where a greater satisfaction is expressed it is likely that the people need to deny the painful feeling that 'all is not well'. Byrne (1964) has called 'repressers' people who deny painful situations and conflicts, 'sensitizers' people who, on the contrary, ruminate over failures and events which activate their anxiety. Both extremes are maladjusted modes of experiencing. It will be important to take into account such processes when we come to consider how women value themselves as mothers.

A third area where reappraisal takes place is the husband–wife relationship. From the psychoanalytic point of view, at the time of having a child, the woman must get in touch with her femininity; she becomes more clearly different to her husband; as for their relationship it must be modified allowing for a third person to be part of the family (shift from a dyadic to a triadic unit). In a more social psychological framework we could say that each partner takes on a new role, that of mother and of father. Particularly in our society these new roles increase the differentiation between the partners since the woman usually takes on the full-time care-taking role, while the man becomes the sole bread winner.

The two main areas mentioned above, identification with a good mother image and role differentiation, lead on to two other notions which have been mentioned in connection with a healthy adjustment to childbearing. 'Acceptance of pregnancy' refers to the woman's real wish to have a child at this time. It describes more than a purely verbal expression of acceptance which may reflect a wish for social approval and an attempt to reduce feelings of guilt if the child is not wanted.

'Acceptance of femininity' is the other notion. The birth of a child helps a woman to get a 'greater sense of psychological femininity' (Rheingold). This again is vague if we don't have a clear notion of what is meant by femininity. If we take a biological orientation then the healthy woman is one who is able to accept and become more aware of her female body with the birth of her child.

My research is an attempt to contribute to an understanding of the psychology of the normal woman. This is not complete without an understanding of childbearing. I am trying to show that the birth of a first child is not a static event in the psychological life of a woman but that it is accompanied by processes which can be adaptive or maladaptive. Adaptive processes, I hypothesize to be the ones mentioned above: identification with own mother and more specifically with a good mother image, satisfaction with oneself in the mothering role, increased differentiation with partner, acceptance of pregnancy and increased sense of femininity. These processes may be adaptive in terms of the biological aspect of childbearing or they may be purely adaptive to a sociological situation. After I have explored which of these processes do in fact occur, I will discuss this point again.

I would like to stress again that when I refer to well-adjusted and ill-adjusted women I am only talking about two extremes on a continuum. Furthermore I am referring to adjustment at a particular point in time and in relation to a particular experience. Unfortunately psychiatry has often tended to consider psychological conflicts and difficulties as immutable and the ill person as ill forever. Added to this, Western culture has associated psychological disturbance with badness or lesser value or something to be ashamed of.

Research procedure

In order to test these processes I interviewed a number of women at the beginning of their pregnancy, towards the end of it and in the postpartum period. It was not feasible to interview women before they got pregnant. I also chose to interview a group of women who were not pregnant. Since all persons – whether pregnant or not – are engaged in long adaptational processes of which all too little is known, I felt it advisable to be able to compare the processes occurring in the childbearing group with those occurring in the non-childbearing group. I could thus compare each woman with herself at different points in time, well-adjusted primiparous women with ill-adjusted primiparous women and pregnant women with non-pregnant women.

The primiparous women were interviewed as soon as possible after they first presented at the maternity hospital which was generally in their third or fourth month of pregnancy (I excluded from my sample women who were more pregnant than this). A duplicated sheet was given to primiparae asking them to fill it in if they were willing to participate in my study. A brief description of the study was given and a space was left for them to fill in some personal details. Although I was reluctant to do this, I decided to select women who belonged to classes 1, 2 and 3 of the Registrar General's Classification (this classification in terms of occupation involves five categories). These three classes include both 'working-class' and 'middle-class' women while at the same time excluding those women who have the added stress of a particularly difficult financial situation. There is evidence for the effect of poor dietary conditions on the physiological state of mother and baby. This would confuse the issue when considering the psychological processes. The class distinction was in fact rather loose as the description of occupation was often vague.

I also eliminated women who were not married or about to be married since in our society this still generally involves not having a stable relationship, sometimes living with the parents, an unwanted pregnancy, plus the additional stress linked to being an 'unmarried mother'. This would also be a confusing variable making results harder to interpret.

Apart from this I interviewed all the women who returned the sheets, visiting them in their own home that same week. I visited them again about 10 weeks before the expected date of delivery (roughly 7 months pregnancy) and again 10 weeks after the actual date of delivery. My foremost concern was with the first and last interviews since the study was about the changes occurring with the birth of a first child. Ten weeks postpartum, I felt, would go beyond transient changes related to the actual experience of childbirth and the recent biological upheaval.

The 'non-pregnant' group was composed of women without children, under 35 years of age (so as to be comparable with the other group), married for at least ten months (so as to eliminate the factor of a very recent marriage). It proved rather more difficult to find these women. An advertisement in a local newspaper provided three volunteers. The other women were working in the institution I was at and their names were given to me by acquaintances. Although the background and social class of these women were on the whole quite different this was not too important as the main interest was change over time. In any case these women were often different, in the sense that many had decided not to have children at this time in their life, or even not to have children at all. I started seeing the women in this group slightly later than the pregnant women so that I could calculate the average span of time between the first and second interview for the latter. This span was about 15 weeks. The non-pregnant women were therefore seen for the second time 15 weeks after the first session and for the third time 20 weeks after the second session (to equate with the 10 weeks prepartum and 10 weeks postpartum of the pregnant women).

There were sixty women to start off in the 'pregnant group'. However three women left the area, and four refused to continue with the interview. Quite a number of women moved homes during this time, it was not always easy to find out their new address so I was surprised that in the end my sample didn't completely dwindle away! For one woman the data was incomplete and two women had miscarriages; so this leaves for the main analysis fifty women. There were twenty-two women in the control group. None of them dropped out. This probably reflects the fact that the situation was less threatening as they were part of the 'control' group and that many of them were themselves involved in research (as research assistants, secretaries, wives of students, etc.). During those nine months a number of them also went through important life events such as deaths or separations.

The average age in both groups is 24 years, ranging from 18 to 32 in the pregnant group and 20 to 31 in the non-pregnant group. The average length of marriage is 2 years 1 month in the pregnant group, the longest time of marriage being 11 years, and 2 years and 7 months in the non-pregnant group, ranging from 10 months to 9 years and 6 months. The two groups are thus comparable on these two variables. Husband's age minus wife's age ranged from -3 to $+17$ years for the pregnant group (with an average of 3·2 years) and from -3 to $+9$ for the non-pregnant group (with an average of 1·5 years). This reflects the cultural tendency for men to be older than their wives. The larger difference in this direction for the pregnant group probably relates to their slightly different social background and class.

I had to collect two sorts of data:

A. Processes of change

When I came to choose the methods I would use for this study I took into consideration not only the kind of information I wanted to elicit but also my wish to get a balance between rigour and freedom for the subject. The whole point of an empirical study is to put one's ideas to the test. This requires a systematic approach to the situation, such as for instance, similar elicitation for everybody. However, psychological research has often been carried away by the desire to be 'scientific' to the extent that 'subjects' are more like 'objects' and treated as if they had no individuality, or at least not beyond the limited categories offered to them.

'Rigour as an end in itself is self defeating' (Kelman, 1968). Yet, even idiosyncratic data require ordering in some systematic fashion. 'Because human existence is structured, there is also something general about it and thus it is a phenomenon that can be studied in a rigorous or systematic manner' (Giorgi, 1970).

This dual concern with fidelity to the phenomena and with systematic structure suggested to me the use of Kelly's Repertory Grid technique as my main method. Kelly developed this method out of his experience in working with psychiatric patients and his wish to explore the ways in which they construed the world around them which would tell him something about the kinds of conflicts they experienced and the ways in which they should modify their construction if the conflicts are to be reduced or resolved. This method is designed to explore how people see themselves, how they order their experience, how they appraise and reappraise their experience and give meaning to it. Kelly was interested in the particular way in which each person makes sense of their universe. What is important is not an actual event, but the person's construing of it. For example if we think of the interview situation with the women in this study, I might have been construed by one woman as a friendly observer, by another as an intruder keeping a watch on her, by a third as a person trying to help, by a fourth as an envious woman, by a fifth as a psychologist doing her job, by a sixth as a woman interested in understanding more about femininity. Each person perceives the event through his or her own way of construing the world around them. Kelly suggests that a person is essentially 'a form of motion, that is, that a person continually reconstrues the environment as predictions are validated or invalidated.

For Kelly, a person is not the victim of his biography, since similar events can be construed differently, but he may become enslaved by his interpretation of it. 'It is not what happens around him that makes a man experienced; it is the successive construing and reconstruing of what happens, as it happens, that enriches the experience of his life' (Kelly, 1955). One can argue that this approach evades the question of why this person construes in such a way and we would be back to looking at the biography, and such a causal approach may not be suitable if we want to do justice to the complexity of a person. Even the analyst in his consulting room can only understand with the patient the infantile feelings as they are expressed in the 'here and now' situation and how they relate to the patient's personal mythology which may be very different from what actually did happen in childhood. Indeed patients' reconstruction of their childhood often is modified at different points in therapy. Freud who first attributed the neurosis to the repressed memories of actual events of sexual seductions in childhood, later came to understand these early seductions which had often probably never taken place, as part of the 'psychical reality' of the patient. So that the main question the analyst can ask himself in such a case is: what is the meaning of this recounted seduction for this patient and why is he telling me about it now? In this sense, as Rycroft (1968) said, the procedure Freud engaged in was not 'the scientific one of elucidating causes but the semantic one of making sense of it. It can indeed be argued that much of Freud's work was really semantic and that he made a revolutionary discovery in semantics, viz. that neurotic symptoms are meaningful disguised communications, but that owing to his scientific training and allegiance, he formulated his findings in the conceptual framework of the physical sciences.'

It is in this sense that I feel Kelly's approach is compatible with psychoanalysis if one sees the latter not as a causal theory but as a semantic one. In both cases one is looking at the way a person construes his environment, be it past or present.

In my particular research I will be looking at the processes as they occur and the ways in which the women construe and reconstrue their environment. In this sense it is compatible both with Kellian ideas and with psychodynamic notions.

REPERTORY GRID TECHNIQUE

In order to look at the way in which a person construes his environment Kelly devised a method which he called the Repertory Grid technique. Very simply the technique is as follows: the person is asked to list a number of important people relating to categories such as family members, liked person, disliked person, teacher who has influenced you, trusted friend etc. These are called 'elements'. The person is then asked to compare three of these elements at a time, finding a way or ways in which two of them are similar and

Self	Mother	Father	Husband	John	Mary	Ann	elements / constructs
2	3	1	6	5	4	7	Friendly
1	6	3	2	4	5	7	I like
7	6	2	3	1	5	4	Hard-working
3	5	6	4	2	1	7	Sympathetic
1	2	7	6	4	3	5	Conscientious
1	3	6	7	4	5	2	Shy
5	3	7	4	2	1	6	Warm
7	5	3	6	1	2	4	Lazy
5	4	3	7	2	1	6	Supportive
7	6	5	4	3	1	2	Haphazard
1	5	3	2	4	7	6	Submissive
7	1	3	2	5	4	6	Humorous

Figure 1: *Example of a Grid: 7 Elements rank-ordered on each construct.*

different from the third one. For example the person says 'I like Jim and John and I dislike Mary' for one of the triads, and 'Jane and Karen are unfriendly whereas Jack is friendly' for the second triad. The descriptive terms elicited in this way are called 'constructs' (and Kelly's theory is called personal construct theory). Once the constructs have been elicited the person is asked to rate or rank all the elements chosen on each of these constructs. Figure 1 gives an example of a 'grid' where the elements are rank-ordered on each of the constructs.

From the grid obtained it is possible to get different sorts of information. First it is possible to look at the kind of words (constructs) the person uses. Secondly it is possible to look at how these constructs relate to each other. For instance if all the people who are liked are also the people who are seen as friendly and all the people who are not liked are seen as unfriendly, we could say that for this group of elements anyway, the two terms are used synonymously. Or we might discover that all the people he likes are those that he sees as submissive which would tell us something about his need to be in control in a relationship. Thirdly one could look at the ways in which a person construes his environment. For instance we may find that half of the constructs are used in a similar fashion. All the people who are seen as friendly are liked and seen as kind and sympathetic, and warm and supportive whereas the unfriendly ones are also unliked, unsympathetic, cold and unsupportive. We would say that this cluster is the main dimension on which the person discriminates amongst his acquaintances, a sort of good–bad dimension. We might then find a second slightly less important cluster which refers let us say to being hardworking and conscientious versus being lazy and haphazard. This second dimension would be separate from the first as some liked people would be hardworking whereas others would not be. We might then find that there are a number of much less important dimensions. We could say that this person construes his environment mainly in terms of whether or not he likes people and whether or not he finds them hardworking. (The statistical measure which tells one how far two constructs are linked is called a correlation and the analysis which gives the different dimensions and their relative importance is called a principal component analysis.) Finally, one can look at where the person places the different elements in his construct system. For example we may find that his parents are seen as disliked and hardworking whereas people of his generation are seen as liked and happy-go-lucky. Or, in my first example, we may find that all the people he likes and finds friendly are women because they are also the ones he feels he can dominate. Or we may find that he sees women as belonging to two separate groups, the domineering women he dislikes like his mother and the submissive women who he can relate to. The girl friends or wife might, depending on the time of the relationship, belong to one or the other group! (see Graph 1).

We could also say something about how similar or how different

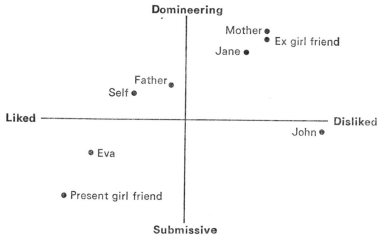

Graph 1 : *The two axes represent the two main dimensions. Elements are placed in relation to these two dimensions.*

he feels himself to be from certain other people. In the above example we could say that he is most similar to his father.

The use of this technique seemed appropriate for my research since it combines freedom for the person to portray an individual picture of him or herself while at the same time enabling the search for general processes. It is suited to exploring how each woman sees herself in relation to significant people in her life. It allows looking at such things as an identification with the woman's own mother after the birth of the child. Identification will be evidenced by an increase in similarity between the perception of self and that of the other person. In some ways this definition of identification is more restricted than the psychoanalytic one since the latter is meant to include unconscious elements; the Repertory Grid mainly taps conscious and preconscious aspects, that is those that are retrievable into consciousness. However, it is also possible that the process of construct selection includes an unconscious element. The fact that one construct rather than another is chosen to compare people at a particular time may be partly determined by unconscious processes. This is why I chose to elicit constructs afresh at each of the three testing sessions rather than ask the woman to re-evaluate the people on the constructs she had chosen the first time. In such a way, maximal change can be expressed, encompassing both a change in the perception of people on certain constructs and a change in the constructs themselves. At times, a new experience produces new constructs rather than distinguish people differently on previously used ones; forcing the use of old constructs for the sake of an easier test–retest analysis would, in such a case, preclude identifying change. If you think of someone for instance who becomes one day politically aware, his construct system might become completely modified because he will now use a whole new set of constructs such as 'capitalist', 'reactionary', 'liberal', 'prejudiced', 'opportunist', 'male chauvinist', etc., which may differentiate between people he knows in a whole new way. If he had been asked to re-evaluate people on his prepolitical constructs (e.g. 'kind', 'lazy' . . .) there might not have been much change.

Most people who have done studies of change using Repertory Grids have asked subjects to use the same constructs over again. This seems to me to limit greatly the possibility of picking up change. A few studies did however allow for a change of constructs. Tippett (1959) for instance administered the Repertory Grid to patients in psychotherapy at 3-month intervals. She found that the verbal designation of constructs changed as well as the way in which people were evaluated on these constructs. Which constructs changed depended on whether the therapist emphasized past or present. If the therapist emphasized the past, the constructs formed on figures important in early life were changed, if the therapist emphasized the present, constructs formed on figures who played a role later in life were changed.

As emphasized by Bannister (1967) no one Repertory Grid can sample the whole construct system of an individual and therefore a particular Grid is devised to sample a subsystem. For one thing, a person could be asked to elicit constructs from a group of objects (paintings or sculptures for instance) or situations (a frightening situation, a happy situation, etc.) or events (your marriage, the birth of your sister, etc.). In the case of people, the construct system may be different depending on which people are selected. I therefore chose the 'elements' (the people being compared in repertory grid jargon) in functions of the particular area I wanted to investigate bearing in mind the fact that I wanted the grids to be small enough not to be too tiresome to complete. I chose the following seven elements:

1. Yourself
2. Your mother

3. Your father
4. Your husband
5. a person you consider very motherly (to be named)
6. a person you consider very immature (to be named)
7. your notion of the ideal mother

Elements 5 and 6 are meant to provide similar categories for everyone while eliciting relevant constructs. I do not plan to look at these particular elements in themselves. With element 7 I stressed that what I wanted was a personal conception of what a mother should be like rather than a stereotyped cultural notion.

Once the seven elements had been named, I elicited constructs by the method of triads described earlier. The person is asked to think of a way in which two of the three elements presented are similar to each other and different from the third one. Since I was focusing on self-concept, rather than choose triads at random, I decided to select all the triads which included the self as one of the elements. With six elements (excluding the ideal mother), the number of combinations is ten. In addition to this I asked each woman what she felt was the most important quality for a mother. This provided the eleventh construct which I will refer to as the 'maternal construct' or the 'motherhood construct'. In contradistinction to the others, it remained the same throughout the testing sessions in order to help me identify change over time in the grid. I emphasized each time that this was what they had said was the most important quality for a mother. They would thus more likely use the word in that sense again. A change in meaning of motherliness could be picked up from the constructs associated with this one.[1]

Once the constructs had been elicited, the woman was asked to rank the seven elements on each one of the eleven constructs. Rank ordering, I felt, would be more meaningful than rating on a five-point scale, for instance (it makes more immediate psychological

[1] It could be argued that the maternal construct would have changed had I allowed this. I hoped to record the change in meaning from the constructs associated with it. The fact that I emphasized each time that it refers to the most important quality for a mother means that whatever the term used it would refer to this. One woman asked if she could use a different word to describe the most important quality for a mother. I asked her to use both the new and the old one. On analysing the grid I found that it made very little difference to the total picture.

sense to say that X is kinder than Y than to say that X rates four on kindness).

DRAWING COMPLETION TEST

The Repertory Grid will allow me to identify processes of change in relation to significant others and provide information on women's conception of motherliness during pregnancy and postpartum.

I now needed a way of understanding women's feelings about their femininity and somehow measure changes in sense of femininity. This is no easy task since practically all so-called masculinity–femininity tests tap socially defined femininity and masculinity (in Gough's Brief Femininity Scale for instance, if you prefer a shower to a bath you are seen as more masculine).

The only test I came across which differed from this and made a claim to be culture-free was the Franck Drawing Completion Test. According to Franck, the FDCT taps the more latent aspects of masculinity and femininity and, in particular, aspects of the body image (see end of Chapter 2). Since this test does discriminate between men and women and yet does not relate to masculinity–femininity tests tapping attitudes, and since it involves drawings rather than words, its claim to relate to body image seemed plausible and the test suitable for my purposes.

The Franck Drawing Completion Test is made up of thirty-six incomplete drawings which the person is asked to complete any way they like. Each drawing is scored male or female according to two sets of criteria. The number of female scores constitutes an individual's score. As there are thirty-six drawings, an individual's score can range from nothing (most masculine) to thirty-six (most feminine). One set of criteria refers to formal properties of the drawings. Drawings scored female are those which are for instance internally elaborated, or left open, or rounded, or made into two separate units. Drawings scored male are those which are for instance expanded outward or upward, or closed off, or angular, or protruding. The other set of criteria refers to the content of the drawings. Furniture, windows, doors, houses, human figures and 'passive containers' (i.e. containers and objects capable of movements with outside assistance only such as kites, vases, sailboats, etc.) are scored female. Tall buildings, tunnels, bridges, 'active containers' (i.e. containers and objects capable of motion or locomotion without further aid from without such as ships, cars, etc.) are scored male. These criteria were developed empirically by Franck who administered a very large number of tests to men and women and noted which properties distinguished their drawings. Like Erikson's findings concerning boys' and girls' play constructions, Franck felt that there was a correspondence between these spacial relations and the morphology and modes of function of the sex organs, that is, 'exterior location and intrusive mode in the male, and interior location and

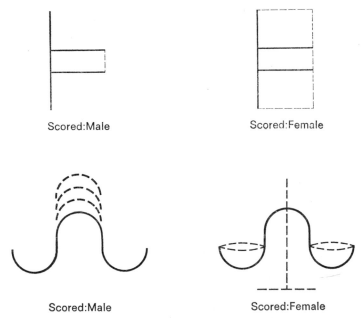

Scored:Male   Scored:Female

Scored:Male   Scored:Female

Figure 2: *Example of scoring on Franck Drawing Completion Test.*

inceptive mode in the female' (Franck, 1946). Actually, when faced with the drawings, scoring is not so clear-cut and I spent a lot of time combining and elaborating the two existing manuals. The tests were then scored by myself and another psychologist, A. Ostell, independently. Our scoring was sufficiently similar.[1]

Most researchers using the Franck Drawing Completion Test administered it once and looked at how this measure related to other variables. There has been a less frequent attempt to look at this measure of masculinity–femininity in developmental terms. Lansky in

[1] Inter scorer reliability: $r = 0.84$.

particular concluded that 'it is quite likely that sex-role identification – at least as measured by standardized tests – may not be quite as stable as our theoretical models would suggest' (1964). He got interested in the vicissitudes of sex role identification in adults, 'particularly as these changes are reactions to the development of the children and thus bring about changes in parents'. He found that the relationship between scores obtained by mothers and by fathers, or between these scores and other variables, varied systematically in families with different structures (sex and number of children). For instance, in families with all girls, he found that the older the eldest daughter was, the more masculine the mother's Drawing Completion Test score was.

I hoped that my own use of this test at different times during the childbearing period would further our understanding of changes in sense of femininity.

TAT

Finally I wanted a measure of acceptance of pregnancy which was free from a socially desirable answer. The Thematic Apperception Test (TAT) is a 'projective test'. It is composed of fairly ambiguous pictures around which the person is asked to invent a story. The analysis is done in terms of the wishes, fears and conflicts projected onto the pictures and of the details of the picture which are not perceived or misperceived. One of the cards depicts a country scene with two women and a man. One of the women is young and carries some books under the arm. The other woman is older and pregnant; she is leaning against a tree. The older woman is not always reported to be pregnant. The perception of the pregnancy by a pregnant woman might well say something about the woman's acceptance of her own pregnancy. This idea is given some support by two different studies. Davids and DeVault (1962) using this test in their research showed that pregnant women who are 'selectively tuned' to perceiving cues suggestive of pregnancy in ambiguous stimuli (that is who perceive the older woman as pregnant) appear to experience little difficulty with the process of childbirth. Of the fifty-three women who later had normal delivery room records, 60% told a story during pregnancy involving the perception of a pregnant woman as opposed to 21% of the twenty-eight women with abnormal delivery room records. The likelihood of finding such a difference by chance alone is less than 1 in 1000. In his study of married and unmarried primiparae, McDonald (1965) found that a greater percentage of married women perceived the woman as pregnant than unmarried women. The likelihood of obtaining such a difference by chance was also small in this case (less than 1 in 100). However he found that, in the case of unmarried women, a certain amount of repression and denial (expressed through the non-perception of the pregnancy on the card) was probably adaptive. In this group, the women who had normal deliveries tended to see the woman as pregnant on the TAT card less often than did those who had abnormal deliveries. This idea was confirmed by the fact that these unmarried women who belonged to the normal delivery group relied more on repression and denial as measured by Byrne's Repression–Sensitization scale than those belonging to the abnormal delivery group. Byrne's scale distinguishes between people who tend to deny problems and difficulties and people who ruminate excessively over them.

With this idea of repression and denial in mind I decided to define acceptance of pregnancy as the perception of the older woman as pregnant on the TAT card. Since, in my sample, all the women were married, I surmised that repression and denial would not be adaptive. It would reflect the wish not to be pregnant or a great deal of conflict over the pregnancy.

Davids and DeVault and McDonald administered this test when the women were about seven months pregnant. I decided to do the same. This will allow comparisons of my data with theirs. At this time, body changes are quite considerable but the actual delivery is not yet impending. The actual instructions were: 'I would like you to tell me a story connected with this picture. It need not be very long, but should have a beginning and an end'.

The different methods I have just described (Repertory Grid Technique, Franck Drawing Completion Test and TAT card 7) are chosen in an attempt to capture the adaptive and maladaptive processes in women with the birth of their first child. In order to identify different patterns of change in women whose psychophysical adjustment is satisfactory from those in women whose psychophysical adjustment is deficient, it is now necessary to describe the criteria that were chosen to measure adjustment.

B. Criteria of adjustment

Psychoanalysts have emphasized how conflicts and difficulties can manifest themselves in many different ways both emotional and somatic. The mode of expression may depend on the particular conflict and may be a symbolic representation of it or on certain constitutional weaknesses of the person or on a combination of these. They have shown that if you remove a symptom without resolving the underlying conflict, a different symptom will most likely develop. It is with this conception of the person as a totality that I felt it would be important to explore the different ways in which women might express their conflict over childbearing and the different difficulties experienced which would affect their feeling about childbearing. I wanted to cover the pregnancy period, the labour and delivery and the postpartum period. I also wanted to cover both the women's subjective feelings and some more objective aspects of their childbearing. Finally I felt it was important to get some assessment of the mother–baby relationship. I hoped that these different areas would cover all possible difficulties. I could then identify a 'very healthy group', free from any difficulties. Once this group has been identified it will be possible to see if healthy pregnancy and childbirth sets in motion the processes I hypothesize. It is possible to combine such different sorts of criteria since no causal explanations are sought. Indeed what I am saying is that it is important to consider the person as a whole and therefore when one talks about difficulties it is necessary to consider all possible sorts of difficulties. I am not saying that a difficult delivery for instance is caused by a particular conflict or that a difficult delivery causes a particular conflict postpartum. There is most probably an interaction between the two. Neither am I attempting to separate out physiological or hormonal from psychological elements in a postpartum depression. Here again there is probably an interaction. What I am trying to do is to identify the adaptive and the maladaptive processes accompanying childbearing.

DOCTOR'S REPORT

The women's obstetricians were given a form to complete for each woman. This form is divided into three parts relating respectively to pregnancy, labour and delivery, and health of the baby (see Figure 3). Each of these sections ends with a three-point scale on which the doctor rated the woman for adjustment and a space in which he can write the reason he chose this rating. A score of 1 reflects a healthy adjustment, 2 reflects mild difficulties and 3 severe difficulties. These scales are very crude but sufficient to identify those women who experienced no difficulties at all. They were the ones who were given a score of 1 on all three scales. Other details such as length of labour, weight and sex of the baby are also recorded on this sheet.

DEPRESSION SCORE

As mentioned in Chapter 2, Brice Pitt devised a questionnaire (see Figure 4) to identify women who suffer from postpartum depression. Most questionnaires rely on relative scores between subjects which means that for instance a person will be rated as more disturbed than another one if he has a tendency to give high ratings generally, or less disturbed than another if he has a tendency to minimize his difficulties. The great advantage with Pitt's questionnaire is that each woman is compared with herself rather than with another woman. The questionnaire is given once in late pregnancy and once postpartum. Pitt found that for most women the scores tended to drop after the birth of the child, in other words that they gave evidence of having more symptoms and fears during pregnancy than postpartum. Those women who presented the reverse pattern, that is who gave evidence of more symptoms and anxieties postpartum, turned out, on interview, to present clinical signs of postpartum depression, which was not true of the former women. Therefore, what is important here, is not the score obtained by a woman on the initial test (it may be low or high) but whether it increases or decreases postpartum. Apart from it making more sense to compare each woman with herself than with another woman, this is more in line with the idea of process which my study is all about. Indeed there is no such thing as x amount of depression; what is important is how a person feels at one time in relation to how he or she feels at another time. Any increase in score from time 1 to time 2 I considered to reveal some difficulty although Pitt considered an increase of 6 points only to be a sign of postpartum depression. He classified women whose scores increased by less than 6 points in a doubtful group. However, as I explained earlier, I wanted to delineate a very healthy group and therefore I deemed even possible or mild depression to be relevant.

BABY QUESTIONNAIRE

This questionnaire, actually called the Neonatal Perception Inventory, described in Chapter 2, gives an idea of how a woman feels about her child and how she feels he or she compares to the average baby. It comprises two sets of five scales (see Figure 5). One set refers to 'the average baby'; it is given first. The other refers to 'your own baby'. The differential score gives a measure of the mother's evaluation of her baby. This test thus taps some aspects of the complex interaction between mother and child. On the one hand, it relates to the child's actual behaviour (crying, vomiting) which will, in part, reflect the interaction between them; on the other hand it relates to the mother's perception of his or her behaviour which is coloured by her feelings about the baby and about herself. Since these women are having their first child and often have little experience with babies, the differential score should, in large part, reflect their personal feelings about the baby. So here again no causal relationship is stipulated but the mother's perception of her baby should relate to the complex interaction between mother and child. Whether the child is actually experiencing difficulties, either for constitutional or for environmental reasons, or whether the mother perceives him or her as problematic, all we can say is that there is a problem here. Balint (1968) has emphasized the need to look at both partners and the 'fit' between them. 'The cause of the early discrepancy may be congenital, i.e. the infant's biopsychological needs may have been too exacting . . . or may be environmental such as care that is insufficient, deficient, haphazard, overanxious, overproductive, harsh, rigid, grossly inconsistent, incorrectly timed, over-stimulating, or merely un-understanding or indifferent. As may be seen I put the emphasis on the lack of "fit" between the child and the people who represent his environment.' In other words the same woman may be a good mother to an active lively child and not be able to deal with a more passive and unresponsive child who makes her feel unwanted for instance. To come back to the questionnaire, the woman who says that her child is worse than average is also saying something about her inability to tolerate the child's crying, vomiting, etc., as well as about the child's difficulties.

This criterion is scored positively (healthy adjustment) when the difference between own baby and average baby is positive, i.e. when own baby is seen as better (however slightly) than the average baby.

The assumption behind this is that a positive evaluation of the baby is part of the healthy adjustment to motherhood. The mother needs to feel that she has produced something 'good', for a positive relationship to develop between mother and baby.

INTERVIEW

Interviews accompanying each testing situation formed an important part of the overall research design. They were vital in creating a relationship which allowed the women to share their experience with me. They were also designed to record factual information, as well as allow each woman to bring to the fore the problems and feelings which most preoccupied her. Although this information did not have a role to play in the main hypotheses I hoped that these interviews would provide material for the exploratory aspect of this study. The interviews combined both the area of processes of change and of criteria of adjustment. The former refers mainly to such things as breast-feeding and sex of the baby. A prospective study is appropriate for studying changes in feelings, the working of memory and rationalizations as well as the effect of additional conflict. For instance, how does a woman cope with having a baby girl when she wanted a baby boy? Does she change her mind about breast-feeding after the birth of the baby? Some of the questions I asked also related to adjustment, albeit in a looser way than the criteria previously described. For example, I asked each woman at the last interview to tell me what was the one thing that stuck most in her mind from the first time I saw her until now. The women were often surprised by such a question, and uncertain of the kind of answer I expected. Precisely because I gave no clue about this, I could obtain an indication as to whether the experience had been felt to be predominantly positive or negative. I could also record which aspect of the process had been most important.

Summary of the research procedure

(a) *Pregnant women*

Time of contact	*3–4 months pregnant*	*10 weeks before expected date of delivery*	*Delivery*	*10 weeks postpartum*
Type of Data				
Processes	Interview	Interview		Interview
	Grid	Grid		Grid
	Franck Drawing	Franck Drawing		Franck Drawing
	Completion Test	Completion Test		Completion Test
		TAT card 7		
Criteria		Depression questionnaire	Doctor's report	Depression questionnaire
				Baby questionnaire

(b) *Non-pregnant women*

Time of contact	*X*	*X + 15 weeks*	*X + 35 weeks*
Type of data			
Processes	Interview	Interview	Interview
	Grid	Grid	Grid
	Franck Drawing	Franck Drawing	Franck Drawing
	Completion Test	Completion Test	Completion Test
		TAT card 7	

. . . The moment the membranes were cut, the contractions began in earnest. Three or four student nurses whipped me on to a stretcher and wheeled me into the delivery room, a large bare room next door that looked like any operating room. Here they more or less assisted me on to the table and strapped down my wrists. I protested again. They said it was to keep my hands off the sterile sheets. I privately thought I had enough self-control to keep my hands where they belonged, but I let them strap me down anyway. My legs were lifted on to two metal supports; they were beginning to feel crampy, and I asked the doctor to rub them, which he did. That was my only real discomfort, and it went away as soon as my legs were properly supported.

By this time I knew I could not have a sedative; the doctor had told me there would not be time enough for it to work, and because gas is almost instantaneous, he had called in an anaesthetist, a jovial chap, who patted my hand and asked me coaxingly if I wouldn't like 'just a little whiff'. This annoyed me very much, but I realized that everyone thought I was in agony; even the doctor had remarked, 'She must be in real pain now', at just about the time the pain stopped.

Someone switched on a dazzling light overhead; there was a mirror diagonally above me in which I could have seen myself if I hadn't been afraid to try. Below this mirror was a ring of bent-over doctors and nurses in masks, just like a movie. For a moment it seemed so unreal I almost laughed. Then there came an enormous contraction; I let go and hung on and pushed, and felt the baby come halfway out – and stop.

'Wouldn't you like just a little whiff now?' the anaesthetist pleaded.

'No, Leave me alone', I said, waiting for the next contraction.

'It's going to hurt,' the doctor said.

'It feels fine', I said.

'Take some gas. I have to get this little girl out of here,' he said.

'But it doesn't hurt', I said.

'It will hurt,' he shouted. I remembered that Dr Read said most unenlightened doctors carried on in just this way, and I stuck to my guns. 'Take some gas – it's for the baby's sake' the doctor said finally.

'Just a whiff' said the anaesthetist, slipping a mask over my face.

O.K. I thought, if it will please you, just a whiff. As he clamped the mask down I knew he meant to put me out, and I thought to myself: A real sell. I've been had.

'. . . Stuck halfway', the doctor said from a distance.

I twisted my face away from the mask. 'If you'd just let me push,' I said with painful articulation.

'You'll push anyway', he said, and then, as I went under, I thought: Of course – he has to cut me. Why on earth didn't he say so? . . .

*I asked to see Nick; the doctor, who was on his way out (back to his party?) told me I could not go down just yet but that he would tell Nick everything was all right. I thanked him as best I could; I guess we were still a little angry at each other over the anaesthetic business. But I realized suddenly that I was being ungrateful; that, in spite of being annoyed because he had not forewarned me about the cutting, I was glad he had been there and could not have gone through with it alone.
Perhaps that seems rather obvious, but in the exalted state I was then in I was so proud of myself for having done well that I felt as if I had done it all. And then suddenly he was just a tired man going home at midnight after a long day's work, and I wished I had been able to tell him what his work meant to me . . . Abigail Lewis*

Chapter 4
What I found

1. What is normal pregnancy and childbirth?

I would like to talk first about the kinds of difficulties encountered by the women in my sample. In the previous chapter I described three 'criteria of adjustment' aimed at picking up on any problem a woman might encounter during the period I was studying. Two of the measures are self-report measures (i.e. filled in by the women themselves) and one is given by the obstetrician.

The highest proportion of difficulties was reported by the obstetrician in regard to somatic difficulties during pregnancy, difficulty with labour and delivery, problems with the baby. More than half the women had at least one symptom reported on their sheet – to be exact twenty-eight out of the fifty-one women (55%). Out of these twenty-eight women, four had symptoms on more than one of the three scales.

The proportion of difficulties is similar for the other two criteria. Eighteen women (35%) showed some sign of difficulty with the baby and seventeen women (33%) were at least mildly depressed 10 weeks postpartum – roughly one-third of the sample in both cases.

DOCTOR'S SHEET

Let us look more closely at the specific difficulties encountered. Most of the problems reported by the obstetrician referred to the labour and delivery.

The most frequent difficulty was uterine inertia and forceps delivery. There were three breech deliveries (when the baby is in the bottom first position which makes birth more difficult) and one caesarian section. Other difficulties were: postpartum haemorrage (bleeding) of 800 ml; labour induced for mild toxaemia; long labour and forceps delivery due to a large baby; hypotension during labour and use of forceps.

The average length of labour for this group of women was just under 15 hours (the shortest labour was $4\frac{1}{2}$ hours, the longest $34\frac{1}{2}$). The average length of the first stage of labour was just over $13\frac{1}{2}$ hours.

The most frequent symptom reported during pregnancy was hypotension, then came vaginal bleeding, then anaemia and oedema (fluid retained in the tissues) and finally urinary infection. Symptoms in the infant were such things as sticky eye (infection in the eye causing the eyelids to stick together); clicking of hips (baby born with a hip joint which does not articulate normally); baby small for dates; baby irritable for a few days postpartum; rash; baby febrile; baby slightly cyanosed at birth.

These various symptoms were generally given a rating of 2 on the three-point scales. In only three cases were there extreme ratings. One was the caesarian delivery. The two others were cases where the woman's fear was mentioned. One of them was given an epidural injection (injection of anaesthetic which numbs the lower part of the body), the other a general anaesthetic. These were the only cases where the woman's emotions were mentioned.

A rating of 2 on *any* of the three scales classed a woman amongst the women who had difficulties according to the doctor's criterion. Mrs Tisman[1] for example (see Figure 3) is one of them. These measures, as I pointed out earlier, are very crude but sufficient in that I am only distinguishing two groups of women, those with even minor problems and women with no difficulties at all. Since a number of different doctors were involved in the ratings, only such a crude measure would be acceptable in any case.

DEPRESSION QUESTIONNAIRE

One-third of the sample gave some evidence of depression 2–3 months after the birth of the baby. Depression is used here as a shorthand term since anxiety and somatic manifestations are included (Pitt whose test I used calls it 'atypical depression'). Depression is defined by an increase in score on the questionnaire after the birth

[1] For reasons of discretion names and certain other personal details have been changed.

D

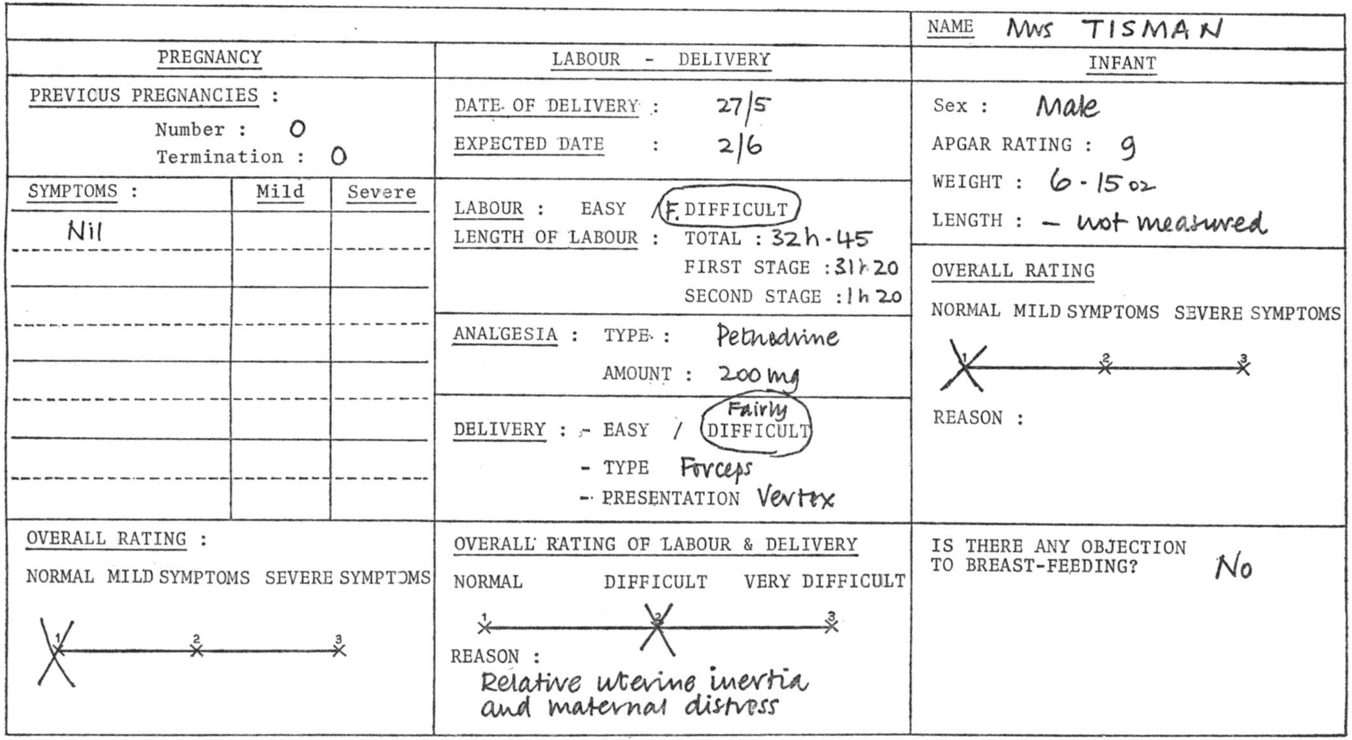

PREGNANCY	LABOUR – DELIVERY	NAME _Mrs TISMAN_
		INFANT

PREGNANCY

PREVIOUS PREGNANCIES :
Number : 0
Termination : 0

SYMPTOMS :

	Mild	Severe
Nil		

OVERALL RATING :

NORMAL MILD SYMPTOMS SEVERE SYMPTOMS

X̶̶̶̶̶ ²X ³X

LABOUR – DELIVERY

DATE OF DELIVERY : 27/5
EXPECTED DATE : 2/6

LABOUR : EASY / F. DIFFICULT
LENGTH OF LABOUR : TOTAL : 32 h · 45
FIRST STAGE : 31 h 20
SECOND STAGE : 1 h 20

ANALGESIA : TYPE : Pethedrine
AMOUNT : 200 mg

DELIVERY : – EASY / (Fairly) DIFFICULT
– TYPE Forceps
– PRESENTATION Vertex

OVERALL RATING OF LABOUR & DELIVERY

NORMAL   DIFFICULT   VERY DIFFICULT

¹X̶̶̶̶̶X² ³X

REASON : Relative uterine inertia
and maternal distress

INFANT

Sex : Male
APGAR RATING : 9
WEIGHT : 6 · 15 oz
LENGTH : – not measured

OVERALL RATING

NORMAL MILD SYMPTOMS SEVERE SYMPTOMS

X̶̶̶̶̶ ²X ³X

REASON :

IS THERE ANY OBJECTION
TO BREAST-FEEDING?   No

Figure 3

Date: Mrs TISMAN   time: prepartum   Confidential

We are asking you these questions in order to find out how you feel about things during this time of having your baby. We want your answers to tell us how you feel at the present time, that is today, or over the past few days.

Please read the questions carefully and then answer as frankly and honestly as you can. Just answer "Yes" or "No" putting a circle round your own answer. If you really cannot make up your mind you may put a circle round "Don't know", but try to avoid this if you can.

Don't spend too much time on any one question, but please don't miss any out. After you have finished the questions you are invited to write a few of your own words about the way you feel in the blank space at the bottom of this form.

At the present time -
1. Do you sleep well?   (Yes)   No   Don't know
2. Do you easily lose your temper?   Yes   (No)   Don't know
3. Are you worried about your looks?   (Yes) No   Don't know 2
4. Have you a good appetite?   (Yes) No   Don't know
5. Are you as happy as you ought to be?   (Yes) No   Don't know
6. Do you easily forget things?   Yes   (No)   Don't know

At the present time -
7. Have you as much interest in sex as ever?   Yes   (No)   Don't know 2
8. Is everything a great effort?   Yes   (No)   Don't know
9. Do you feel ashamed for any reason?   Yes   (No)   Don't know
10. Can you relax easily?   (Yes)   No   Don't know
11. Can you feel the baby is really yours?   (Yes)   No   Don't know
12. Do you want someone with you all the time?   Yes   (No)   Don't know

At the present time -
13. Are you easily woken up?   (Yes)   No   Don't know 2
14. Do you feel calm most of the time?   (Yes)   No   Don't know
15. Do you feel that you are in good health?   (Yes)   No   Don't know
16. Does food interest you less than it did?   (Yes)   No   Don't know 2
17. Do you cry easily?   (Yes)   No   Don't know 2
18. Is your memory as good as it ever was?   (Yes)   No   Don't know

At the present time -
19. Have you less desire for sex than usual?   (Yes)   No   Don't know 2
20. Have you enough energy?   Yes   (No)   Don't know 2
21. Are you satisfied with the way you're
        coping with things?   (Yes)   No   Don't know
22. Do you worry a lot about the baby?   (Yes)   No   Don't know 2
23. Do you feel unlike your normal self?   (Yes)   No   Don't know 2
24. Do you have confidence in yourself?   (Yes)   No   Don't know

Is there anything you want to add about your feelings at the moment? If so please write it here.

Total = (18)

Figure 4

relative to before.[1] Mrs Tisman's score (see Figure 4) is higher postpartum than prepartum (the score prepartum is eighteen; the score postpartum is thirty-two)[2]. Postpartum, in addition to the

[1] Brice Pitt used a stricter criterion than I did. He only classified as depressed those women whose score increased by more than six points after the birth of the baby. I, on the other hand, considered together *any* increase in score. Here again I am concerned with even minor difficulties.

[2] Brice Pitt's scoring procedure: 'The pattern of morbid answers is easily remembered, viz:

    1st 6 questions: No, Yes, Yes, No, No, Yes

Date: **Mrs TISMAN**   time : *Postpartum*   Confidential

We are asking you these questions in order to find out how you feel about things during this time of having your baby. We want your answers to tell us how you feel at the present time, that is today, or over the past few days.

Please read the questions carefully and then answer as frankly and honestly as you can. Just answer "Yes" or "No" putting a circle round your own answer. If you really cannot make up your mind you may put a circle round "Don't know", but try to avoid this if you can.

Don't spend too much time on any one question, but please don't miss any out. After you have finished the questions you are invited to write a few of your own words about the way you feel in the blank space at the bottom of this form.

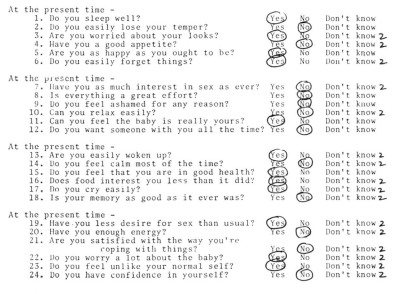

At the present time -
1. Do you sleep well? (Yes) No Don't know
2. Do you easily lose your temper? Yes (No) Don't know
3. Are you worried about your looks? (Yes) No Don't know 2
4. Have you a good appetite? Yes (No) Don't know 2
5. Are you as happy as you ought to be? (Yes) No Don't know
6. Do you easily forget things? (Yes) No Don't know 2

At the present time -
7. Have you as much interest in sex as ever? Yes (No) Don't know 2
8. Is everything a great effort? Yes (No) Don't know
9. Do you feel ashamed for any reason? Yes (No) Don't know
10. Can you relax easily? Yes (No) Don't know 2
11. Can you feel the baby is really yours? (Yes) No Don't know
12. Do you want someone with you all the time? Yes (No) Don't know

At the present time -
13. Are you easily woken up? (Yes) No Don't know 2
14. Do you feel calm most of the time? Yes (No) Don't know 2
15. Do you feel that you are in good health? (Yes) No Don't know
16. Does food interest you less than it did? (Yes) No Don't know 2
17. Do you cry easily? (Yes) No Don't know 2
18. Is your memory as good as it ever was? Yes (No) Don't know 2

At the present time -
19. Have you less desire for sex than usual? (Yes) No Don't know 2
20. Have you enough energy? Yes (No) Don't know 2
21. Are you satisfied with the way you're coping with things? Yes (No) Don't know 2
22. Do you worry a lot about the baby? (Yes) No Don't know 2
23. Do you feel unlike your normal self? (Yes) No Don't know 2
24. Do you have confidence in yourself? Yes (No) Don't know 2

Is there anything you want to add about your feelings at the moment? If so please write it here.

Total = (32)

Figure 4 *continued*

problem areas she mentions the first time, Mrs Tisman mentions a poor appetite and bad memory, a difficulty to relax, be calm, have confidence in herself and cope with things.

An example of a very large increase in depression score is Mrs

---

2nd 6 questions: No, Yes, Yes, No, No, Yes
3rd 6 questions: Yes, No, No, Yes, Yes, No
4th 6 questions: Yes, No, No, Yes, Yes, No
A morbid answer scores two points, "Don't know" one, and a healthy answer nothing. The maximum score is forty-eight points.'

Ramsey. Her score increases by twenty-four points.[1] The problems reflected in such an increase, she describes in her own words: 'I feel confused most of the time – with thoughts of birth and life in general. . . . I think of the miracle of life: how something can come out of nothing. It's not a pleasant feeling'. Other women have expressed similar concerns but have not described it as unpleasant. She feels she cannot cope with things and fears to be on her own with the baby.

What areas of difficulty are in fact being tapped by the questionnaire? A 'principal component analysis' is a statistical analysis which enables one to find out which questions 'clump' together and which clusters of questions are more important for a particular group of people. During pregnancy, the most important cluster referred to confidence and anxiety. Questions such as 'Do you feel calm most of the time?' (Question 14) and 'Do you have confidence in yourself?' (Question 24). The second most important cluster related to sex: 'Have you as much interest in sex as ever?' (Question 7), 'Have you less desire for sex than usual?' (Question 19). The third component related to what I called ergic tension: 'Do you easily forget things?' (Question 6), 'Is your memory as good as it ever was?' (Question 18), 'Have you enough energy?' (Question 20).

Postpartum the most important cluster refers to confidence: 'Do you have confidence in yourself?' (Question 24); anxiety is less relevant now. The second cluster relates to sex again but also this time to food ('Does food interest you less than it did?' – Question 16) and to shame ('Do you feel ashamed for any reason?' Question 9). The third cluster is quite different. It relates to the acceptance of motherhood: 'Can you feel the baby is really yours?' (Question 11) and 'Do you want someone with you all the time?' (Question 12).

The main differences between pregnancy and postpartum are the association of shame, sex and food on the second component postpartum and the composition of the third component which refers to a relationship postpartum, the feeling of being a mother and of coping with the situation and being the responsible one. Also, whereas before the birth of the child the area of main concern involved anxiety as well as self confidence, after the birth of the child, when the women are no longer anticipating a situation but are actually confronted with it, self confidence remains important but anxiety is no longer very

[1] Since a morbid answer scores two points, this means that twelve more questions give evidence of difficulties postpartum.

relevant. This makes sense if we think of anxiety as a state in which a danger, particularly an unknown one, is anticipated.

To sum up:

	Pregnancy	Postpartum
Component 1	Anxiety and confidence	Confidence
Component 2	Sexual interest	Drives (food and sex) and shame
Component 3	Memory and energy	Acceptance of motherhood

During pregnancy more than half the women said they were easily woken up (Question 13), that they cried easily (Question 17), that they had less desire for sex (Question 19) and not enough energy (Question 20). Postpartum more than half the women were worried about their looks (Question 3) and were easily woken up (Question 13).

The main shifts for this sample are as follows: after the birth of the child many women become more interested in sex, find they do not cry so easily and find that they are more like their normal self. The latter is interesting. More women feel unlike their normal self during pregnancy than after the birth of the baby – a conception of pregnancy as an abnormal state since the question is not 'Do you feel unlike your usual self?' but 'Do you feel unlike your normal self?'. I should imagine that this response is at least in part culturally determined.

BABY QUESTIONNAIRE (Neonatal Perception Inventory)

Just over one third of the women gave evidence of some difficulty with their baby. This is defined by a worse rating for 'own baby' than for 'average baby'.

Mrs Millard, for example, had an easy labour and delivery though she had to be induced for postmaturity. She was disappointed when the doctor said she would have a large baby as she would prefer a little one: 'the little ones are more cuddly – you miss out if they are big'; she had worked as a nurse with premature babies and 'loved the babies there'. With all this concern about prematurity and post-maturity, I found it amusing when, as I arrived for the last interview, she said to me: 'you're dead on time' (reminding me of Mrs Temple who greeted me in late pregnancy with 'you haven't changed').

Mrs Millard rated her baby as having more difficulty than the

AVERAGE BABY   *Mrs Millard*

Although this is your first baby, you probably have some ideas of what most little babies are like. Please check the blank you think best describes the AVERAGE baby.

How much crying do you think the average baby does?

_____ _____ _____ ___✓___ ___ 2
a great deal   a good bit   moderate amount   very little   none

How much trouble do you think the average baby has in feeding?

_____ _____ ___✓___ _____ ___ 3
a great deal   a good bit   moderate amount   very little   none

How much spitting up or vomiting do you think the average baby does?

_____ _____ _____ ___✓___ ___ 2
a great deal   a good bit   moderate amount   very little   none

How much difficulty do you think the average baby has in sleeping?

_____ ___✓___ _____ _____ ___ 4
a great deal   a good bit   moderate amount   very little   none

How much difficulty does the average baby have with bowel movements?

_____ _____ _____ ___✓___ ___ 2
a great deal   a good bit   moderate amount   very little   none

How much trouble do you think the average baby has in settling down to a predictable pattern of eating and sleeping?

_____ _____ _____ ___✓___ ___ 2
a great deal   a good bit   moderate amount   very little   none

Total   15

Average baby minus your baby = 15 - 20 = (-5)

Figure 5

average baby in the areas of crying, vomiting, bowel movements and settling to a pattern. The total score was negative (see Figure 5) Mrs Millard breast-fed her baby for two weeks but 'he wasn't satisfied; he cried every two hours'. She is disappointed because he is not a 'good baby' and hadn't expected him to be so 'naughty'. She experienced difficulty with food herself: throughout pregnancy she vomited and this continued even after the baby was born. Just as she expected her baby to be a perfect baby, this woman expects herself to be a perfect mother; being a good mother to her implies 'not enjoying myself' and not 'being interested in life'.[1] Mrs Millard's

[1] These are descriptive terms given on the grid.

YOUR BABY   *Mrs Millard*

You have had a chance to live with your baby for about 2 months now. Please check the blank you think best describes your baby.

How much crying has your baby done?

a great deal	a good bit ✓	moderate amount	very little	none

4

How much trouble has your baby had feeding?

a great deal	a good bit	moderate amount ✓	very little	none

3

How much spitting up or vomiting has your baby done?

a great deal	a good bit	moderate amount ✓	very little	none

3

How much difficulty has your baby had in sleeping?

a great deal	a good bit	moderate amount ✓	very little	none

3

How much difficulty has your baby had with bowel movements?

a great deal	a good bit ✓	moderate amount	very little	none

4

How much trouble has your baby had in settling down to a predictable pattern of eating and sleeping?

a great deal	a good bit	moderate amount ✓	very little	none

3

Total 20

Figure 5 *continued*

negative score on the baby questionnaire seems to me to reflect a problematic relationship on a background of rigid expectations.

COMBINING THE THREE CRITERIA

The relationship between these criteria is loose: this means that a low score on one of them does not predict a low score on the others. Therefore different areas of difficulties are being tapped as I had anticipated. The criteria served to form three groups:

1. *a well-adjusted group:* women in this group showed no evidence of disturbance on any measure. There are eleven women in this group (22%).
2. *a medium-adjusted group:* women in this group showed evidence of disturbance on any one of the three criteria. There are twenty-one women in this group (42%).

3. *an ill-adjusted group:* women in this group showed evidence of disturbance on two or all three criteria. There are eighteen women in this group (36%).[1]

The women in each of these groups are broadly comparable in terms of age (mean age in all groups is 24) and length of marriage (mean length of marriage is 1·8 years in the well-adjusted group, 2·4 in the medium-adjusted and 1·9 in the ill-adjusted group). There is however a slight tendency for the ill-adjusted women, though the mean age is similar, to be either younger or older than the women in the well-adjusted group; the youngest and the oldest women almost all belong to the two problem groups. Seven women are 20 years of age or younger. Five out of the seven belong to the group encountering most difficulties, and the two others to the intermediary group. Of the five women in their thirties, two belong to the group with most difficulties, two to the intermediary group and one to the group without difficulties. This latter difference is probably only due to the difference in size of the groups. In the case of the younger women, however, there does seem to be a difference worth noting – perhaps a greater susceptibility to experiencing difficulties. Since the women should be physiologically well fit for childbearing, it may be that they are not psychologically ready to have a child. The five women in the ill-adjusted group who were 20 or younger all said at the first interview that the child was not planned, three of them conceived before they were married. One of the two women in the medium-adjusted group said that the child was not planned (both these women were married). It is the combination of a conception before marriage (possibly precipitating a marriage which might not have taken place) and a young age which seems important. In the well-adjusted group two women were unmarried at the time of conception but both of them were over 20 (one was in her thirties).

The actual planning of the pregnancy does not seem important. Actually a higher proportion of women in the ill-adjusted group reported at the first interview that this pregnancy was planned (66%) than in the well-adjusted group (54%) or the medium-adjusted group (57%). The question of planning is complex. There is a difference between the woman who gets married and uses no contraception though she doesn't particularly want a child at this time, and the woman who stops using an effective method of contraception

[1] As the data is incomplete for one woman the total sample is 50.

in order to conceive. Yet both might respond that the child is planned. What about the woman who is using a not very effective method of contraception? She might say that the child is not planned, and yet, she might in some ways have wished the child. I didn't in fact systematically ask about contraception but a number of women conceived within a month or two of marriage which suggests that they were either using no contraceptive measure or a very ineffective one; and yet when asked they said that this pregnancy was un-planned. In such cases it is difficult to say if it is a question of an 'unconscious wish to have a child' or, more likely, in the case where it is not planned and there is no contraception, a sort of splitting off of sexuality from conception, or a denial of an internal reproductive system. Actual real lack of information seems fairly unlikely in this group of women. Perhaps saying that the pregnancy was unplanned in some cases reflected the feeling that they had not decided that it would be this particular month rather than the last or the next (which says something about the need to always be in control, even of our bodies, in our present culture).

So I don't think that to ask if the child is planned says very much about the wish to have a child though it may say something about what a person feels they ought to be saying – the more insecure women being more likely to say in doubtful cases that it was planned.

Let us come back to the figures presented earlier: 22% of the women gave no evidence of difficulty around the time of childbearing. This means that 78% of the women presented some problem. In fact this is probably a conservative estimate if we consider the fact that the criteria refer to specific points in time. For instance, those women who were not depressed by the time of the last interview might have gone through a phase of depression earlier on. If we think of 'nor-mality' as referring to what is the norm, then we could say that it is normal to experience difficulties at this time. What it is probably more correct to say is that women are, at this time, in a state of particular stress and upheaval and therefore particularly sensitive to experiencing difficulties. It may not in any case be appropriate to talk about pathol-ogy if problems are so prevalent at this time. It is however important to compare those women who seem free from psychological and physiological difficulties with those who have the greatest difficulties. This will help towards an understanding of the processes involved in a healthy adjustment to the birth of a first child. As Maslow (1969) points out, there is a place in psychology for the study of the healthiest people rather than of the average if we are to understand human potentialities.

2. Changes in self-concept and perception of family members, changes in preoccupations

For the purpose of clarity I will describe separately the changes in self-concept and perception of family members and in preoccupations which took place in the well-adjusted group of women and those which took place in the ill adjusted group of women. The statistical analysis was in fact done in terms of a comparison between these two extreme groups.[1]

Let me remind you briefly how I looked at these changes. Each woman was given a 'Grid' early in pregnancy, late in pregnancy and 10 weeks after the birth of the baby (we will here be considering the first and last ones). Each Grid consists of descriptive terms chosen by a particular woman at a particular time and the rank ordering of seven people (self, mother, father, husband, a motherly person, an immature person, the 'ideal mother') on each of these personal descriptive terms. One of these descriptive terms refers to what the woman thinks is the most important quality for a mother ('motherhood construct').

In the findings I will now present, I am interested in two main things: Firstly how a woman sees herself in relation to another person regardless of what terms she uses to describe these people (that is, how similar or different she thinks she is from this person at a particular time) and how this changes over time; Secondly in what ways she perceives herself and others at a particular time (that is, what words she actually uses) and how this changes over time, how she tends to structure her environment and what motherliness means to her at different times. I will give examples of particular cases to illustrate the general processes I have found to be operating. I will also describe cases which did not follow these processes.

A. WOMEN IN THE WELL-ADJUSTED GROUP

The women in this group see themselves as *more similar to their own mother after the birth* of the child than they did early in pregnancy.

This is as predicted.

[1] See the Appendix for the actual analysis.

Mrs King, a young woman of 24, only just married, described her mother, at the beginning of pregnancy, as 'selfish' and 'ambitious', 'inclined to spoil children too much' and 'doesn't believe in punishing children'. She sees herself at this time as more easy-going and less selfish than her mother.[1] After the birth of the child she now describes her mother and herself very similarly. Both are 'concerned for others', 'careful with money' and somewhat 'overconcerned with children'. The change lies in her perceiving her mother and to some extent herself as much less selfish postpartum, and in the introduction of a new factor, the financial aspect.

In the case of Mrs Rand, aged 23, married for nearly two years and like Mrs King involved in nursing, things are reversed. Early in pregnancy she describes herself as more selfish than her mother, as 'irresponsible' but gifted with a 'good sense of humour'; she sees her mother as patient, intelligent, commonsensical and hardworking. After the birth of the baby, as with Mrs King, she and her mother move together but unlike her, she and her mother are now both seen as neither generous, commonsensical nor intelligent.

In both cases, self and mother become more similar after the birth of the baby but in the first case Mrs King's mother, from being seen in negative terms is now described more positively, whereas in the second case Mrs Rand's mother becomes described more negatively. In both cases other factors appear or disappear; for Mrs King, being careful with money is important postpartum, for Mrs Rand, having a sense of humour ceases to be a factor of consideration.

There is a problem, however, in that what I describe as a positive quality may not necessarily be what the woman herself considers to be a positive quality, or at least not when it comes to the area of motherliness. Furthermore, when I describe how a woman sees herself or her mother I pick out the salient words (given by the statistical analysis); but there are other words which, though less important perhaps, go to make the total picture. For these reasons I introduced the notion of the 'ideal mother' – 'your own personal view of a good mother'; this will enable me to talk about positive and negative evaluation of self and mother in the woman's own eyes. I can now refine

[1] When I describe how a woman sees herself and others I am referring to the two-component graph given by a principal component analysis. This graph gives a picture of the two main dimensions in which a person thinks and where he or she places people in terms of these two dimensions. See Graph 1 (page 69) for an example of a two-component graph.

the previous hypothesis. I predicted that:

When a woman sees *her own mother as a good mother*[1] *after the birth* of the baby, whether or not this is the case during pregnancy, she describes *herself and her mother* as becoming *more similar* to each other after the birth of the baby. On the contrary, when her *mother is described as a bad mother after the birth of* the baby, whether or not this is so during pregnancy, she perceives *herself and her mother* as becoming *more dissimilar* after the birth of the baby.

This prediction is indeed confirmed. This process occurred for eight out of the eleven women in this group.

There are four different possible patterns.

1. The woman perceives her mother to be a good mother both early in pregnancy and in the postpartum period. She perceives herself and her mother to be more similar to each other after the birth of the child than during pregnancy. This is the most frequent pattern, followed by four women.

   Mrs Marshall belonged to this subgroup; both during pregnancy and postpartum her mother and the ideal mother (seen as 'interested in the home' and 'not dominant') are relatively similar; they become slightly more similar to each other in the postpartum period.

2. The woman perceives her own mother to be a bad mother when she is first interviewed, but at the last interview she comes to see her as a good mother with whom she identifies. This is the second most frequent pattern, followed by three women.

   Mrs Longman, an actress and singer in her mid-twenties very recently married, illustrates this process. Early in pregnancy she says that she 'laughs at things', 'likes to tell jokes', is 'eccentric' and 'romantic'. Her mother she sees as 'jealous', 'has more give and take', 'never classifies anything as "mine" in the family. In a sense, her mother is more involved in the family than she is. The ideal mother is placed between these two poles, but much nearer herself. After the birth of the baby, mother and ideal mother have come together and are now both described as 'homely', 'understanding', 'motherly' and 'loving'. Her perception of herself is now more similar to that of her mother; this is due more to a change in her perception of her mother than of herself who she describes as 'jovial', 'forward' and 'musical'.

---

[1] Statistically, 'good mother' means that the distance between mother and ideal mother is smaller than a random distance between two elements on the grid, 'bad mother' means that the distance between mother and ideal mother is equal or larger than a random distance between two elements on the grid.

Mrs King described earlier also belongs to this subgroup. In her case the change in her perception of her mother is even greater; from being seen as selfish during pregnancy she is seen as concerned for others postpartum.

3. The woman perceives her mother to be a good mother early in pregnancy. However, in the postpartum period she now sees her as a bad mother from whom she becomes more dissimilar. One woman follows this pattern.

Mrs Line is in her thirties. She owns a shop. During pregnancy her mother, the ideal mother and herself are all described as 'precise', 'aware', 'artistic' and 'able to cope on their own', though her mother tends to be more 'highly strung' and 'independent' than the other two. After the birth of the child she sees herself and the ideal mother as 'responsible', 'organized', 'diligent' and 'understanding', the ideal mother being more 'affectionate', 'unselfish' and 'realistic' than she is. Her mother is now seen as very different from either herself or the ideal mother and at the opposite end to any of the descriptive terms used. She is neither affectionate nor easy going, nor mechanically minded, etc. No word is used to describe her directly. Actually Mrs Line's mother died not long before she conceived and it is possible that the recent death and the changes during her own pregnancy have come to blur and confuse her picture of her mother. Her father, who died a number of years prior to her mother, is described very similarly both times. Perhaps she had more time to come to terms with his death and reconstruct for herself an image of him.

4. The woman sees her mother as a bad mother both early in pregnancy and after the birth of the child. She sees herself as more dissimilar to her mother in the postpartum period. None of the women in the well-adjusted group followed this pattern.

Three out of the eleven women follow none of these four patterns.

For Mrs Down and Mrs Craft, their own mother is seen as a good mother both early in pregnancy and later on after the birth of the baby, and they see themselves as less similar to her in the postpartum period. However the move is very small so that, in both cases, even after the child is born, self and mother are still perceived quite similarly. The process therefore is almost like pattern 1.

The third woman, Mrs Laing, shows a different pattern. Early in pregnancy her ideal mother is 'understanding' and 'modern in thoughts'. She herself is neither of these but on the contrary is 'reserved', 'quiet' and 'inclined to take things said against the family in the wrong way'. Her mother is different from herself or the ideal mother; she is 'experienced', 'careful with money', 'inclined to worry' and 'not interested in modern clothes or pop music'. After the birth of the baby, she describes her mother and ideal mother similarly: 'understanding', 'interested in family life' and 'inclined to worry'. She is now herself at polar opposites to her mother, she is 'modern in outlook' and 'enjoys music'. The following has happened: her view of the ideal mother has changed considerably and become more like that of her own mother. She has herself moved considerably: she becomes more carefree and less interested in family life. When I interviewed Mrs Laing for the third time she was living with her parents because, she said, 'my husband is away a lot'. Mrs Laing's mother was there and told me about the time when she had had her children. Perhaps the grid reflects Mrs Laing's giving over of the mother role to her own mother with whom she is now living again while she becomes the carefree daughter. This would explain the changed conception of the ideal mother who, like her mother, becomes more involved in family life, and her own disinterest in this.

Out of these eleven cases, seven women see their mother as a good mother at the beginning of pregnancy. After the birth of the child, only one woman, Mrs Line (who's mother died shortly before her pregnancy) does not perceive her mother to be a good mother. There is therefore a tendency for these well-adjusted women to view their mothers positively early in pregnancy and, when this is not the case, to re-evaluate them at this time so that they perceive them positively after they themselves become mothers.

We can also look at how each woman sees herself in the mothering role. I predicted that after the birth of the child the well-adjusted woman would see herself as *more in the good mothering role* than early in pregnancy. This is the case. There is for the group as a whole an increase in similarity between self and ideal mother. It is true of eight women. For one woman the distance remains identical. In three of the eight cases the move is considerable.

During pregnancy, Mrs Dare thinks the ideal mother is 'patient', 'able to show feelings' and 'hospitable'. The reverse is true of herself; also she tends to be 'smothering' and 'cautious with money'. After the birth of the baby, Mrs Dare slightly reconstrues the ideal mother now seen as 'patient' but also 'conscientious' and 'careful with money' (feelings are no longer involved). This is fairly similar to her present description of herself though she is more 'happy-go-lucky' and 'scatter brain' than the ideal mother. Smothering does not come into the picture this time. The redefinition here involves both herself and the ideal mother.

In the two cases where the distance between self and ideal mother increased, this distance in fact remained small postpartum, in other words they still saw themselves as good mothers at this time.

Combining the two previous processes (the changed perception of self in relation to mother depending on whether the latter is seen as a good or a bad mother, and the increase in similarity between self and ideal mother) we find that seven of the women move in the predicted direction (64%).

The two patterns which now occur are the following:

1. mother is seen as a good mother both early in pregnancy and postpartum and there is, postpartum, a greater similarity between self and mother and between self and ideal mother (four women).
2. mother is seen as a bad mother early in pregnancy; postpartum however she is reconstrued as being a good mother with whom the woman can identify as well as see herself as more similar to the ideal mother (three women).

Adding this second criterion (increased similarity between self and ideal mother) one woman drops out. This is Mrs Line, the only woman who followed the third pattern (she came to consider her mother postpartum as a bad one and moved away from her). She sees herself as more dissimilar to the ideal mother postpartum.

In sum, women who adjust well to the birth of their child tend to perceive their own mother positively, at least postpartum and through this are able to value themselves as mothers. The psychoanalytic idea of the 'internalized mother' is relevant here: what is important is not so much the actual parent as the image the person has of the parent. The 'good mother image' is part of the woman's psychological makeup and she can use it in her mothering of her child. Those women who can conjure up such an image are more likely to value themselves as mothers. In nine of the ten cases where mother is seen as a good mother postpartum, the woman also views herself as a good mother. In the one case where mother is seen as a bad mother postpartum, the woman sees herself as less like the ideal mother postpartum (although she still views herself as a fairly good mother).

I predicted that the women in the well-adjusted group would perceive a *greater dissimilarity between themselves and their husbands* after the birth of the child than in pregnancy. This is indeed the case.

Nine out of the eleven women (81%) perceived themselves as being less like their husbands postpartum.

Early in pregnancy Mrs Down describes herself and her husband similarly though she is more 'reserved' and 'understanding of children' than he is. After the birth of the child she and her husband are described quite differently. He is a 'good mixer' and 'not so children oriented'; she is 'more settled', 'home oriented', 'understanding of children' and 'carefree with money'.

Mrs Marshall also ascribes to a traditional division of roles. Early in pregnancy when she still lives at home (she conceived before marriage) she describes herself, as 'interested in the home', 'likes to be at home' and 'a person one can talk to'. Her husband is 'ambitious', 'sporty', 'aware of what is going on', 'domineering' and 'likes to go out different places'. The descriptions are fairly similar postpartum but the difference between the partners is even greater.

In other cases something different from this role differentiation seems to be operating. There is a process whereby one partner is feeling well while the other one is experiencing difficulties.

Mrs Dare describes herself and her husband similarly early in pregnancy though she sees him as somewhat more like the ideal mother than she sees herself. After the birth of the baby, she is 'happy-go-lucky' and relatively 'patient' while he becomes 'moody' 'bad tempered', 'inhospitable' and 'vain' and much less like the ideal mother than she now is.

A similar process takes place with Mrs Cooper. From seeing herself and her husband both as 'extrovert', 'like to have a drink' and enjoy to travel' she comes to see herself, postpartum, as 'easy going', 'enjoys her work' while her husband becomes 'moody' and 'unreasonable'.

Mrs Dare has been married for two years, Mrs Cooper for four so it seems more likely that indeed the husbands are experiencing difficulties rather than that the women change radically their perception of them.

In two other cases the reverse takes place.

Mrs Craft describes herself and her husband similarly early in pregnancy; both 'tend to have an inferiority complex'; he is somewhat more 'adventurous' and 'possessive', she is slightly 'kinder' and 'independent', 'home loving' and 'patient'. After the birth of the baby they become very different from each other. He is 'placid' and 'kind' whereas she is 'moody', she 'worries' and 'nags'.

Similarly with Mrs Rand who sees both her husband and herself as 'irresponsible', 'intellectual' and as having a 'sense of humour', early in pregnancy. Postpartum, her husband is 'intelligent' 'friendly' and 'generous' (not very different from the ideal mother) while she is none of these things.

Both Mrs Craft and Mrs Rand have been married for nearly two years.

In these last four cases, the increased dissimilarity between self and husband is not due to a role differentiation but must have another meaning. As seen by the women, one of the partners expresses the difficulties postpartum while the other is free from conflict. It is striking that in these four cases, husband and wife are described very similarly during pregnancy. It may be that the relationship was a very close rather symbiotic one which had more difficulty in tolerating the arrival of a third person; one of the partners feels excluded and becomes bad tempered. Mrs Craft actually used the word 'possessive' as one of her descriptive terms. This may be reflecting a concern with sharing.

Content

Up till now I have been considering the changes in perception of self and family members. Let us go on to look at the *content* of the construct systems.

Maternal dimension. If you remember, each woman produced in the first session a 'maternal construct' in response to my question about the most important quality for a mother. At subsequent testing sessions I gave each woman her maternal construct back reminding her that she had chosen it because she felt this was the most important quality for a mother. This enables me to find out which of the other constructs in each woman's grid are used in a similar fashion to this one (in statistical terminology, which of the constructs correlate significantly with the maternal construct). I call this set of constructs the 'maternal dimension'. It can contain from one (when no other construct is used in this fashion) to eleven constructs (when all are used similarly).

I predicted that the women in the well-adjusted group would *increase their use of constructs relating* in their own mind *to motherliness*, since they would become more accepting of motherhood after the birth of the baby.

This is not the case. The average number of constructs in the maternal dimension is 3·8 early in pregnancy, and 3·4 postpartum. I will discuss this later when I come to consider the ill-adjusted women.

Looking at the actual *verbal designation of the constructs in the maternal dimension*, there is a decrease, after the birth of the baby, in words relating to feelings and relationships. Such words as 'loving', 'has give and take', 'thinks of others' come up twice as frequently early in pregnancy in comparison to postpartum. On the contrary such words as 'diligent', 'hardworking' and 'reliable' come up postpartum only.

The table opposite gives the number of times each of the different categories of words are used (I will only give the most frequently used categories).

During pregnancy, the important qualities are seen in more idealistic terms (give and take, unselfish etc.) than postpartum when the ability to work well and hard, an interest in home and in children become more focal. This is facing reality!

Mrs Dare feels that the most important quality for a mother is 'patience'. Early in pregnancy this is associated with being 'hospitable', 'able to show feelings, in particular affection' without being smothering. This is no longer the case postpartum, when patience becomes associated with being 'conscientious' and not being 'scatterbrain'.

This switch from the emotional to the more practical aspect of the

Table 1: *Most frequently used constructs by the well-adjusted women within the maternal dimension.*

	Early pregnancy (Number of times the category is used)	Postpartum (Number of times the category is used)	
Loving, affectionate, kind, motherly	6	4	*
Has give and take, not smothering, someone you can talk to, able to make a relationship	3	1	*
Thinks of others, not selfish, not self-centred, understanding, sympathetic, tactful, considerate	9	4	*
Patient, tolerant	6	6	
Diligent, hardworking, reliable, responsible, conscientious, not scatterbrain, not lazy	0	5	†
Home loving, settled, homely, domesticated	1	3	†
Understands children, sentimental about children, child oriented, knows about babies	3	4	†

* Decrease postpartum   † Increase postpartum

mothering role is interesting and says something about the idealized culturally encouraged conception of motherhood versus the reality of the situation of caring for a small child.

The maternal dimension can be considered to form a grid on its own and the other constructs disregarded. On this new grid (which is a partial grid) similar processes take place as those described for the total grid. There is a tendency for self and mother to be described more similarly and for self and husband to be described less similarly on this maternal dimension postpartum than during pregnancy.

However, contrary to the total grid, self and ideal mother are described less similarly postpartum. This seems to reflect an increased self criticalness in relation to the maternal role. I will discuss this too when I come to look at the ill-adjusted group.

Total grid. I put together and categorized all the constructs elicited except the maternal construct (since it remained the same throughout) in order to see if the content of the grids tended to be different postpartum. This time I will list the categories in order of importance separately for early pregnancy and postpartum. I will list the percentage of time each of the categories is used for the total sample

Table 2: *Most frequently used constructs in the well-adjusted group at Time 1.*

	Well-adjusted group Time 1 %
1. Old fashioned, not modern, traditional taste, fashion conscious, square	5·4
2. Wrapped up in children, show affection to children, gets on with children, family person, like to have a nice cosy family, settled, domesticated, interested in the home, likes settling down, satisfied staying home	4·5
3. Enjoys life, carefree, gay, easy going, jovial, jolly, free and easy, happy-go-lucky, gay, likes going out, fun loving	5·5
4. Motherly, kind, soft, loving nature, affectionate, generous, shares, would help someone	3·6
5. Selfish, thinks of him-or herself only, steps on others, self-centred, uses people, is not helpful, does not do a lot for others	3·6
6. Mind of her or his own, independent, stands up for her or himself, does not need someone else, can talk outright, outspoken, self reliant	3·6
7. Likes meeting people, extroverted, sociable, gregarious, mixes with people well, likes social life, hospitable	3·6
8. Mature, adult, not childish, not adolescent	3·6
9. Good at handling money, worries about money, saves money, careful with money, has money, mean with money, spends a lot of money	3·6
10. Reserved, shy, does not show feelings, not open, not demonstrative, inhibited	3·6
11. Moody, temperamental, snaps at slightest thing, quick tempered, not placid	2·7
12. Agitated, not calm, highly strung, nervous, not relaxed, not patient, nervous	2·7
13. Stubborn, dogmatic, obstinate, does not make concessions, unreasonable, can't talk things out, not flexible, not receptive, won't give in, cannot see reason, does not give in easily	2·7
14. Sense of humour, tells jokes, quick witted	2·7

Table 3 : *Most frequently used constructs in the well-adjusted group at Time 3.*

	Well-adjusted group Time 3
1. Moody, temperamental, snaps at slightest thing, quick tempered, not placid	6·3
2. Wrapped up in children, shows affection to children, gets on with children, family person, likes to have a nice cosy family, settled, domesticated, interested in the home, likes to be at home, likes settling down, satisfied staying at home	5·4
3. Likes sports, likes cars, likes driving, mechanically minded	5·4
4. Not lazy, diligent, tidy, keeps at things, organized, conscientious, hardworking	5·4
5. Enjoys life, carefree, gay, easy going, jovial, jolly, free and easy, happy-go-lucky, gay, likes going out, fun loving	5·4
6. Motherly, kind, soft, loving nature, affectionate, generous, shares, would help someone	4·5
7. Good at handling money, worries about money, saves money, careful with money, has money, mean with money, spends a lot of money	4·5
8. Responsible, sense of duty, dependable, reliable, faithful, keeps promises, honest, sincere	3·6
9. Likes meeting people, extroverted, sociable, gregarious, mixes with people well, likes social life, hospitable	3·6
10. Worries, does not take things lightly	2·7
11. Old fashioned, not modern, traditional taste, fashion conscious, square	2·7
12. Tolerant, broad-minded, not petty-minded	2·7

(To make this more directly readable I have sometimes phrased the constructs the other way round. For instance 'not lazy' rather than 'lazy' to go with 'diligent'—since the direction is not relevant)

(there are 110 constructs for these 11 women at each testing time). I will only list categories used more than 2·5% of the time.

As can be seen from the tables above, the greatest change involves the swelling of the category referring to moodiness and quick temper. These become the most frequently used constructs post-partum. The increased preoccupation with the more practical qualities such as diligence and the decreased preoccupation with more idealistic notions of unselfishness which I noted in connection with the maternal dimension, are also evident when the total grid is considered.

An overview

Having looked at specific aspects of the grids let us now consider each woman's grid in its totality and understand the kinds of changes taking place for this group of well-adjusted women.

Two women construe things similarly during pregnancy and after the birth of the baby. Both of them construe the maternal role in very traditional terms and give no evidence of any conflict with this role.

Mrs Marshall, just like her mother and her ideal mother, is 'interested in the home' and 'likes being at home'. On the contrary both her husband and her father 'like going out places', are 'domineering' and 'have tempers'. After the birth of the baby there is a similar split between herself, her mother and the ideal mother who are 'happy to be in the house' and 'not dominant' and her husband who is 'ambitious' and 'enjoys sports'.

This satisfaction and identification with a traditional role is also present with Mrs Down. After the birth of the baby even more so than before, there is a clear division between, on the one hand her mother and herself who, like the ideal mother, are 'soft where children are concerned', 'home birds', 'understanding of children' and 'settled', and her husband and father who are neither keen on animals nor children but like travelling and cars.

Four other women do not change much their overall perception but they do modify their conception of what a good mother should be like.

During pregnancy, Mrs Longman, thinks that the ideal mother is 'loving', 'romantic', 'affectionate', 'artistic' and 'has more give and take'. After the birth of the baby the ideal mother is 'homely' as well as 'jovial'. She seems to have been able to integrate the sense of family which her mother had ('never classes anything as "mine" when the family is concerned') and her own eccentricity and ability to entertain which were previously somewhat separate; 'homely' and 'jovial' are now linked. This may make it possible for her to continue without conflict her career as an actress as she wishes to.

For Mrs Cooper there is a marked conflict early in pregnancy. The ideal mother she perceives to be neither independent, nor interested in going out to work, nor interested in travelling or having a drink. Mrs Cooper clearly feels rather ambivalent about the mothering role: she construes the ideal mother as 'mature' but also 'neurotic'. Although after the birth of the baby the same split still operates between being a good mother and having an interest in social life, the ideal mother is no longer seen as neurotic. Mrs Cooper can identify more with the role seen in this new light and is quite happy since she now sees herself as 'easy going', 'enjoy my work', 'not moody'.

During pregnancy, the ideal mother is 'even tempered' and has a 'sense of humour' for Mrs Soper. Postpartum she is 'patient' and has 'stamina'.

Mrs Laing's conception of the ideal mother changes radically. She first describes the ideal mother as being 'understanding', 'modern in thoughts' and 'lively' and 'not inclined to worry'. After the birth of the baby, the description is diametrically opposed. The ideal mother is now 'not modern' and 'inclined to worry' and 'involved in family life'. If you remember Mrs Laing came to live with her parents after the baby was born and I felt she was taking on the more adolescent role while the mothering role was taken on by her own mother. Postpartum the ideal mother is described more like she describes her own mother both in pregnancy and postpartum.

In all the other cases (five) there is a more general change in the structuring of the human environment as well as a changed conception of the mothering role.

Mrs King structures her world very simply at first, mainly in terms of people being 'affectionate', 'soft hearted', 'easy going' and 'understanding' like the ideal mother, or on the contrary 'lacking in feelings', 'ambitious', 'out for themselves regardless of anyone else' and 'selfish'. The second component refers to spoiling children too much and never punishing them (which is not the case for the ideal mother). After the birth of the child she no longer thinks of people in terms of softness versus selfishness. Though it is still a factor, other considerations come in such as being careful with money, thinking before acting and being sensible. The ideal mother who was earlier on affectionate and didn't spoil children too much is now sensible, capable of thinking before acting, of fighting rather than giving in and is not overconcerned with children.

The change is along similar lines for Mrs Rand. Her main concern early in pregnancy is whether people are 'practical', 'placid', 'patient' and 'commonsensical' like the ideal mother or on the contrary 'selfish', 'conceited' and 'intellectual'. After the birth of the child, she sees people as either 'secretive' and 'broadminded' or as 'sensitive' and 'fussy'; generosity, friendliness and commonsensicalness, the qualities of the ideal mother, are secondary; these qualities are no longer in conflict with intellectuality and, as was the case for Mrs King, no longer involve selflessness. As regards the construct 'secretive' which has gained in importance and is an attribute of the ideal mother, it may account for the fact that no negative attributes are named this time.

Things go in a somewhat opposite direction for Mrs Line since the idea of affectionateness and unselfishness are only introduced after the birth of the baby. At this time two clusters appear, both characterizing the ideal mother: the more important one refers to the practical aspect of things such as diligence and responsibility, the other one to the more emotional aspect such as affection and unselfishness. Things were different early in pregnancy, when Mrs Line felt it was most important for a mother to be calm rather than highly strung and the ideal mother should also be artistic and be able to cope on her own. In the case of Mrs Line therefore it seems that the conception of motherliness and the mothering role is seen more traditionally *after* the birth of the child than during pregnancy. As we will see later, it is a pattern more common amongst the ill-adjusted women.

Mrs Dare's construction of her environment changes from a concern with whether people 'show feelings' or on the contrary are 'childish', to a concern with whether people are 'conscientious' and 'careful with money' or on the contrary 'scatterbrain'; the idea of moodiness, bad temper and worry also appear postpartum.

Placidity as opposed to moodiness is something which is also important for Mrs Craft's ideal mother, after the birth of the child. During pregnancy her main construction of the human environment follows a traditional sex role conception: 'kind', 'likes looking after people', 'home loving' like the ideal mother versus 'adventurous' and 'loud'. Postpartum this distinction no longer appears. The ideal mother is now 'kind' and 'placid' rather than 'moody' and 'undependable'.

Looking specifically at the mothering role we see that in this group of well-adjusted women, two women are satisfied and identify with a very traditionally defined role, and the nine others reconstrue the mothering role. In nearly half of these nine cases the reconstruction involves defining the mother role in a less stereotyped and traditional way (that is, not in terms of selflessness and interest in the home). In two more cases, the definition of the ideal mother is more traditional postpartum (one of these women seems to be abdicating some of her mothering role to her own mother). In the last three cases the role is defined neither more nor less traditionally but just differently.

B. WOMEN IN THE ILL-ADJUSTED GROUP

The processes in this group are opposite to the processes taking place in the group of well-adjusted women. I will describe these processes and take the opportunity of making some comparisons with the well-adjusted women.

The women in this group see themselves as *less similar to their own mother after the birth* of the child than early in pregnancy.

Taking into account the way in which each woman perceives her own mother, one can see that *when her mother is perceived as a good mother* after the birth of the child she will see herself as becoming *increasingly different from her*, and *when her mother is perceived as a bad mother* she will see herself as becoming *increasingly similar to her*. This is true regardless of how the mother is perceived early in pregnancy.

There are four different possible patterns:

(a) The woman perceives her mother to be a good mother both early in pregnancy and after the birth of the child. She perceives herself and her mother to be less similar postpartum than during pregnancy. This is the most frequent pattern in this group, followed by six out of the eighteen women (33%).

Early in pregnancy, for Mrs Jones, a young telephonist only just married, her mother and the ideal mother are 'understanding' and 'domesticated'; she is neither of these things herself.

After the birth of the baby, she thinks the ideal mother is 'understanding' and 'patient' and her own mother 'satisfied staying at home'. Again she is neither of these things herself. On the contrary, she 'enjoys going out' and 'has a tendency to do what she wants even if it hurts someone'. The dissimilarity between herself and her mother has increased.

(b) The woman perceives her mother to be a bad mother early in pregnancy but changes to thinking of her as a good mother after the birth of the child. She perceives herself and her mother to be less similar postpartum than during pregnancy. This is the next most frequent pattern, followed by four women (22%).

Mrs Sanders, a young dressmaker aged 19, describes the ideal mother, early in pregnancy, as 'patient', 'mature' and 'organized' whereas her mother and herself are 'likely to be moody', 'emotional, tend to get depressed', her mother being somewhat less 'outspoken' and more 'tactful' than she herself is. After the birth of the baby, her mother resembles the ideal mother; both are 'patient', 'practical' and 'generous'. She remains 'moody' and 'inclined to worry'.

(c) Both before and after the birth of the baby, the woman perceives her mother to be a bad mother and sees herself becoming increasingly similar to her. Three women followed this pattern (17%).

Early in pregnancy, Mrs Cox feels that her mother who is 'moody' and 'immature' is the opposite of what a mother should be, which is 'easy going', 'kind and gentle' and 'sympathetic'. She describes herself more like her mother than like the ideal mother, though more 'sentimental' and less 'moody' than her mother. It may be relevant to mention that her mother is actually a step-mother. After the birth of the baby she still sees her mother as 'temperamental', 'domineering' and 'inconsistent' and now describes herself in very similar terms. Both are very different from the ideal mother who is 'considerate', 'easy going' and 'not selfish'.

(d) From being seen as a good mother, the woman perceives her mother to be a bad mother after the birth of the child and identifies with her. No woman followed this pattern.

Five out of the eighteen women follow none of these patterns. In two cases the woman thinks her mother is a good mother both before and after the birth of the child and identifies with her mother. In two more cases it is only after the birth of the child that the woman sees her mother as a good mother and she identifies with her. Finally in one case, the mother is seen as bad both before and after the birth but the woman perceives herself to be increasingly different from her mother. These patterns belonged to the well-adjusted ones. We will see later how other features distinguish them from the well-adjusted women.

Out of these eighteen women, eight see their mother as a good mother early in pregnancy. Postpartum, fourteen of the women see their mother as a good mother. We can see from the table below that this is a smaller percentage, at both times than in the well-adjusted group. In both groups though there is a tendency for more women to see their mothers as good mothers after they themselves become mothers.

Table 4: *Percentage of 'good mothers'.*

	Well-adjusted group %	Ill-adjusted group %
women who see their own mother as a good mother early in pregnancy	63	44
women who see their own mother as a good mother postpartum	90	77

Let us now consider how the women in this ill-adjusted group valued themselves as mothers. Relative to the well-adjusted women there was a greater tendency for these women to *value themselves as mothers less positively after the birth* of the baby than during pregnancy.

As shown in the table overleaf, nearly three-quarters of the women in the well adjusted group saw themselves as more similar to the ideal mother after the birth of the child, only just over half did so in the ill-adjusted group. As a group, the well-adjusted women viewed themselves much more positively than did the ill-adjusted women at this time.

All but one woman in the well-adjusted group saw herself as a good mother[1] postpartum (90%) while only twelve out of the

1 Small self to ideal mother distance.

Table 5: *Percentage of self as a good mother.*

	Well-adjusted group %	Ill-adjusted group %
women who saw themselves as more similar to the ideal mother after the birth than before	72	55
women who saw themselves as good mothers postpartum	90	66

eighteen women in the ill-adjusted group saw themselves as good mothers postpartum (66%).

It is possible to combine the previous areas. Let us consider together the following adaptive processes described earlier when the well-adjusted women were being considered: the four well-adjusted patterns involving self, mother and ideal mother (see pages 96–7), and the perception of self as a good mother after the birth of the child (self more like ideal mother postpartum than during pregnancy – see page 98).

Sixty-four per cent of the women in the well-adjusted group changed in accordance to these two sets of processes as opposed to 11% of the women in the ill-adjusted group. This is a considerable difference.

Mrs Salmon, a secretary in her late twenties, married for a number of years, describes the ideal mother as 'easy going', 'understanding' and 'having a mind of her own', early in pregnancy. She sees herself as not too different from this ideal though more interested in dancing and in cars. She is diametrically opposite to her mother who 'likes sports' and is rather 'obstinate'. After the birth of the baby the ideal mother is still 'understanding' but also this time 'placid' and 'good mannered'. Her mother, still described as a 'sport type' is now much more like the ideal mother. She is herself now very different from both mother and ideal mother; she is 'gay', has a 'good temperament', 'likes social life, going out' and has a 'mind of her own'.

The different changes are interesting: mother is described more positively as well as being more similar to the ideal mother after the birth of the baby; a new definition of the ideal mother is given postpartum: she no longer has a mind of her own and becomes more like the cultural image of the controlled, self-sacrificing mother; she now describes herself as having a mind of her own and liking to go out but feels it is incompatible with good mothering; an increased split between self affirmation and self restriction defines the increased distance between self and ideal mother.

A similar process but with a different content takes place for Mrs Ramsey, a 25-year-old social worker. Early in pregnancy, for her, the ideal mother is 'patient', 'interested in welfare and health', has a 'broad outlook on life', 'likes social activities and meeting people'. This is true of herself too, to a lesser extent. On the contrary she thinks her mother is 'immature'. After the birth of the baby, two somewhat separate clusters appear: 'patience', 'interest in health and welfare' typified by the ideal mother; and 'broad minded', 'artistic', 'serious minded', 'eccentric', 'likes music' typified by her husband and herself. Her mother is now more like the ideal mother and less like herself.

As with Mrs Salmon therefore there is a modified conception of the good mother which becomes separated from the more 'outside' or 'non-helpful' activities.

The only two women in this ill-adjusted group who both followed one of the well-adjusted patterns in relation to mother and ideal mother and became more similar to the ideal mother postpartum were both 18 years old (the youngest age group), both conceived before marriage and both were first interviewed at their parents' home. Both were to some extent acting against the parents' will.

Mrs Pyke, a clerk, had wanted to get engaged but her mother said she was too young. She told me that she had many times thought she was pregnant; it seems a not too great assumption to say that she wished to get pregnant in order to get married – which is what happened.

The other woman, Mrs Leach, a dressmaker, implied that she got on poorly with her parents and that her mother had wanted her to 'get rid of the baby'; she definitely wanted to have the child; this her mother could not understand.

Mrs Pyke described herself, early in pregnancy, as 'gullible', 'relaxed', 'emotional' and 'soft'; at this time she perceives her mother and the ideal mother to be more mature and more sensible than herself. After the birth of the baby she still sees herself as 'soft' but also now 'fashion conscious' and 'fun loving'. Mother and ideal mother are 'loving', 'sentimental' and 'sensible'. Although she tends to see herself more like she sees her mother and the ideal mother after the birth of the child, the move is very small indeed and at both times she is still very different from either of them; also she creates postpartum a conflict between being 'fashion conscious', 'complicated', 'fun loving', 'able to take things lightly' on the one hand, and 'sensible', 'loving', 'has more responsibilities' on the other. These two poles constitute the main criteria according to which she now distinguishes between people. Her husband, previously seen as similar to the immature person and described as 'easy going', changes radically to being 'sensible', 'bossy', and having 'more responsibilities'. When I asked her if she felt that she had changed she replied that her husband had changed more than she had. She also told me that she was moving soon and was worried about being far away from her mother. This suggests that her husband and her mother have perhaps assumed the mothering role more than she has.

Mrs Leach follows the one well-adjusted pattern (pattern 4) which in fact none of the well-adjusted women followed (see page 97). She and her mother are both very different from the ideal mother early in pregnancy. Both are more 'adolescent', 'selfish', 'immature', 'spoiled' and 'emotional' than a mother should be. After the birth of the baby she still sees her mother as a bad mother who 'likes her own way', is 'lazy' and 'selfish'. She is now different from her mother, is more 'understanding', more 'sympathetic' and does not have such 'a temper'; this is more like the ideal mother.

If you remember there was only one woman in the well-adjusted group who perceived her mother negatively after the birth of the baby (her mother had died recently). It may be that the truly adaptive processes to the birth of a first child involve a woman being able to call on a positive image of her mother postpartum and identify with her (patterns 1 and 2) and view herself more positively as a mother. This is in line with the psychoanalytic notion of an 'identification with a good mother image'. This is the case for more than half of the women in the well-adjusted group (64%) as opposed to only one out of the eighteen women in the ill-adjusted group (5%).

Let us come back specifically to the *perception of self in relation to the ideal mother.*

Although there is a decrease in similarity between the perception of self and of the ideal mother for the ill-adjusted women as a group, only in fact eight out of the eighteen women value themselves less positively as mothers after the birth of the baby relative to before. When I set out the areas to explore, I mentioned the possibility of two opposite responses from women experiencing difficulties: either rumination over the problem and self-depreciation or, on the contrary, denial of any problem at all. This is indeed the case: in the ill-adjusted group women tend to see themselves as either *more* or *less* like the ideal mother postpartum than do the women in the well-adjusted group; that is, in the ill-adjusted group there are women who are more satisfied with themselves as mothers and others who are less satisfied with themselves as mothers postpartum than in the well-adjusted group.

As predicted, there is *not a tendency* for women in this group *to see themselves as less similar to their husbands* after the birth of the baby as is the case in the well-adjusted group.

Ten out of the eighteen women in this group perceived themselves as less similar to their husbands after the birth of the baby (55%); this was the case for nine out of the eleven women in the well-adjusted group (81%).

In the ill-adjusted group none of the women show the kind of role differentiation that was present in the other group. When there is, postpartum, a split between 'outside' and 'home life' both husband and wife come closer together postpartum. This is the case with Mrs Salmon, Mrs Ramsey and Mrs Bruce.

The clearest example is Mrs Bruce. After the birth of the baby, Mrs Bruce perceives herself almost identically to her husband. Both now have an 'interest in travelling', 'cultural interests', 'professional interests', 'left-wing attitudes' (this was more true of her husband than of herself early in pregnancy).

Although on the whole they tend to see a greater similarity

between themselves and their husbands postpartum, Mrs Leach and Mrs Pyke both add the descriptive term 'likes to be the boss' or 'bosses' to characterize their husband. If you remember both these women got married during their pregnancy, and the modified perception may here relate more to the new experience of living with their husband than to the birth of the baby.

As with the group of well-adjusted women, in a number of cases there is a tendency for one of the partners to experience or be thought to experience more difficulties postpartum (what could be called the 'problem partner').

Mrs Longford, a seamstress in her mid-twenties, describes herself, both during pregnancy and postpartum, as 'dependable', 'down to earth', 'reliable'. Her husband, 'self-assured' at first becomes 'lazy', 'selfish' and 'needs someone else' after she has had the baby.

Similarly, Mrs Sanders who saw herself as much more 'moody' and 'inclined to depression' than her husband during pregnancy, perceives him to be more moody and inclined to worry than she is postpartum.

Both these women have been married for more than two years, so that if indeed the husbands change in the way their wives describe it, it is probably due to the birth of the child.

Content

Maternal dimension. Let us now turn to the 'maternal dimension'. If you remember I predicted wrongly that the women in the well-adjusted group as opposed to those in the ill-adjusted group would use more constructs closely associated with the maternal construct after the birth of the baby than during pregnancy.

In fact it is the women in the ill-adjusted group who increase their use of such constructs. The maternal dimension is made up, on average, of 4 constructs during pregnancy and 5·2 postpartum. The average number for the well-adjusted women postpartum is 3·4.

I interpret this finding as follows: the ill-adjusted woman is more preoccupied postpartum with the notion of motherliness than is the well-adjusted woman for whom it is not such a problem. It is as if much more of her differentiation of people revolves around being a good or a bad mother. The well-adjusted woman on the contrary is more open to new experiences.

Looking at the verbal designation, there is an increase in words referring to feelings and relationships such as loving, understanding and unselfish. The reverse was true for the well-adjusted women. The words that did come up more often in the well-adjusted group such

Table 6: *Most frequently used constructs as part of the maternal dimension.*

	Number of constructs from each category given by the women in the ill-adjusted group at	
	Time 1 (early pregnancy)	Time 3 (postpartum)
Understanding, sympathetic, tactful, considerate, thinks of others, not selfish	14	17
Loving, affectionate, kind, motherly	13	16
Diligent, hard working, reliable, responsible, conscientious, not scatterbrain, not lazy	10	9
Calm, doesn't lose their temper, self control, placid	6	8
Can see reason, not set in ideas, not obstinate, not domineering, not stubborn	6	5
Patient, tolerant	4	8
Understands children, sentimental about children, child oriented, knows about babies	4	3
Practical, commonsensical, down to earth, organized	3	4
Easy going, happy-go-lucky	2	3

as diligence, understands children and domesticated, either decrease in use or are practically not used in the ill-adjusted group.

Patience and self control and similar words are also used considerably more often in the ill-adjusted group.

For the women in the ill-adjusted group, there is, after the birth of the child, an increased preoccupation with motherliness construed in more idealistic terms as loving, kind, patient, unselfish and never losing their temper. This corresponds to the stereotype of the perfect-all-sacrificing-contented-never-angry-mother. It is the classical smiling mother and baby representation which the advertisers exploit and perpetuate. For the well-adjusted women, on the contrary, this image becomes less important after the birth of the child when a good mother is felt to need diligence, hard work, reliability and a liking to be at home and with children. This more realistic picture of the situation takes into account the ability to cope with the work involved while being basically satisfied with domesticity.

Mrs Carter, a teacher in her early twenties, belongs to the ill-adjusted group. She feels that the most important quality for a mother is to be 'loving of children'. Early in pregnancy she relates this to 'knowing about babies', being 'able to relate things to oneself', 'enjoying life' and being 'able to make stable relationships'. Mrs Carter experienced difficulties in many areas; she was quite ill during pregnancy, had a difficult labour and delivery, became depressed and had a hard time with the baby who cried a lot and would not settle. Postpartum she still feels it is important to be loving and capable of stable relationships but it is also now important to be 'patient', 'kind', 'unselfish', 'not stubborn', and not to 'lose one's temper quickly'. Enjoyment of life is not mentioned this time.

As I mentioned earlier when talking about the well-adjusted women, the maternal dimension can be considered to form a grid on its own, the 'partial grid'.

The interesting finding refers to the women's perception of themselves in relation to the ideal mother. Whereas on the total grid the well-adjusted women tend to show a greater satisfaction with themselves as mothers after the birth of the baby and the ill-adjusted women a greater dissatisfaction with themselves as mothers after the birth of the baby, the reverse is true if we consider the partial grid only.

I see this finding as linked to the previous one (increase in the number of constructs in the maternal dimension for the ill-adjusted group). Both reflect the complexity of a conflictual situation. The women who experience most difficulties during this period, tend to be overpreoccupied with motherliness (thus producing more constructs relating to motherliness) while defending themselves by 'protesting too much'; whereas the well-adjusted women can admit to imperfection where motherliness is concerned, the ill-adjusted women need to describe themselves as quite good mothers, in the area where I had specifically asked them to describe themselves as mothers. The woman who has coped with the situation may be able to express the natural difficulties with conforming to an ideal in the face of the real situation and the demands of the baby; the expression of imperfections does not entail too great a threat to her self-esteem. The slight increase in dissimilarity between herself and the ideal mother in this case may reflect her realization of the infantile unrealistic nature of the 'ideal-mother' image. On the other hand, the woman who has experienced many difficulties may find the need, in order to preserve her self-esteem in the face of her perceived inadequacy, to react by describing herself as a good mother. This is particularly striking if we consider the much more unrealistic character of the qualities which tend to constitute the 'maternal dimension' for the women in the ill-adjusted group.

I am therefore suggesting that total grid and partial grid tap two different levels, the conscious level in the partial grid and the more unconscious, or at least subconscious, level in the total grid. The latter reflects what the woman feels about herself, the former what she is wanting to communicate about herself (since I have here stressed that it has to do with the most important quality for a mother). Some support is given to this idea by the fact that where self-esteem and social desirability are not involved, for example in the similarity between self and husband, the total and partial grids show no discrepancy in results.

The ill-adjusted women are, in a sense, stuck with the experience of childbearing: postpartum they are preoccupied with the idea of motherliness, and in particular with an idealistic conception of it, and the need to assert their good mothering qualities. The well-adjusted women are not so preoccupied with motherliness which they tend to see in more realistic terms, and do not have to 'protest too much'.

Total grid. Let us go on to look at the content of the whole grids. This time in the table I will give the percentage of times a category is used for the total group, and I will list the categories in order of importance separately for pregnancy and postpartum. I only list those categories used more than 2·5% of the time.

Table 7: *Most frequently used constructs in the ill-adjusted group at time 1.*

	Ill-adjusted group Time 1 %
1. Enjoys life, carefree, gay, easy going, jovial, jolly, free and easy, happy go lucky, gay, likes going out, fun loving	5·5
2. Stubborn, dogmatic, obstinate, does not make concessions, unreasonable, can't talk things out, not flexible, not receptive, won't give in, cannot see reason, does not give in easily	5·5
3. Moody, temperamental, snaps at slightest thing, quick tempered, not placid	4·4
4. Mature, adult, not childish, not adolescent	3·9
5. Motherly, kind, soft, loving nature, affectionate, generous, shares, would help someone	3·3
6. Responsible, sense of duty, dependable, reliable, faithful, keeps promises, honest, sincere	3·3
7. Worries, does not take things lightly	3·3
8. Stable, can make stable relationships, not neurotic, stable mind	2·8
9. Old fashioned, traditional taste, not modern, square, does not like pop music and clothes	2·7
10. Likes meeting people, extroverted, sociable, gregarious, mixes with people well, likes social life, hospitable	2·7
11. Wrapped up in children, shows affection to children, gets on with children, family person, likes to have nice cosy family, settled, domesticated, interested in the home, likes to be at home, likes settling down, satisfied staying at home	2·7

From this table we can see the change in emphasis from pregnancy to the postpartum period in this group of women. Important is the large increase in use of constructs referring to moodiness and temper, which become, postpartum, the most frequently given constructs. Constructs which are important during pregnancy but not postpartum are 'mature', 'adult', etc., 'worries', etc., 'neurotic', etc. The two latter ones may be related to the anxiety present during pregnancy. Postpartum the constructs becoming more frequently used are 'not lazy', 'selfish', 'agitated', etc.

In both well- and ill-adjusted groups, moodiness becomes the most

Table 8: *Most frequently used constructs in the ill-adjusted group at time 3.*

	Ill-adjusted group Time 3 %
1. Moody, temperamental, snaps at slightest thing, quick tempered, not placid	7·2
2. Enjoys life, carefree, gay, easy going, jovial, jolly, free and easy, happy-go-lucky, gay, likes going out, fun loving	6·1
3. Not lazy, diligent, tidy, keeps at things, organized, conscientious, hardworking	5·5
4. Motherly, kind, soft, loving nature, affectionate, generous, shares, would help someone	5·0
5. Responsible, sense of duty, dependable, reliable, faithful, keeps promises, honest, sincere	3·9
6. Wrapped up in children, show affection to children, gets on with children, family person, likes to have nice cosy family, settled, domesticated, interested in the home, likes to be at home, likes settling down, satisfied staying at home	3·8
7. Selfish, thinks of him or herself only, steps on others, self centred, uses people, is not helpful, does not do a lot for others	3·8
8. Agitated, not calm, highly strung, nervous, not relaxed, patient	3·3
9. Likes meeting people, extroverted, sociable, gregarious, mixes with people well, likes social life, hospitable	3·3
10. Practical, down to earth	2·7
11. Reserved, shy, does not show feelings, inhibited, not demonstrative, not outgoing	2·7

frequently used concept postpartum. This probably reflects the 'postpartum blues'. Again in both groups the practical aspect of hard work and diligence becomes important postpartum though as I mentioned earlier it is less related to the qualities necessary for a mother in the ill-adjusted group. As in the case of the maternal dimension, selfishness is a preoccupation only for the ill-adjusted women. Two categories which are important for the well-adjusted group but do not appear in the ill-adjusted group concern money on the one hand, and the more active and traditionally considered masculine interests (cars etc.). In the first case it may be that here again the concern of the well-adjusted women is with a more realistic problem, the financial aspect, rather than with their own competence as mothers. My later discussion of femininity may throw some light on the well-adjusted women's use of constructs relating to 'masculine' activities.

An overview

I will go on to consider the kind of changes taking place for this group of women.

In the largest number of cases (nine out of the eighteen women in this group) there is, postpartum, some sort of *conflict between the way they see themselves and the way in which they construe the mothering role.* In some cases the conflict is present during pregnancy and is unresolved or even increased postpartum; in other cases the conflict only appears postpartum after a restructuring of the construct system. I will look at cases in this order.

> Mrs Boulton, a business woman in her mid-twenties, perceived some conflict with the mothering role. Early in pregnancy the ideal mother is perceived to be 'loving and protective' (the most important quality for a mother) and to have 'old-fashioned attitudes to the role of wife'. She and her husband, on the contrary, are 'ambitious', 'like to enjoy him- or herself', 'like to go out, abroad, live it up'. After the birth of the baby, the grid still presents a split between 'love and protection', the mothering quality, now associated with being 'more conventional', and 'likes to go out', 'more ambitious', 'better mixers with people', 'more initiative'. Mrs Boulton now places the ideal mother next to herself, on the ambitious side. I suspect that there is no real resolution of the conflict since the construct system still highlights the split. After the birth of the child, she told me she thought she had changed in that now she was less ambitious and not so bothered to be at home. In 'grid language' this would have meant a similar system with a move of the self towards the ideal mother on the more 'conventional' side; on the contrary there is a move of the ideal mother towards the self and the more 'ambitious' side. This incongruity could reflect a wish not to appear to be too bad a mother.

In three cases, *the conflict* which is present during pregnancy *increases* after the birth of the baby.

Mrs Bruce, a young woman who gave up her studies because of the pregnancy, splits the world during pregnancy between people who are 'domesticated' and 'wrapped up in children' like her own mother and those who have 'outside interests' and 'academic interests' like herself. The conflict is not total since the mothering quality, 'fond of children' is not synonymous with 'domesticated' nor is the ideal mother altogether domesticated. However she does not see herself as 'fond of children' but on the contrary as 'irresponsible'. After the birth of the baby, the split increases. At one pole we find 'domesticated', 'settled', now joined by the maternal construct 'fond of children' and at the other pole 'interest in travelling', 'cultural interests', 'professional interests' and 'left-wing attitudes'. The ideal mother is now more definitely on the 'domesticated' side while she is herself on the 'outside interests' side.

In the case of four women, *the conflict only occurs postpartum when the construct system is changed and a new conception of the ideal mother appears.*

Mrs Mills, a telephonist in her early twenties, moves from a fairly complex view of things to a very simple construct system. Early in pregnancy Mrs Mills perceives the ideal mother to have 'self control and even temper', the maternal quality, but also a 'mind of her own' and the ability to 'see things the way they are'. Postpartum, the maternal quality 'self control and even temper' is almost synonymous to 'organized', 'experience parent-wise' 'responsible', 'placid', 'loving nature', 'affectionate', 'not so quick tempered' and diametrically opposed to 'carefree' and 'irrational'. The ideal mother, placed at the first pole, is now defined in a much more culturally stereotypical way than she was in pregnancy. From this she differs more than she did during pregnancy.

In the case of Mrs Salmon, a secretary in her late twenties, there is also postpartum a more traditional conception of the mothering role. Early in pregnancy Mrs Salmon sees the ideal mother as having a 'sense of understanding', the maternal quality, 'a mind of her own', a 'sense of humour' and as being 'easy going' and 'placid'. After the birth of the baby for Mrs Salmon too there is a split between the mothering qualities and a liking to go out and have a social life. But more than this the qualities of the ideal mother now include on top of a sense of understanding and placidity a need for 'good manners'. This is separate from 'likes social life and going out', now associated with 'gay', 'good temperament', 'has a mind of her own', the qualities which characterize herself, now further removed from the ideal mother. To be a good mother now means to be placid and controlled and to deny one's needs – the cultural image of femininity. The change is here particularly striking and evident through the displacement of the construct 'mind of her own' which initially described the ideal mother but later became antithetical to her.

For three women, *the construct system is similar, the conception of mothering is similar,* but there is with the birth of the child a maintained or an increased *dissatisfaction with herself as mother.*

For four women part of the problem seems to be reflected in the *perception of their husbands.*

Mrs Saunders describes her husband during pregnancy as 'outspoken', 'not much tact' whereas postpartum he is 'moody' and 'inclined to worry' which is how she tends to describe herself at both times. Mrs Saunders' husband is engaged in a profession generally considered feminine and we might hypothesize a difficulty for him in his identification with women at this time. The story she gives to the TAT card gives some support to this idea: the man is seen as hesitating between the two women: 'he had to decide and decided for the one who is pregnant because *she is more like him*'.

Two women, Mrs Tisdam and Mrs Greenson, give evidence of *some resolution of conflict.*

Mrs Tisdam perceives herself to be more similar to the ideal mother after the birth of the child. Both are 'loving', 'like to keep something when he or she has it', are 'self confident', 'think about security and future'. On closer inspection however part of the increased satisfaction with herself as a mother involves the following: early in pregnancy she uses four constructs referring to preoccupation to describe herself ('worries', 'worries about the family', 'worries rather than takes things as they come', 'works when upset'); at this time this cluster is separated from the maternal construct. Postpartum 'worries' becomes closely associated with 'thinks about security and future' which is one of the maternal qualities. Mrs Tisdam has modified her conception of motherliness to englobe her own insecurity.

For Mrs Greenson, a clerical worker in her thirties, there seems to be no conflict postpartum. She sees herself and the ideal mother both as 'down to earth', 'practical' and as having 'a sense of responsibility' as opposed to 'inhibited', 'lacking in confidence' and 'romantic' like her husband. One point to consider however is that early in pregnancy she describes herself as 'unwilling to make a fuss'; this suggests at least the possibility that her adjustment is more apparent than real.

Whereas in the group of well-adjusted women, the majority of women either are satisfied and identified with a very traditionally defined mother role postpartum, or reconstrue the mother role in a less stereotyped way with which they can be satisfied, the majority of women in the ill-adjusted group perceive the mother role postpartum in a *more* traditional or idealized way involving a greater conflict with outside interests or a greater dichotomy between good and bad qualities (perfect selflessness for the ideal mother). In some cases, the conception of the mother role remains similar and the difficulties are expressed in terms of the woman's and/or her husband's greater moodiness and inability to be 'good'.

It is difficult to say what makes one woman able to reconstrue the maternal role while another woman finds herself at odds with her definition of the role to which she feels she ought but cannot ascribe. Looking at the group of ill-adjusted women it seems that the definition of this role with which they are in conflict is a very idealistic one[1] – one to which the well-adjusted women no longer ascribe. This image of the all-sacrificing mother is a cultural one, but it is also one which results from a very primitive psychological mechanism involving the separation of good and bad qualities which are then ascribed to different people – the fairies and the witches of childhood (it is the process called 'splitting'). The women in the ill-adjusted group seem less able at this particular time to reach back to a realistic image of the good mother who is neither idealized nor denigrated. One can only conjecture that they have less often come to terms with their conflicting feelings towards their own mothers. In fact the women in this group less often perceive their mothers to be good

[1] The fact that the difference is striking between the two groups precludes the idealized picture being an artifact of my use of the term 'ideal mother'—which by the way I stressed referred to 'your personal view of what a good mother should be like'.

mothers than the women in the well-adjusted group and the idealized image of the good mother which they evoke at the time of their own child's infancy may be the counterbalance for the kind of mothering they received or felt they received.

I would say that the picture of the all-sacrificing perfect mother is largely culturally determined during pregnancy but that postpartum it persists or increases in women for more personal psychological reasons relating to their own experience of being mothered.

Earlier on in this book I talked about the problem of 'adjustment'. In what sense can we say that some women are 'well adjusted'? I think it is possible to say from looking at the findings I have presented that some women are well adjusted in the sense that they experience no conflict with the social environment and the traditional roles it defines but that others are well adjusted in the broader, less constricted sense that they are at peace with a more personal definition of their role and that they are able to call forth a more realistic appraisal of their human environment where positive and negative qualities are integrated.

The processes of identification with parental images obviously occur throughout life. Some of the processes I described in this chapter probably take place before early pregnancy with the decision to conceive and with the knowledge of the pregnancy. The women in the 'pregnant group' tend to see themselves as more similar to their mother than the 'non-pregnant group' of women I tested, even in early pregnancy. This is particularly true when the similarity is considered for the 'maternal dimension' only. Also in terms of these qualities relating to the maternal role, the pregnant women on average tend to see themselves as being more like their mothers than their fathers whereas the non-pregnant women tend to see themselves as being more like their fathers than their mothers. This was true both in early pregnancy and postpartum.

A note on the criteria of adjustment

The three measures I combined to distinguish between well-adjusted and ill-adjusted women are very different. Two of them are based on questionnaires filled in by the women, the third is a report given by the obstetricians. The latter refers to the pregnancy, the birth and the baby's health after the birth; the baby questionnaire refers mainly to the third month postpartum; the depression questionnaire compares pre- and postpartum. The person reporting varies, the time of reporting varies, the period assessed varies, the nature of the problems investigated varies.

One could wonder if the kind of changes in self-concept and perception of family members which I described earlier really only relate to one or two of the measures. I therefore analysed the changes occurring in women who showed some disturbance versus the women who showed no disturbance on each of the measures separately. On the doctor's report criterion, twenty-eight women showed some evidence of disturbance versus twenty-three who did not. On the depression questionnaire seventeen women showed some evidence of disturbance, versus thirty-four who did not. On the baby questionnaire eighteen women showed some evidence of disturbance, versus thirty-three who did not. Three separate analyses were performed opposing well- and ill-adjusted women on each of the three criteria. The various changes which I had predicted and described in relation to the extreme groups identified when the criteria were combined (perception of self in relation to mother, to ideal mother, to husband) hold true but to a lesser extent. For example, for each of the criteria, there is a greater dissimilarity in perception of self in relation to mother after the birth of the child for the women who experience difficulties, and a greater similarity in perception of self in relation to mother after the birth of the child for the women who experience no difficulties. However, although in all three cases the women with no difficulties tend to see themselves as more like their mother postpartum than do the women with difficulties, the difference is in fact rather small (and reaches statistical significance in one case only).

It could be argued that the two measures which rely on the woman's own report and which are comparable in timing (since the second depression form and the baby questionnaire are administered at the same time), are more likely to be capturing a similar process. I combined the depression criterion and the baby criterion and separated a well-adjusted group of twenty-four women who experienced difficulties on neither of these two criteria, and an ill-adjusted group of eighteen women who experienced difficulties on both of these criteria. However, here again, although the processes tended to be similar they were not as clear cut and extreme as when the three criteria were taken into account. Only the satisfaction with self as a mother (similarity between self and ideal mother) was more extreme in opposite groups when these two rather than the three measures were combined.

This supports the idea of combining such different criteria, based on the notion that difficulties can be expressed in different ways and that difficulties in different areas will have similar meanings and repercussions. Physical symptoms as rated by obstetricians are equally important when the self-concept of the mother is the focus of interest. How a woman physically experiences pregnancy and childbirth and the state of the baby will be important in shaping her conception of herself as a mother; conversely, it is possible that a woman who, for whatever reason, cannot modify her self-concept or see herself as a mother will encounter difficulties at a somatic level in connection with bearing a child.

The fact that combining criteria proved fruitful points to the complexity of the processes and interactions involved and the futility of searching for a causal explanation.

The three criteria I used were fairly crude and limited in time. It is likely that more sensitive and extensive measures would make the processes more evident still.

Chapter 5
Conflict and acceptance of pregnancy

'That lady is pregnant, isn't she?
Her husband went off and got killed. He used to work there in the field.
And she just stands there in the field, thinking of him all the time.
Well, you can't say anything more, can you?' (Story given by
Mrs S., after she had a late miscarriage)

Inspired by David and DeVault's findings that women who are
selectively tuned to perceiving a pregnant woman in an ambiguous
stimulus, are likely to have easier deliveries, I chose to consider such
a perception as indicating greater acceptance of the pregnancy. At the
second interview, 10 weeks before the expected date of delivery, I
presented women with the TAT card mentioned earlier (country
scene with a man, a young woman carrying books and an older
pregnant woman). I predicted that women who were to present a
healthy adjustment would more often describe the woman as
pregnant than would the women who were to experience difficulties.

This is not the case. Between 60 and 70% of the women in either
group describe the woman on the picture as pregnant. David and
DeVault's ill-adjusted group is more restricted than mine and only
comprises 'abnormal delivery-room records' which is meant to
include both difficult deliveries and abnormalities in the baby. I
attempted to use a similar criterion to split my sample into two groups,
according to the obstetrician's ratings of the woman on the labour and
delivery scale and on the health of the baby scale. With this new
criterion twenty-three women are ill-adjusted and twenty-seven well
adjusted. There is still no difference between these groups in the number of women who perceive the woman as pregnant on the TAT
card, but there is a tendency for the women who perceive the pregnant woman to have shorter labours. It has been shown (McDonald

et al., 1963) that less anxious women tend to have shorter labour times than more anxious ones. It could be that the women who perceive the pregnancy tend to be less anxious. However too much should not be made of this as the association between perception of pregnancy and labour time is rather loose.[1]

As a tentative explanation of these negative findings I suggest that the acceptance of pregnancy is only one of the factors involved in the perception of the pregnant woman, and that for some women, conflict and anxiety may be a sensitizing factor to the stimulus, while it would be an inhibiting factor for others. The method of coping with conflict, what psychoanalytic theory calls 'defence mechanism', would be as or more important than the intensity of the conflict. The notion of 'acceptance of pregnancy' is actually a complex one if we think that a person can accept something at one level but reject it at another level. It is also difficult to predict what might cause greater difficulties, an open rejection of the baby, an unconscious rejection of the baby or a great conflict over the baby. Mrs James, a woman in her thirties, is the only woman in my sample who openly rejected her pregnancy. She had thought she would never have a child and got pregnant accidentally but she did not want an abortion. 'I hate children, I thought I would never have any, I went quite mental when I found out', she said the first time I saw her. At the second interview, talking about her expectations of baby care: 'I suppose you shove it in the bath and shove food into it . . .' After the birth of the baby, at the last interview, she said her first thought about her daughter was 'I don't like her much'. She felt very depressed the first two weeks and wanted to throw the baby out of the window. Still she is relieved not to have a boy, the thought of which is even worse. She still does not like children and will not have any more. And yet in reply to my asking if she felt she had changed she said 'no, except I didn't think I could pick her up, change her and in fact I don't mind, I suppose because she is mine'. This openly rejecting mother perceived the pregnant woman on the TAT card. In this case one could say that she was only too sensitized to the pregnancy. The story she tells involves a young student on holiday who comes across the pregnant peasant woman and the farmer. They look poor. 'She rushes off and studies like mad so that she doesn't have to end up in a situation like that.' Perhaps she is referring here as much to the pregnancy as to the poverty. Mrs James did not in fact belong to the ill-adjusted group,

[1] $r = .24$; $p < .10$ (2 tailed).

but to the middle group, comprising those women who showed difficulties on one of the criteria only, in her case the doctor's report (she experienced a difficult pregnancy and delivery).

In any case, whether or not the perception of the pregnant woman on the TAT card is in part connected with the acceptance of pregnancy, this 'acceptance' might be best considered in more dynamic and interactive terms. Indeed, the acceptance of pregnancy may modify and be modified by other processes, somatic and experiential, throughout pregnancy and the postpartum. The one time testing during pregnancy does not allow the recording of such a process. It may be, for example, that conflict is greater and healthier in early pregnancy than it is in late pregnancy and postpartum. This is a view taken by Hanford (1968) who suggests that the pregnant woman's mental conflict will decrease through the nine months. This explains why nausea and vomiting which are generally considered to be emotional reactions, occur with greatest frequency during the early months of pregnancy. After the first trimester there is for most women a drop in symptomatology.

This TAT card has been called the 'oedipal card' because of the three-person situation: a man, an older and a younger woman which evokes the situation of the girl in relation to her parents; the story the woman tells is felt to reflect how she resolves the conflicts involved in this triangular situation. Out of the twenty-nine women in the two extreme groups I have been considering, ten gave a story expressing the conflict. In some stories the young girl is jealous or envious of the older woman. 'The woman that looks pregnant looks a lot older than the man. I should think it's a farming family and I would say from the features that the two women are sisters and one is married to the man. The one against the tree (the older one) is married to the man who is ploughing. Very contented life. The girl, judging from the look on the face has a lot of affection for the man but is very envious. But she is proud and would never say it. She would wait for the sister's baby to be born and give her love to the baby. She is not happy, like jealousy. She has capable hands like the other' (Mrs Longman, one of the well-adjusted women). Sometimes the younger woman feels left out 'These two are married (older woman and man). She's quite a hard woman; she's going to have a baby. This girl (young woman) is at college and she has liked him for a while and she follows him home and sees he's married and works hard on the farm and is going to be a dad and she is sad over it. She knows she can't get anywhere with him. She didn't know he was married, she'd just seen him, so she is going to try and forget him and that will be the end of it. He looks quite nice from the back view.' (Mrs Pyke, one of the ill-adjusted women.)

In two cases the man walks off with the younger woman. 'There is the girl who's always loved him (young woman). There, his nice confident pregnant wife (older woman) who admires him looking all muscley and brown. She knows the other girl likes him which is why she is looking so smug. I should think he'll probably go off because she looks as if she is getting a bit bovine. I can't really think of a story, it's just a situation. This one (older woman) will probably have a sad end, walk away and pine for him' (Mrs Phillips, a woman in the ill-adjusted group). Or this dramatic story: 'A man out ploughing, working on the land and the two women who love him standing there. One, a sort of earth mother figure (older woman) – it looks as if she is pregnant – who perhaps he is living with, and the other the modern intellectual hardy girl with clean clothes and clean looks, both admiring the man and the strength. I think she is jealous. And he is torn between the two and doesn't know which way to turn and eventually winds up with the farm woman but always part of him hankers after the one on the left (young woman) and finally he might leave one for the other, like Jude the Obscure, but she doesn't have the sensuality and warmth of the farm woman. The other woman (older one) commits suicide. He returns to the farm and lives not very happily ever after.' (Mrs Carter, an ill-adjusted woman.)

In all the other nineteen cases there is no such rivalry in the story. Other conflicts are expressed mainly between education and country life, career and childbearing. 'Small farm. This man and woman work on the farm that belongs to the girl's father. She is about 16. She has a very good education. She looks nice and tidy. Her parents say: don't associate with farming boys; just do your studies. You don't want to become like the farmer's wife. One day she sees this woman is pregnant. She thinks this woman looks so happy she wonders if what her parents taught her is right or wrong.' (Mrs Temple, an ill-adjusted woman.) 'Probably the girl is looking at the woman and wondering whether she wanted to be a career girl rather than settle down and have a family. She is a bit wilful and she doesn't know whether she is doing the right thing. Whether she would be best settling down instead of making a career for herself. The wife looks very proud and satisfied with herself.' (Mrs Boulton, a woman in the ill-adjusted group also clearly showed this conflict on her grid.) In a number of cases no conflict at all is depicted. 'They don't look as if they belong to the same period. The girl has been sitting on the hill, reading the books. She is looking at the view and imagining what happens in the books. The man is ploughing and the wife is standing there, obviously pregnant. She is going home to her tea now. She looks quite peaceful. The man will lead the horse into the shed. They will all be going home.' (Mrs Longford in the ill-adjusted group). In this story the conflict is perhaps avoided by construing the people as unrelated to each other. In other stories it is avoided by omitting one of the characters or making them non-human. 'I don't know much about farming: is it spring or harvest? I guess they plough at both times. I don't know what to say about this. Harvest is over and she looks very satisfied with herself and ploughing the land for the following year, to start all over again.' (Mrs Salmon in the ill-adjusted group.) 'Is it supposed to be on a plantation? I suppose she (younger woman) could be a school teacher. Is that a pregnant woman there (older woman)? It looks like they are waiting for something to happen but I can't put a story to it, not really . . . they look a bit like statues. Something lacking in the photograph. They are waiting for something; maybe it's happened. I don't know.' (Mrs Jones in the ill-adjusted group.)

An unusual story was given by Mrs Ramsey, a woman in the ill-adjusted group: 'She (older woman) looks as if she has just started labour by the looks of it and he is just leaving his horse to go towards her. He has just called out and the girl looks as if she is going to turn around. I should think he will send her to get help. . . . I should think he takes her (older woman) to the house and waits for help. She probably gives birth to a lovely baby boy, which is what I want.' Mrs Ramsey did give birth to a boy but she had a difficult and very long labour (34 hours); forceps had to be used because of inertia. Another story suggested to me some anxiety about the delivery, though in this case represented symbolically. The story was given by Mrs Kahn, a woman in the middle group. 'Is that a statue (woman against the tree)? Do you want any names? I'll call her Jane (young woman). Jane was a young school teacher and she taught fairly young children and all respected her and paid attention in class. She went to school one morning and two of the little boys were missing in their seats and she inquired and the other children said that they didn't know and a while later the parents of the two children turned up very distressed and explained that their sons had gone out the evening before to the sea shore and hadn't returned. A search party had been sent out but to no avail. Jane asked if they had contacted the police – they said yes. So Jane had the idea to take the other children to the sea shore and they would do their own search because she knew some caves. All the children got hats and coats and went to the seashore and she divided them into little groups and told them to go searching. She took a party of four with her and went to the caves. She went inside, it's very dark and all the children had torches and ropes and they went further and further calling every now and then the names of the boys. One of the other children told her to be quiet because he thought he heard someone calling. They stopped still and heard someone. They made their way very carefully in the direction of the voice but came to a dead end because there had been a cave in. Jane called out and the boys answered and said they were trapped but not badly hurt. Jane sent one of the children for help and very soon all the rubble etc. had been dug away and the boys were free.'

The fantasy expressed here could be interpreted along psychoanalytic and particularly Kleinian lines.

Melanie Klein has described the girl's wish to rob her mother of the babies and the father's penis seen in fantasy as being inside mother (the missing children are boys) and the anxiety and guilt associated with this (she asks the distressed parents if they have contacted the police). The guilt over her fantasy that she has stolen the baby from mother (the mother/pregnant woman is interestingly enough blotted out of the picture by being made into a statue, which makes her harmless) makes her fear what will happen to the baby inside her own 'cave' (the boys are trapped but not badly hurt). Mrs Kahn's mother died when Mrs Kahn was in her teens which may have increased her guilt in relation to her mother. Like Mrs Jones, Mrs Kahn had a long labour (17 hours) and a forceps delivery (one can't help relate this to the last part of her story). The obstetrician wrote on her form, 'Maternal distress and slow progress in the second stage.' Mrs Kahn told me that she had a dream three weeks before the baby was born that he would be born on the second day of the following month. This is when the labour started (a week before the expected date of delivery).

There is a somewhat greater tendency for the women in the ill-adjusted group than in the well-adjusted group to give a story with neither a conflict between people nor an internal conflict in one of the people. This was the case for six out of the eighteen ill-adjusted women (33%) but only two out of the eleven well-adjusted women (18%).

For both well- and ill-adjusted women when the story involves a three person situation where one person is left out (for instance the man is married to the older woman and the younger one is left out or rejected) or one person feels jealous or envious of the other one, the older woman is *always* perceived to be pregnant. This is only the case in roughly half (52%) of the other stories (involving no conflict at all or a conflict over education versus country life or education and career versus motherhood). There is therefore some connection between not perceiving the woman as pregnant and not perceiving a three-person rivalrous situation. It seems fair to hypothesize here the avoidance or the denial of such a conflict especially since the picture is selected to evoke such a situation. The following story given by Mrs Craft, a woman in the well-adjusted group, illustrates an almost conscious avoidance of this conflict, though she does perceive the pregnancy. 'Is she pregnant? she must be. You could make a really nasty story, couldn't you? That one, Alice, was brought up on a farm and then sent to study to town but her love was for the country and here she is dreaming of ploughed fields and peasant women, hoping that one day she will return to where her heart really belongs, and she hopes that she will be a pregnant lady, like this woman in the corner, and lead a peasant's life – that is all in her dream.' We never find out what the 'nasty story' is and this is ensured by making the pregnant lady into the young woman's dream of what she will become. The man is not mentioned. The three-person conflict is avoided.

This idea connects up with another finding. I argued that if perception of the pregnant woman in the stimulus card is used as an indicator of the acceptance of this pregnancy, and if the acceptance of pregnancy entails a reappraisal of roles within the family, then it should be possible to show a reappraisal of roles by the women who perceive the older woman on the TAT card as pregnant. In particular the reappraisal of roles would involve a modified perception of the husband in his new role of father. This should appear on the grid as increased similarity between father and husband. This is the case. For the 'perceivers', there is a tendency to see father and husband as becoming increasingly similar to each other from early pregnancy to postpartum; for the 'non-perceivers' there is a tendency to see father and husband as becoming increasingly dissimilar from early pregnancy to postpartum. Postpartum, as a group, the 'perceivers' see their husbands and fathers as much more similar to each other than do the 'non-perceivers'. Similarly I felt that there would be a greater tendency for 'perceivers' to differentiate between male and female roles. Indeed the 'perceivers' at all three times tended to see the husband as less like the ideal mother than did the 'non-perceivers'.

These findings support the notion that the defence mechanism of denial (the process by which either some painful experience, or some aspect of the self is denied) is taking place in some women. It is generally the same women who both avoid seeing the pregnant woman as pregnant and avoid seeing the newly acquired similarity in roles between father and husband. It could be either that these women experience particular conflict over this pregnancy or that they are women who tend to use denial as their way of coping with a threatening situation. The latter, or a combination of the two, seems most likely, since these women, as a group, do not give evidence of greater difficulty with childbearing.

The conflict which is almost never mentioned by the women who do not see the pregnancy situation on the card or perceive an increased similarity between father and husband, is the rivalrous situation between the two women. These women would be coping with the rivalry situation between mother and daughter to which they are sensitized at the time of becoming mothers by turning it into a situation where there is no pregnancy and no rivalry between the women, in the same way as they see no similarity or see a greater dissimilarity between their husbands and their fathers.

. . . Nervousness makes me feel about babies something like the way I feel about a piece of ceramic sculpture I have just finished and am proud of; that since they are very liable to be broken anyway, it is almost better to break them immediately and end the suspense. She looked so fragile; it was as nerveracking as being in bed with a large and delicate egg. I felt that some kind of violent action, like jumping out of the window, was called for, but all I could do was sit there and try to meet the unwavering stare of those violet eyes. With what does one bridge the gap between the newborn and one who has gone through twenty-five years of life? Surely she was drawing some immense conclusion from this first impression that would affect her whole life; what could I do to impress her favourably?

I suppose if I'd made up my mind to breast-feed her this social embarrassment wouldn't have arisen; there would have been something to do beside stare at each other. But I haven't – I can't. Maybe if I had milk I could decide but it seems so impossible to decide about something which isn't even there yet. Maybe it won't come at all either. Oh dear, I don't even want to touch her much; how can I submit to such an animal contact? But all my reason is on the pro side.

. . . The moment I woke I knew my milk had come in. What a curious sensation! Where there was nothing yesterday, suddenly today there is milk, and my breasts are very swollen. No, not really milk, but a nasty, thin, brown-looking stuff – the colostrum, I suppose.

So, with a kind of desperation, I thought: Now it's here, why waste it? I'll blame myself always if I don't at least try.

. . . I hadn't realized a natural process could be so painful. It is as if blinding light were poured into the eye, or a deafening noise into the ear; an organ sensitized to one kind of stimulus (touch in this case) has the same kind of stimulus, but much too strong, applied to it.

The nurse said lovingly that the baby was a 'good little nurser', meaning, I suppose, the way she rose to the breast with a snap of a hungry trout. After the first bite, however, it was not so bad; rather pleasant, in fact. I could feel my uterus contract and a purely physiological peace and warmth ran through me. This I had expected, but there is a psychological peace, too, which I didn't expect . . . Abigail Lewis

Chapter 6
On the psychology of women and femininity

If you want to know more about femininity, you must interrogate your own experience, or turn to the poets, or else wait until science can give you more profound and more coherent information. S. Freud

I would like to proceed slightly differently in this chapter. I will discuss the meaning of 'femininity' and how one can get an understanding of femininity. I will present my own findings when they are relevant. I will start with the Freudian view of femininity not because one should always start with Freud but because his view is so coloured by and has so coloured the cultural notion of femininity.

It is fair to point out that Freud was much more cautious about his assertions than his critics generally think. He was also much more contradictory and complex in his statements than his critics and sometimes his followers suggest. His understanding of cultural influences is greater than is generally acknowledged. He writes: '. . . we must take care not to underestimate the influence of social conventions, which also force women into passive situations.'

In his paper on the 'Psychology of Women' (1933) Freud begins cautiously: 'even in the sphere of human sexual life, one soon notices how unsatisfactory it is to identify masculine behaviour with activity and feminine with passivity'. He then goes on to make a distinction between passivity and passive aims – 'One might make an attempt to characterize femininity psychologically by saying that it involves a preference for passive aims. That is naturally not the same as passivity; it may require a good deal of activity to achieve a passive end.' In the next sentence, however, passivity and passive aims are linked again: 'It may be that the part played by women in the sexual function leads them to incline towards passive behaviour and passive aims, and that this inclination extends into their ordinary life to a greater or less degree, according to whether the influence of their sexual life as a model is limited or far-reaching.'

Besides a preference for passive aims, femininity is characterized by masochism. Masochism, Freud writes, is due to the repression of aggressiveness which is imposed on women by society and by their constitution. 'Masochism is . . . truly feminine.'

According to Freud, the little girl lives a masculine life, obtaining pleasure through the excitation of her clitoris and directing her sexual wishes often of an active character towards her mother until she discovers the anatomical difference between the sexes. 'The discovery of her castration is a turning-point in the life of the girl . . . (she) finds her enjoyment of phallic sexuality spoilt by the influence of penis-envy.' The little girl then gives up clitoritic masturbation. 'Her passive side has now the upper hand, and in turning to her father she is assisted in the main by passive instinctual impulses. You will see that a step in development, such as this one, which gets rid of phallic activity, must smooth the path for femininity.' At first she turns to the father for the penis she feels her mother has refused her. 'The feminine situation is, however, only established when the wish for the penis is replaced by the wish for a child.' Freud then goes on to suggest that the masculine wish for the possession of a penis is perhaps essentially feminine. So that we get the paradoxical situation that femininity involves the wish to be male. Niles Newton's study quoted earlier, shows that the 'culturally feminine' women generally wished to be men, as opposed to the 'biologically feminine' women who were satisfied with being female. It seems very tortuous indeed to believe that true femininity involves rejection of one's biological sex!

As early as 1932, Freud's phallocentric view was criticized by Ian and Jane Suttie:

> Freud . . . makes little of the father's jealousy of the mother's re-lation to the child. . . . Women, he says, envy masculinity . . . not seeing that the girl's desire to be a boy expresses, not so much a sexual wish, as the desire to be preferred by her mother and so retain union with her. In fact the whole Freudian theory looks suspiciously like an expression of the father's jealousy both of mother and of child, converted, on the principle of 'sour grapes', into an apotheosis of the paternal position and function. The envy

and associated aggressiveness are then projected upon woman and child respectively in the following manner. 'Not I, the father' – it would run – 'envy them; they envy me. I would never harm the child, or grudge it its infantile pleasures. These do not appeal in the least to a man who has "put away all childish things". It is the child who envies me, the father, my sexual powers and privileges. So also it is not I who envy the mother her breasts and her power to bear children, it is she who envies me the penis.'

Clara Thompson, amongst others, emphasizes the fact that 'penis envy' symbolizes and refers to the actual position of power of males in our society rather than to any inherent envy of the penis.

Another interesting passage in Freud's paper 'The Psychology of Women' refers to the little girl's wish to have a child which occurs 'before the phallic phase was interfered with', that is before the 'discovery of her castration'. At this early stage Freud says, the meaning of her playing with dolls is not really an expression of her femininity; 'it served, in identifying her with her mother, the purpose of substituting activity for passivity'. This suggests that the mother as mother is masculine, the 'phallic mother' Freud talks about – not just in the little girl's imagination but the actual active mother (since identifying with her makes the girl masculine). Helen Deutsch takes up and emphasizes Freud's position devoting a special chapter of her book on *The Psychology of Women* (1945) to 'each of the three essential traits of femininity – narcissism, passivity and masochism'.

Female passivity is the cornerstone of the Freudian notion of femininity. Physiology and anatomy are given as the basis for this equation of femininity with passivity. 'The ovum is relatively motionless, passively expectant, while the spermatozoid is active and mobile. The behaviour of the sexual partners during intercourse continues this differentiation between masculine-active and the feminine-passive. The anatomy of the sex organs leaves no doubt as to the character of their aims: the masculine organ is made for active penetration, the feminine for passive reception. The objection that many and even most normal women develop a high degree of activity during sexual intercourse does not refute the view presented here. There are facts that seemingly contradict the natural law but are nevertheless of great significance. They are secondary forms of behaviour, for the most part psychologically determined. Woman's protest against her passive role and her tendency to identification may play a part in this active behaviour'. Similarly, Helen Deutsch goes on to dismiss Margaret Mead's study of a primitive tribe in which women play an active and aggressive role, while the men perform social functions regarded elsewhere as feminine, as 'exceptions (which) cannot change the general principal'.

This notion of female passivity is linked to the distinction between clitoral and vaginal eroticism. According to Freud (1931) 'the sexual life of the woman is regularly split up into two phases, the first which is of a masculine character, whilst only the second is specifically feminine; this split corresponds to the renouncing of the clitoris in favour of the vagina'.

Masters and Johnson conclude from their recent research that there is no such thing as a vaginal orgasm distinct from a clitoral orgasm, that the clitoris always participates and the nature of the orgasm is the same regardless of the erotogenic zone stimulated to produce it. In a recent book, Irving Singer (1973) rejects the notion that all female orgasms are similar and adopts a pluralistic approach: 'By "pluralism" I mean the refusal to assume in advance that nature prescribes a unitary model for male and female responses, that there is any one norm which could indicate how all men or women must behave in order to function properly, that there is a unique mode of consummation that satisfies male or female sexuality, that there is a universal condition which constitutes or structures sexual response in all people on all occasions, or that there is a single instinct or biological system basic to human sexuality'. Singer argues that Freud as well as Masters and Johnson suffer from a wish to describe a norm of sexual responsiveness. On the contrary there are different kinds of sexual responses in different women or in the same women at different times. Such a pluralistic approach certainly takes better account of the different subjective experiences reported by women. Singer plausibly argues that Masters and Johnson's findings are determined by the fact that their observations were done in a laboratory situation, thus limiting the kind of orgasmic responses produced.

In any case, what is important to retain from both Masters and Johnson and Singer is that the clitoris belongs intimately to female sexuality and not, as Freud suggested, to a masculine component of sexuality. Gillespie (1969) puts it as follows:

. . . we should reconsider very carefully the question of whether clitoral excitation is necessarily associated with the urge to penetrate and act the male; may not clitoral excitation on the contrary lead to the wish to be penetrated in order to satisfy its proper erotic aim in the physiological manner that has been described? In the former case, penis envy indeed seems an inevitable and therefore normal consequence of anatomy; but in the latter case, penis desire, i.e. the desire to be penetrated and so stimulated both vaginally and clitorally, is the outcome to be expected in a normal female psychosexual development.

From their study of the physiological responses during intercourse Masters and Johnson have shown that the vagina is not passive or purely 'receptive' (a term Sylvia Payne prefers to use). During intercourse 'the engorged vaginal barrel, gripping the penis, holds the semen in the vagina after ejaculation. Equally important, the "ballooning" of the vagina during a woman's sexual response . . . provides a useful cup-like receptacle for semen. . . . Following his ejaculation, a pool of semen collects in this receptacle; and as her sexual tension subsides, her cervix promptly dips down into this pool of semen. At about the same time, the opening in the cervix, known as the cervical os, enlarges. All this, it seems likely, makes it easy for the sperm cells to swim up through the os into the uterus, and up the Fallopian tubes to meet a descending ovum and fertilize it.' (R. and E. Brecher, 1968). In certain cases of infertility Masters found that some factor in the vaginal fluids (which he called 'the lethal factor') is capable of inactivating sperm cells within seconds. Studies I mentioned earlier (Chapter 12) speculated on other possible mechanisms of infertility such as expulsion of the semen or spasm of the Fallopian tubes. Bardwick and Behrman (1967) conducted an experiment with a view to studying changes in the contractions of the uterus in response to sexual and non-sexual stimuli. Before the experiment, each of the subjects was given some psychological tests and two groups of women were identified: those who were passive and sexually anxious and those who were neither passive nor sexually anxious. Uterine contractions were measured by means of a small water-filled balloon inserted in the uterus. They found that the high anxious women extruded the intra-uterine balloon and the low anxious women had uterine spasms. The extrusion of the balloon (which occurred without the women being aware of it) by the passive and sexually anxious women occurred when they were confronted with the sexual stimuli or shortly afterwards. The authors interpret the extrusion as a way of ending the experiment (without having to express anger directly) and ending the anxiety situation – for women who are sexually anxious and passive, i.e. unable to express anger directly. Under the same conditions, the women who were not passive or sexually anxious, revealed brief uterine spasms when they were presented sexual stimuli. 'Other experiments suggested that these muscle spasms might be the normal response of the uterus during coitus and could have the effect of increasing the probability of conception. The expulsive pattern of the anxious women would seem to have the opposite effect.' If this is so, then different responses of the uterus would either prevent or facilitate conception.

These kinds of findings suggest that it is important to consider the active aspects of female sexuality and that it takes more than just the male's activity if conception is to take place.

I do not personally feel that it is at this level that we should look for the answer to femininity but it is important to mention this aspect of sexuality since it is at this level that claims to female passivity have been voiced. Indeed Freud says: 'Nature has paid less careful attention to the demands of the female function than to those of masculinity. And . . . this may be based on the fact that the achievement of the biological aim is entrusted to the aggressiveness of the male, and is to some extent independent of the cooperation of the female.' (1933).

The other important characteristic of femininity, according to Freud, is masochism, which he views as both constitutionally and socially determined. 'We must not overlook one particularly constant relation between femininity and instinctual life. The repression of their aggressiveness, which is imposed upon women by their constitutions and by society, favours the development of strong masochistic impulses, which have the effect of binding erotically the destructive tendencies which have been turned inwards. Masochism is then, as they say, truly feminine.' Helen Deutsch, who accepts this idea, emphasizes that feminine masochism is different from moral masochism (which serves as self punishment) and from conscious masochistic perversion (where the person gets erotic pleasure from having pain inflicted on him or herself). She suggests that masochism is part of the woman's sexuality as evidenced by the pain of defloration and childbirth. The little girl, she tells us, 'gives up her aggressions partly as a result of her own weakness, partly because of the taboos of the environment, and chiefly because of the love prize given her as compensation. Here we come to a development that again and again takes place in the woman: activity becomes passivity, and aggression is renounced for the sake of being loved. In this renunciation the aggressive forces that are not actively spent must find an outlet, and they do this by endowing the passive state of being loved with a masochistic character. Earlier we have tried to explain feminine passivity on the basis of the anatomic difference between the sexes. The same explanation applies to feminine masochism. The absence of an active organ brought the turn toward passivity and masochism in its train. It is noteworthy that the processes in the ego and the instincts, the constitutional, anatomic, and environmental factors, all seem to work together to produce femininity.'

Helen Deutsch's postulation of a feminine masochism rests on the notion of the girl's switch to passivity when she becomes aware of her 'castration'. But even if we were to accept this as being the prime factor in the development of femininity (which I don't, as I will discuss later on) it seems like a rather fortuitous jump to make from lack of a penis to masochism. The confusion in her chapter on feminine masochism between the constitutional and the environmental, is summed up in these sentences: 'In his function the father is a representative of the environment, which later will again and again exert this inhibiting influence on the woman's activity and drive her back into her constitutionally predetermined passive role. . . . He appears, without being conscious of it, as a seducer, with whose help the girl's aggressive instinctual components are transformed into masochistic ones.' She describes the role of social factors in the turn from the girl's activity to passivity and masochism but goes on to assume that the latter are constitutional.

In his article on 'The Economic Problem in Masochism' (1924) Freud talks about the similarity between the type of masochism he calls 'feminine masochism' and childish behaviour: '. . . the masochist wants to be treated like a little helpless, dependent child, but especially like a naughty child'. Significant is the fact that in his paper he describes this form of masochism in men. The kind of behaviour which he sees as neurotic in men he assumes to be normal in women.

This view is based on a model which postulates instincts to explain behaviour. Such a model, apart from the fact that it relegates huge chunks of behaviour to the inevitable, depends on too many assumptions to make it tenable. Helen Deutsch has to introduce the existence of another essential trait of femininity, narcissism (self love) to counter-balance masochism (self injury). 'Since the sexual tendencies of woman are directed toward goals that are dangerous for her ego, the latter defends itself and strengthens its inner security by intensifying its self-love, which manifests itself as "narcissism". Woman's sexual goals are dangerous for her ego because they are masochistic in character, and the riddle of feminine narcissism can be solved only if we understand feminine masochism, the aggressor in the inner conflict.' This is very tortuous indeed!

Helen Deutsch describes two sets of phenomena when she refers to female masochism. First her observation that women 'gladly' expose themselves to privations and sufferings leading in its extreme form to prostitution. She interprets this as evidence of innate maso-chism rather than understanding it in psychological and sociological terms. Second, she links the physical pain of defloration, menstruation and childbirth with masochism. This view is one which takes no account of the meaning of the painful situation and of the presence of relationships. To say, for example, that defloration is masochistic – i.e., that it is pain inflicted for its own sake – is absurd. Similarly, labour pains are not an end in themselves and cannot be abstracted from the total context of having a baby. The meaning of the situa-tion is important not only to the ability to tolerate pain but also to the amount of actual pain experienced.

Apart from being based on a model which does not take into account the complexity of the person involved in meaningful rela-tionships and the more tender side of emotional life, this view of femininity as inherently masochistic is inappropriate if the woman is to have a healthy creative relationship with another person. Let us take the woman's relationship to her child, one in which our culture has placed the greatest emphasis on the woman's self sacrifice and suf-fering 'for the sake of the child'. Helen Deutsch takes this up: 'The masochistic components of motherliness manifest themselves in the mother's readiness for self-sacrifice but . . . without demand for any obvious return on the part of the object, i.e. the child, and also in her willingness to undergo pain for the sake of her child as well as to renounce the child's dependence upon her when his hour of libera-tion comes.' This view is one which takes no account of the real re-lationship between mother and child and the need for the mother to be contented if she is to fulfill the child's needs. As Frieda Fromm-Reichman put it: 'We know from psychoanalysis that there are few sacrifices made without resentment. Therefore, we do not think that a mother should give up her own happiness for the sake of her child. The happier the mother can be, the more she will be able to secure happiness and freedom of growth for her child; the more happiness she sacrifices for the sake of her child, the more she will resent the child for whom she did so, thus diminishing her capability to deal with him without hostility and resentment.' Enid Balint (1971) goes even further in saying: 'a child's wish is not only to get, and in my opinion this is much helped if the mother's wish to give is not over-strong.' I find from my own experience with patients in therapy that people's relationships and sense of worth are just as crippled when their mothers are unable to receive as they are crippled when their mothers are unable to give. Furthermore, in the mother–child relationship it is important for the mother as well as the child to be gratified. For example, if the relationship is good, breast-feeding and physical proximity are pleasurable. 'Pleasure in the mutuality' (E. Balint, 1971) is very different from 'sacrifice for the love of the baby', the masochistic attitude. My own findings, mentioned in the previous chapter, that the well-adjusted women had a more realistic view of the qualities necessary for a good mother, whereas the women who experienced difficulties tended to have a notion of a good mother as being perfect and self-sacrificing, are relevant. Also relevant is Lomas's finding (1960) that a masochistic character structure pre-disposes a mother to a postpartum breakdown.

Another point worth thinking about is the incongruity in the Freudian image of the healthy woman. On the one hand she is supposed to be able to have orgasms (vaginal orgasms) while on the other hand she is supposed to be masochistic. It seems to me that the ability to enjoy sexual intercourse involves the ability to enjoy oneself as well as please one's partner, to receive as well as to give – this the masochistic woman cannot do (unless we are in the realm of masochistic perversion, where pleasure involves pain).

The notions of femininity I have discussed up till now are all very negative. Passivity and masochism are negative states: they are the inability to be active and the inability to be assertive. The sense of castration, the cornerstone of Freudian theory is negative. It is the feeling that something is missing. I suggest that in order to under-stand femininity and the psychology of women, we must look at the positive aspects, at what the woman is rather than at what she is not.

F

Femininity refers to the qualities of the female sex, the sex that bears young. I think that it is in relation to the female body and biology only that we can understand femininity. Femininity refers to the awareness and acceptance and valuing of the female body and to the qualities which make for a good adjustment to the bearing of young. This is far removed from the sense of inferiority and the wish to be male of Freudian femininity.

I will stress again that I am far from saying that women should be defined in terms of their biology. I am saying that if we are to retain the word 'femininity' it must refer to the biological aspect of the female. Other aspects of the person cannot be referred to as feminine and masculine unless we are to take a social definition of it. An example of the latter is Helen Deutsch's assertion that 'woman's intellectuality is to a large extent paid for by the loss of valuable feminine qualities: it feeds on the sap of the affective life and results in impoverishment of this life either as a whole or in specific emotional qualities . . . ; everything relating to exploration and cognition, all the forms and kinds of human cultural aspiration that require a strictly objective approach, are with few exceptions the domain of the masculine intellect, of man's spiritual power, against which woman can rarely compete'. All observations point to the fact that the intellectual woman is "masculinized". One can't help wondering if these 'few exceptions' are created for herself!

I will look at three different areas: first at what makes a person feel she is female and how this sense of femaleness develops; secondly at the feelings connected with and the meaning of having a female body; thirdly at psychological states relating to the biological female reproductive function.

The sense of femaleness is what makes a woman know 'I am a woman'. This is called gender identity. Stoller did some very interesting work on this subject (1968). He studied intersexed people, people with defective genitalia and people brought up as members of the opposite sex. These 'natural experiments' gave him evidence for the presence in varying degrees of three factors in producing gender identity: the anatomy and physiology of the genitalia, the attitudes of parents and other environmental forces and a biological force. The latter refers to sources such as the endocrine and central nervous systems. Stoller found that the sense of maleness was present from earliest life and that the penis is not essential to this sense of maleness; similarly the sense of being female is independent of the female genitalia. He describes the case of two girls, one who had no vagina or uterus and the other who had no gonads or female hormones in any physiologically significant amount. Both had been brought up as girls and never questioned their femaleness. Stoller also quotes the work of Money and Hampsons on masculinized females; this masculinization results from excessive adrenal androgens *in utero* which masculinize the external genitalia of female infants. One such girl raised as a girl turned out to be as feminine as other little girls while one raised as a male became a masculine little boy. In support of the notion that besides the environmental factor there is also a biological force operating, he quotes the example of people who grow up convinced that they belong to the gender opposite to the one in which they have been brought up. One child, for example, was apparently a girl and raised as a girl. But from birth on she acted as if she were convinced she should be a boy. The effects of learning of gender left this child untouched. At puberty a physical examination revealed that she was a male with a penis the size of a clitoris.

The two points which seem particularly important for our purposes are, firstly that the sense of femaleness is fixed 'in the first few years of life and is a piece of identity so firm that almost no vicissitudes of living can destroy it', secondly that the presence of a penis or a vagina is not essential for gender identity to develop. This counters the Freudian idea discussed earlier on, that the little girl is masculine until she discovers that she has no penis when she becomes feminine.

A recent paper of Stoller's (1973) in which he distinguishes between transsexuals and transvestites gives an understanding of the processes involved in the formation of gender identity. The male transsexual's gender identity is female, the male transvestite's is male. 'The adult transsexual male has been feminine since earliest childhood, in some cases as early as a year and in all without a phase of masculinity. By 3 or 4 he is already saying that he wants to be a girl. . . . He plays only with girls, is accepted by them (in games in which no other boys are included) and takes only female roles. Usually while still adolescent, this person has already passed successfully as a woman, never recognized to be a male. "Her" femininity is natural, not act or mimicry.' On the other hand 'transvestism is a perversion in the sense that a substitute relationship, instead of a full human relationship, is required for maximum sexual gratification. The sexual act of cross-dressing focuses on the genitals as the most prized and necessary producer of pleasure; it follows that if a man gets his greatest pleasure from his penis and spends much of his time preoccupied with methods of gratifying his sexual needs, then – whatever appearances to the contrary – he prizes his maleness. This is the case with the transvestite, as paradoxical as it seems since he enjoys dressing as a woman.' Whereas the transsexual considers himself to be a female trapped in a male body, the transvestite considers himself to be male. Stoller found that mothers of transsexual boys often considered the son to be a cure to her lifelong hopelessness; she holds the child in an endless embrace; the child does not learn where his own body ends and hers begins. 'A transsexual boy of $4\frac{1}{2}$ draws a picture entitled "Mother and Son", wherein there is no clear delineation of his body from hers. He is without anatomical features, except for eyes, and is represented only as her arm. Both face forward, looking not at each other but at the world as if one.' In a footnote to this article Stoller says 'I wonder if many males are not a bit less sure of their maleness and masculinity than females of their femaleness and feminity; the greater amount of homosexual hallucination and delusion reported in male paranoid psychotics . . . might point to this. Perhaps this is evidence that the core gender identity of males is more endangered than in females; females do not need, and males are unable at first, to escape from having to identify with a female (mother) from birth on.' And later 'Most of the perversions are found in men; is this because men's masculinity is threatened in infancy by closeness to mother and that boys, to become masculine, must separate . . . from mother's femaleness and femininity.' In a way, the reverse process to that described by Freud seems to be happening: a feminine identity is the primary one in both males and females. The experience of 'being' which Winnicott (1971b) describes as the female element in both men and women, is the earliest of experiences. 'This sense of being is something that antedates the idea of being-at-one-with, because there has not yet been anything else except identity. . . . By contrast, the object-relating of the male element to the object presupposes separateness. . . . Henceforth, on the male element side, identification needs to be based on complex mental mechanisms, mental mechanisms that must be given time to appear, to develop, and to become established as part of the new baby's equipment. On the female element side, however, identity requires so little mental structure that this primary identity can be a feature from very early. . . . Either the mother has a breast that is, so that the baby can also be when the baby and mother are not yet separated out in the infant's rudimentary mind; or else the mother is incapable of making this contribution, in which case the baby has to develop without the capacity to be, or with a crippled capacity to be.' Since this female element of being exists in both males and females, one wonders if we should really call being the female element and doing and being done to the male one – it might be best to call them primary and secondary states (thus taking into account other forms of social structures where for example 'mothering' is done by men as well as women).

Sara Winter (1969) conducted a study of nursing mothers' fantasies. A group of women were asked to give stories to a projective test (TAT) while breast-feeding their baby (this was done with a tape recorder); another group of women who were no longer breast-feeding their babies but had done so were asked to do similarly. She found a number of differences between the stories told by the women in both groups. The women who were breast-feeding gave stories where the treatment of time was non-chronological, the activities depicted were performed for the pleasure they yield in themselves, there were more references to positive feelings. On the contrary the women who were not breast-feeding (but had breast-fed their babies in the past) gave stories which were chronologically organized with past, present and future events presented in a deliberate fashion, and concentrated on negative feelings. Activities were more often performed for a reason. 'One way to summarize these differences is that Aroused subjects (breast-feeding) focus on story characters' positive present states of *being*, while Neutral subjects stress organized, carefully considered *doing* over a period of time . . . The stories illustrate further, the direct, immediate, and emphatic quality of the Aroused subjects' response to the pictures. This is in contrast to the Neutral subjects' more detached attitude, in which response to the picture stimulus is mediated by the conceptual activities . . . Thus empathy (literally 'feeling with') appears to be another important characteristic of the nursing experience.' Sara Winter distinguishes two groups in the non-nursing mothers, the ones whose stories most resembled the nursing mothers' stories (high 'Empathic Being Orientation') and those that least resembled them (low 'Empathic Being Orientation'). Eight out of the ten High Empathic Being Orientation mothers had female babies, while only three out of the ten Low Empathic Being Orientation mothers had female babies (this difference is statistically significant). This finding is interesting in that one could speculate that there is a longer period of 'being' of the mother with baby girls than with baby boys, propitious to developing their sense of femaleness. A prolonged state of being with baby boys is what Stoller described in his study of transsexual boys (with a female identity). It is well known that from birth on, mothers treat boys and girls differently though they may not be aware of it (but also that boys and girls have different patterns of activity and reactivity). A prolonged state of 'being' with female babies could result in part from the woman's greater identification with the baby girl.

The sense of femaleness is the very basis of femininity. Next it is important to consider girls' and women's feelings about their female body. This is called the 'body image'. The Freudian picture of the girl's body image is that of a castrated man. This view is one which does not consider the possibility that the girl may have an awareness of possessing a vagina and a uterus. Stoller in his previously mentioned book, *Sex and Gender*, describes the case of a girl born without vagina or uterus.

When she was 10 (four years before she was told that she had no vagina or uterus) she tells how she was taught in school about menstruation. 'I never understood it at all. I even read the books, and I still didn't understand it. I just didn't figure . . . nothing fit in. My mind was just a blank to it. . . . I'll tell you how I thought girls menstruated – from the breasts. But they had explained how menstruation really occurred. I don't know how I thought that.' Obviously a normal girl might also have had difficulty understanding but it is worth considering the possibility of an unconscious awareness of internal organs. Such an awareness would contribute to the girl's feminine identity (though, as mentioned earlier, the possession of a vagina and uterus are not sufficient for a female gender identity).

Some authors support the notion that there is a specifically feminine, primary sexuality. Karen Horney argues, against Freud's assertion that the little girl's vagina remains altogether 'undiscovered', that there is a primary vaginal sexuality. Physicians, she says, often report vaginal masturbation and the introduction of foreign bodies into the vagina. Fantasies of rape occur long before puberty in the guise of criminals who break in through windows or doors, animals which creep, fly or run inside some place, etc. A specific form of anxiety in the girl, described by Melanie Klein, is the 'fear of having her body attacked and her loved inner objects destroyed'. Karen Horney also talks about the girl's fear that the contents of her body will be destroyed, stolen, sucked out.

Penis envy postulated as the basis of feminine development by Freud, is seen as secondary. Although penis envy is still important for Melanie Klein, 'the feminine desire to internalize the penis and to receive a child from her father invariably precedes the wish to possess a penis of her own'. For Karen Horney (1939) the wish to have a penis expressed directly by little girls is no more important than the boy's wish to possess breasts or have a child, nor does it in most cases have any influence on the child's behaviour as a whole. There is also another form of penis envy but this is a neurotic secondary formation which has little to do with the earlier infantile one. It is a reaction and flight against all that is female, a 'flight from womanhood'.

One must also disentangle from this the cultural aspect of penis envy. As Clara Thompson (1943) has pointed out, in a patriarchal society, 'the restricted opportunities afforded women, the limitations placed on her development and independence give a real basis for envy of the male quite apart from any neurotic trends'. But it is necessary to emphasize with Karen Horney (1939) that a person belonging to a less privileged group can use that status as a cover for inferiority feelings of various sources. 'What then are the repressed strivings which are covered up by the wish for masculinity? The answer must be discovered from an analysis of each patient and each situation'.

The denial of a primary female sexuality (denial of an awareness and preoccupation with the vagina, and specifically female fantasies connected with the inside of the body and female biological functions)[1] which is epitomized in Freud's theory of female sexuality is nourished from two sources: a cultural distortion and devaluation of femininity leading to a rejection of femaleness, and a psychological and primitive anxiety about the inside of the body which makes the wish for a penis and masculinity a safe escape. The latter is not free from social influences particularly in the form of guilt and anxiety about the genitals and sexuality; the anxiety can be stronger for the girl since

[1] This primary female sexuality includes the role of the clitoris if we no longer accept the split, vagina – femininity, clitoris – masculinity; the clitoris would only be masculine when it is accompanied by specifically male fantasies and experienced as a penis.

she cannot verify that her inner organs and reproductive capacity are intact. Little girls in our society are not often helped to accept the feelings connected with the inside of their body since they are generally thought of and treated as penisless boys.

The escape from femininity, the awareness and acceptance of femaleness, can lead either to passivity, the culturally sanctioned 'femininity', or to what I would call 'overactivity', in some ways also culturally sanctioned, though reproved, in that it models itself on masculinity (albeit a distorted cultural picture of it). Psychoanalysts have described 'manic defences', the psychological process by which people protect themselves against feelings of guilt, anxiety and depression. Manic defences involve the denial of these feelings, the fantasy that one is in control of situations and the projection of the anxious and depressed parts of oneself onto others. Similarly the overactive woman feels in control of situations while she prevents the emergence of feelings connected with her female body.

A young woman I have seen in psychotherapy illustrates this process well. She reports that as a child she would sometimes wake up from a dream with an orgasm. This would terrify her and she would immediately close her legs to stop the sensations. As a young adult she had difficulty in reaching orgasm during intercourse. The 'overactivity' she exhibits in different spheres is represented in the closing of the legs, which in turn symbolizes the pushing away of feelings and sensations arising from the body; it avoids being receptive to her own feelings and sensations by creating cover-up feelings. When she stops 'closing her legs', being overactive, she has to face the anxieties linked with her female body which she experiences as very vulnerable and which she feels she protects and hides by being plump. The overactivity is nicely expressed in the experiment quoted earlier (Bardwick and Behrman) showing that sexually anxious women tended to extrude a balloon from the uterus when sexually aroused which is probably what they do with the sperm during intercourse. In this case the overactivity is at a specifically physiological level. Coquetry is another possible way of avoiding feelings connected with the inside of the body by overemphasizing the outside of the body. It is another culturally sanctioned defence.

The femaleness which a woman cannot accept in herself, she may look for in another woman. Piera Aulagnier-Spairani (1967) suggests that what the homosexual woman searches for is not the penis, but femininity. 'Ce que l'homosexuelle vénère chez sa partenaire, ce qu'elle se désole de ne pas avoir, ce n'est point le pénis mais la féminité; c'est celà qui lui fait envie; c'est là l'object de son ravissement, dans le double sense du terme: ce qui ravit et ce qu'on voudrait ravir.'[1] In a way this notion that the overactive woman and the homosexual woman cannot accept the feelings connected with their female body is compatible with the Kleinian view; but the latter postulates a number of fantasies to be at the root of this. Paula Heinmann (1955) writes: 'To turn now to the girl: her position in the early stages of the Oedipus complex is in many respects similar to that of the boy. She too, oscillates between heterosexual and homosexual positions, and between libidinal and destructive aims, and experiences corresponding anxiety situations. . . . Our observations are that vaginal sensations occur at this stage, not only sensations in the clitoris. . . . The fantasies associated with vaginal urges have a specific feminine character. The little girl wishes to receive and incorporate the father's penis, and to acquire it as an internal possession, and from here she soon arrives at the wish to receive a child from him. These wishes, partly because they meet with frustration, alternate with the desire to possess an external penis. The masculine component of the sensations and fantasies connected with the clitoris can only be fully assessed if the girl's conflicts and anxieties which follow from her feminine position are taken into account. When jealousy stimulates fantasies of attacking her mother's body, these attacks recoil upon herself, and she feels that her own genital will be mutilated, soiled, poisoned, annihilated, etc., and her own internal penis and children stolen from her by her internalized mother. These fears are the graver because she feels that she lacks the organ (i.e. the external penis) which could adequately placate and restore the avenging mother, and because she has no evidence that in reality her genital organs are unharmed. We consider that there is here a psychological consequence of the anatomical difference between the sexes which is of the greatest significance for the development of the girl. We distinguish several sources for masculine drives in the little girl. Frustration of her feminine desires gives rise to hatred and fear of the father and drives her back to the mother. Anxieties related to her external and internal mother lead her to concentrate on phallic

---

[1] What the homosexual woman most admires in her partner and despairs not having herself, is not a penis, but femininity, *that* is what she envies, what she is fascinated by and would like to steal.

activities and fantasies. Her primary homosexual trends are thus most strongly increased by failure in her feminine position. She then comes to find that her male organ is inferior, that it is not a proper penis, that it cannot rival the father's penis. Because her phallicism is largely a secondary and defensive phenomenon, she comes to develop penis envy at the expense of femininity. She disowns her vagina, attributes genital qualities exclusively to the penis, hopes for her clitoris to grow into one and meets with disappointment. Devaluation of femininity underlies the overvaluation of the penis.' I do not ascribe to the assumptions present in this view: that the anxieties about the inside of the body can always be traced back to an 'Oedipal' conflict and originate in the little girl's fantasies about the parents and that the clitoris is connected with a masculine component (the clitoris cannot be considered as connected with masculine strivings unless it is experienced as masculine or accompanied by phallic fantasies but is well and truly part of the female genital apparatus).

It is important to take into account the factors such as prohibition on sexual feelings, a cultural denial of sexuality and a sexual organ in the little girl, fear connected with sensations arising from a mysterious part of the body, a cultural devaluation of femininity – most of all one must take into account the meaning of her femininity and her sexuality for every individual girl or woman. The patient I referred to earlier told me that her mother used to refer to her vagina as 'your pride'. She was also taught through her religious upbringing that the 'sin of pride alienates you from God'. One can interpret this in terms of forbidden sexual feelings which alienate from God the father, but just as relevant is the confusion she must have felt as a child about her vagina which was to be valued and cherished ('pride') but by this very act meant condemnation and alienation from her religious strivings. Now she says: 'I don't like my vagina because it's mysterious and shapeless and unmasculine. A penis is straight and straightforward.' In a way, for her, the penis is straightforward because it does not involve the ambiguity and contradiction connected with the 'pride'. Her vagina has to become 'mysterious' – perhaps a mystery in the religious sense of sacrifice as an atonement.

The problem which the girl is faced with in her development is one of accepting and being in touch with her female body without having to reject it either by anaesthetizing it (psychological or physical denial of vagina and uterus), by masochistically renouncing its

valuation and enjoyment, or by drowning and masking the awareness in overactivity.

Up till now I have talked about the sense of femaleness and feelings
connected with a female body. I will go on to consider states specific
to women where changes in body image occur. First changes related
to the menstrual cycle, secondly changes related to pregnancy and
motherhood. Such changes are characteristic of women and are an
important component in the sense of femaleness and the female body
image. These states occur at adolescence and later and come to confirm or modify the basic sense of femaleness while adding new elements, particularly a cyclical element to it.

Periodic shifts in hormonal balance are characteristic of women.
The psychoanalyst Therese Benedek (1960) looked at psychoanalytic
records in relation to the hormonal cycle in women (by taking daily
vaginal smears and basal temperature charts). The psychological and
physiological data were collected independently and compared. She
reports that the data coincided and that both methods were able to
establish the different phases in the cycle. 'The gonadal cycle begins,
often during menstruation or soon after the flow ceases, with the
ripening of the follicle which produces oestrogic hormones.
Corresponding with this stimulation, an active object-directed,
psychodynamic tendency characterizes the sexual drive and brings
forth wishes, fantasies and desires of various intensity and from different levels of maturation. The aim of the unconscious motivating
tendency is to bring about contact with the sexual object and achieve
gratification through coitus. When progesterone production comes
into effect, beginning in the preovulative state, the active, out-
wardly-directed tendency fuses with a passive receptive tendency.
Parallel with the peak of the cycle at the time of ovulation the sexual
drive reaches its highest level of integration. . . . After ovulation
and relief of preovulative tension, manifestations of the receptive and
retentive tendencies dominate the emotional life during the progesterone phase of the cycle. This is a high hormone phase, since both
hormones, oestrogen and progesterone, are produced. Yet the active
heterosexual tendency appears masked, overshadowed by manifestations of passive-receptive and retentive tendencies. The content
of the psychological material can be best described as emotional
preparation for motherhood. This evolves parallel with the effects of
the corpus luteum hormone upon the uterus which prepares for

nidation of the impregnated ovum.' This monthly repetition of the physiological process and change in emotional attitudes, in the progestin phase, she feels, is a preparation for pregnancy, when there will be a marked increase in progesterone production.

Ivey and Bardwick (1968) conducted a study aimed at assessing the psychological changes occurring in normal women during the menstrual cycle. Twenty-six women were asked to talk about some experience they had had, once at ovulation, once premenstrually and again in the next cycle once at ovulation and once premenstrually. They found much greater anxiety expressed in the experiences reported premenstrually than at ovulation: death anxiety, separation anxiety, mutilation anxiety, shame anxiety. At ovulation themes are of self-satisfaction and ability to cope. Here is one of the examples Bardwick gives of two reports from the same woman. At premenstruation: 'I'll tell you about the death of my poor dog. Oh, another memorable event – my grandparents died in a plane crash. That was my first contact with death, and it was very traumatic for me. . . . Then my other grandfather died.' At ovulation: 'Well, we just went to Jamaica and it was fantastic. The island is so lush and green and the water is so blue. . . . The place is so fertile and the natives are just so friendly.' One might object that the women were aware of the fact that the experimenters were interested in the menstrual cycle. Bardwick, in response to this, quotes the case of a girl who was interviewed on the fourteenth day of her menstrual cycle but produced material that was much more anxious than the average at ovulation and with references to death, mutilation and separation. The next day she menstruated – two weeks early. Paige (1969) replicated these findings and also showed that in women taking the Combination Pill (where levels of oestrogen and progesterone are constant) there is no such swing in affect. In these women the hormone level is rather constant and anxiety and hostility are correspondingly constant.

These studies are interesting in that they give evidence of the emotional correlates to hormonal levels and the changes through the menstrual cycle in normal women – by the way it is interesting that the fantasies of death and mutilation seem to be linked to the hormonal production rather than to the symbolic meaning of menstruation (that is they occur *pre*menstrually). It would be useful to study the differences in hormone production in the same woman over the months in relation to environmental factors and emotional conflicts. In other words, is it possible to show that the particular levels of hormones in a woman and the corresponding emotional attitudes vary in intensity at a corresponding cycle phase in relation to other emotional components (particular anxiety situations and emotionally charged events). As far as I know, this has not been done. It is of course known that emotional factors are responsible for producing menstrual difficulties such as amenorrhea (abnormal absence of menstruation).

Besides an understanding of the change in feelings through the cycle in relation to hormonal levels and the effect of emotions on hormonal levels, it is important to consider the meaning of the cyclical change on the psychology of women and its meaning for each particular woman. Therese Benedek, in the earlier quoted paper, mentions the fact that women who have undergone a total hysterectomy may show a 'reflection' of the ovarian cycle for years. Such a reproduction of the cycle without the presence of the hormones confirms the importance of its meaning. One could speculate that the presence of these rhythmical changes might make women's sense of time different from men's (though generally covered up by complex social factors). Each woman attaches her own meaning to her menstrual cycle and menstruation. It reassures one woman about her fertility whereas it makes another one feel a slave to her body.

Similarly with pregnancy, one can look at the effect of the changes in hormonal balance during pregnancy and the postpartum period and their psychological concomitants, and one can look at the meaning of the pregnancy for each woman and the way in which she will deal with the hormonal changes.

The meaning of the pregnancy, for example whether a woman thinks of the foetus as something precious or as a parasite, which in turn links to what this particular child represents to her at this particular time in her life, will be important in shaping a woman's psychophysiological adaptation to the pregnancy. Both conscious and unconscious meanings are important here. A nice example of an unconscious awareness and reaction is given by Ann Faraday in her book on dreams. She recounts how during her second pregnancy she had dreams of being pursued by wild cats, dogs and wolves. 'Sometimes, I merely attempted to run away from them, but often I stayed to fight and always succeeded in subduing the animal either by beating it with sticks or cutting it down with a knife.' She interprets this as a counter-balance to her conscious determination not to be overwhelmed by motherhood. 'I was moreover struck by the fact that the first of these dreams occurred only a few days after the baby had been conceived, suggesting that my body was in some way aware of the impending uprush of "animal nature" before my conscious mind even suspected it.'

Although it is important to look at and understand the role played by large shifts in hormonal balance during pregnancy and the postpartum period, there is a danger in relying too heavily on a hormonal explanation of moods. It is a way of robbing the woman of freedom and responsibility. It is also a way for the woman of avoiding an understanding of her feelings and for people around her of avoiding an understanding of their contribution to the situation.

Let me take the example of postpartum blues and postpartum depression. These, in particular the 'blues' are often attributed to hormonal phenomena. This avoids facing the social factors which might be contributing to the depression. I am thinking of the situation in hospitals. The effect of hospitalization with all its associations with illness and death, with all its mysterious and unknown procedures can be a frightening experience in itself. In many hospitals still, natural childbirth methods, through preparation and demystification are discouraged. For some women the experience of the hospital can be responsible for depressive or anxiety reactions. Julian Hall gives the following description: 'Far from being one of the great experiences of a woman's life, having a baby can be made a time of anxiety, disappointment, loss of autonomy and resentment. The mother's confidence in her instinctive reactions and her feelings towards the baby may be undermined. She may be humiliated and made to feel that she is a passive object, submitting to childbirth, not taking an active part in it. At the ante-natal clinic she may be waiting for hours and then be given a very perfunctory examination without time to ask questions. She may see a different person at each visit and never get to know who any of them are. . . . In the hospital, owing to overcrowding she may have no privacy when quite far into labour and in considerable discomfort. Or she may be in labour for a long time with nobody by her at all. After delivery she will be told the baby is normal, but will not necessarily see it. It is not uncommon for a mother to take her baby home without ever having seen it naked.'

For other women, hospital is experienced as a safe place, where one is taken care of and protected; going home with new responsibilities might in this case be experienced as problematic. Mrs Ramsey in my sample, described how well she felt in hospital: 'I didn't mind being in hospital; other women were crying but I didn't mind; I wouldn't have minded staying longer.' When she got home she felt confused and depressed.

Another factor rarely mentioned which can be responsible for depression, is the discrepancy between what the woman experiences and what she is told she should be experiencing. If she doesn't feel immediate love for the baby, if she is insecure about her ability to cope (often reinforced by efficient nurses and the removal of the baby into the nursery) she feels this is unnatural and a reflection on her ability to be a mother; 'every other woman seems to be coping, happy and blooming'. The woman in hospital cannot fight for what she thinks is right (for example keeping the baby with her); she is in too novel a situation to know if she should object to instructions given to her on the right procedures to use with the baby. There is also, in hospitals, a taboo against expressing meaningful feelings. It is all right to be angry or 'weep' for nothing as a result of your hormones but not to have feelings about hospital procedures or feelings about the baby which are not positive (these too must be 'sterilized' like the bottles).

When I read the reports of childbirth experiences transcribed in Sheila Kitzinger's book, *Giving Birth*, I was struck by the fact that only positive feelings towards the baby were described: 'We were both simply delighted with Lucinda, and I'm sure she will very soon become the most beautiful baby in the world.' Sheila Kitzinger similarly comments at the end of the book: 'I realized when I read through these labour reports that the mothers writing in these pages do not report on feelings of horror when they first see their babies. Most insist that they are absolutely beautiful. This is a pity in a way, because it makes them all seem "natural mothers", whereas I am sure they are not.' Earlier on she says: 'But just now she may be looking at it with something approaching horror, both at its own appearance and strangeness, and her own reactions. For it looks like none of the pictures in the baby books she so assiduously studied, cuddly, smooth and scented in the conventional wrapping of human dress. It is something outlandish and weird, its face bearing all the signs of senility rather than newness, scarlet as a boiled lobster, its shriek animal like; it stops crying and she listens to the jerky, spasmodic breathing, the little sighs, grunts and starts and, not surprisingly, she does not feel that she is a "born mother". Her own reactions may alarm and depress her, making her feel afraid of her inner thoughts. She ought, she feels, be overwhelmed with thanksgiving and love – and there is only this!'

The woman feels that other women have no such thoughts since all she is allowed to know about is the smiling mother and baby of the magazines; she feels she is abnormal, becomes depressed which she and others quickly attribute to hormones and give a name to (the 'blues'), and promptly helps to perpetuate the myth of the normal ever smiling mother and baby. It seems that part of the problem then lies in the inability to tolerate the whole gamut of feelings. This is a characteristic of our culture. One can also of course give a more personal analysis of puerperal depression. My purpose here was to show some of the social issues involved and avoided when a hormonal explanation is solely invoked.

I will now come back to my own findings. I was interested in looking at the meaning of pregnancy and the birth of a first child for a woman's sense of femininity. I chose to use the Drawing Completion Test to get some reflection of changes in body image.

This test, which I described earlier, consists of a series of incomplete drawings which the person is asked to complete any way he or she likes. It has been shown that men and women tend to complete these drawings differently both in terms of the form of the drawings and of the content. I argued that, women who adjust well to the pregnancy and the birth of the child as opposed to those who encounter difficulties at this time, would show a greater sense of femininity after the birth of the child than before – in practical terms that their femininity score would increase from the first testing (early pregnancy) to the last time (ten weeks postpartum).

I made no prediction about the late pregnancy testing as I did not know how the drastic body changes would affect the scoring.

The results were exactly opposite to prediction. The well-adjusted women showed a decrease in femininity score from the first to the last testing, while the ill-adjusted women showed an increase. Postpartum, the ill-adjusted women as a group had a much higher average femininity score than did the well-adjusted women. This was true, although to a lesser extent, of the late pregnancy measure. The first testing time revealed no difference between the groups. In order to disentangle this finding, the first thing I did, was to look at the criteria separately; but whether I was concerned with the doctor's report, postpartum depression or the mother–baby relationship, in all cases the well-adjusted women were less 'feminine' postpartum than the ill-adjusted ones. The difference in score was larger when the three criteria were combined.

I then examined the different scoring categories separately. There are twenty-three scoring categories, ten of which are considered male responses. Six of the 'male' categories and eight of the 'female' categories refer to formal properties of the drawings, the rest describe content (see Figure 6). Formal properties are: 'no expansion or internal elaboration', 'open' (area left open or indented), 'roundness' (use of curved lines and blunting of angles), 'twosomes' (unconnected parts of stimuli treated as two discrete units), 'single line modified or supported' (reinforced by doubling, enclosing, or supporting). These are scored 'female'. 'Expansion of stimulus outward', 'closure of stimulus area', 'angularity' (use of sharp angles and protrusion), 'unity' (parts of stimuli connected), 'single line left alone or carrying weight'; these are scored 'male'. There is no greater use of any of these categories or of male versus female categories by the women from either group. The drawings are also scored for content. 'Passive containers' (i.e. containers and objects capable of movements with outside assistance only such as sailboats, kites, vases, boxes), Houses, furniture and interiors, windows and doors, Small faces and human figures; these are scored 'female'. 'Active' containers (i.e. containers and objects capable of motion or locomotion without further aid from without such as cars, ships, fountains); these are scored 'male'. Here there is a difference. There is a large difference for the two main female content categories: 'passive containers' and 'houses, furniture, etc.'; in fact these two categories can really be considered as one since houses and furniture are a type of 'passive container'. The women in the ill-adjusted group made many more drawings scored as passive containers in late pregnancy and postpartum than did the women in the well-adjusted group. This accounts for the ill-adjusted women's higher 'femininity' scores at these times.

In discussing her test, Kate Franck interpreted the greater number of passive container drawings done by women as an expression of feminine nature. The data shows that the use of such drawings differentiates adjusted from ill-adjusted women during pregnancy and the postpartum period, with the ill-adjusted women increasing their use of such representations. This puts in doubt less the test itself than

Male	(a) Formal properties	Female
Expansion	Examples	No expansion Internal elaboration

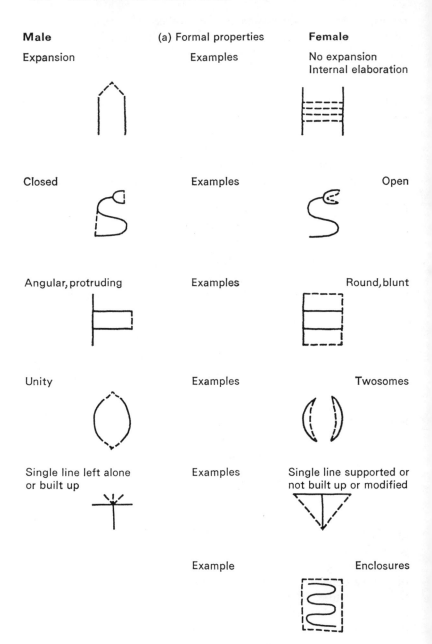

Closed	Examples	Open

Angular, protruding	Examples	Round, blunt

Unity	Examples	Twosomes

Single line left alone or built up	Examples	Single line supported or not built up or modified

	Example	Enclosures

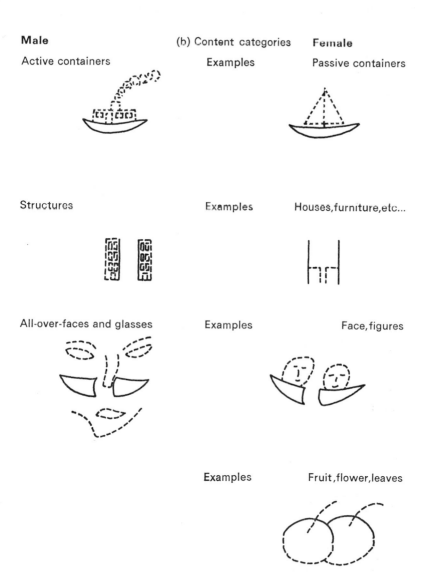

Figure 6: *Franck Drawing Completion Test scoring categories*

the interpretation Kate Franck imposed on its demonstrated power to discriminate between the sexes. It seems legitimate to question this self image of passivity as representing feminine nature, since it turns out to be maladaptive to childbearing, the most feminine activity. Adjustment to pregnancy and the birth of a child is more likely to be linked to a sense of being in control, of being the active partner, being creative, being a giver rather than to a sense of being passive, someone who is held, contained, given to.

I found that the women with low 'femininity' scores responded positively to the question: 'can you feel the baby is really yours?' (one of the questions from the depression questionnaire) while the reverse was true for the women with high 'femininity' scores. It seems possible to interpret this along the passivity/activity dimension, as expressing the feeling of having oneself produced this child (for the women who responded positively to the question). I am reminded here of the women in my sample who had strong anaesthetics (for caesarian sections or certain forceps delivery) and who remarked that it took them a very long time before they felt that the baby was really theirs because they had not had the feeling of having *given birth* to it. This has been one of the arguments in the literature in favour of natural childbirth and active participation from the woman. Different authors have described the cultural elements of this passivity. Lomas (1966) analyses the ritualistic elements in the management of childbirth itself which prevent the mother from 'participating actively and fully in the birth': 'Childbirth is expected to be a painful process. The mother characteristically moans and screams and in general behaves in a rather regressed and helpless way, is spoken to as though she were a child – and often a naughty child who needs a good spank. Frequently the birth is taken more or less out of her hands; she may be anaesthetized and delivered by forceps, not necessarily because of physical abnormality. In some hospitals, the perineum is incised as a routine procedure.' Katie Breen's article on 'Liberation and Pregnancy: a nine month diary' (1971) may also help to understand the passivity which seems to be expressed in the Franck Drawing Completion Test by some women during pregnancy. She describes how the pregnant woman is told through pamphlets what she is supposed to feel: 'Dr Birch outlines my unstable emotional state: he predicts that I will swing from one mood to another, tears and laughter, depression and good spirits. . . . My husband is urged to be indulgent.' The pregnant woman is placed in a child-like, de-

pendent role. 'My varying moods "from high ecstasy to deep depression" must be controlled all the time and many employers will
not make any concession to a pregnant employee whose condition
interferes with her work.' The relationship to the doctor is an infantilizing one in which he scolds the woman if she puts on too much
weight, for instance. Then there is the fact that she is made physically
passive. 'Some books . . . stress the fatigue of the pregnant woman
and recommend a nap in the morning and a nap in the afternoon
throughout the nine months.' Also, by consensus, working should
stop at seven months. Then the woman is asked to stay at home and
just wait. The passivity expressed in the Franck Drawing Completion
Test may be reflecting the child-like emotional state prescribed by
society in which the woman 'needs to be constantly reassured by two
father figures: doctor and husband'. Sheila Kitzinger (1971a) also
refers to the infantilizing aspects of childbirth in our society: 'and
often she is just the uterus on the delivery table, a more or less resist-
ing female body obstructing the birth of the child. Doped, pleaded
with, generally lectured or cajoled, reduced to a state of infantile
dependence, she looks in vain for knowledge, guidance and the skilled
help which could allow her to play her part in labour actively and
with human dignity. As a result, childbirth is turned into an experience of suffering and humiliation, lying waiting, with the great
machinery of the uterus twisting and kneading away, not knowing
what is happening to her, or what she can do to help herself, and not
understanding what the masked figures around her are saying.'
    The connection between my own findings and the sort of feelings
described by these authors finds some support in Rosengren's study
quoted earlier (1961b). Rosengren distinguished women who look
upon pregnancy as an illness from those who see it as a normal state.
He found that women who regarded pregnancy as an illness tended
to have longer labours than those who did not regard pregnancy as an
illness. In my own study the ill-adjusted women tended to have longer
labours than the well-adjusted ones. It may be that the women who
have more difficulty with all aspects of childbearing, more often regard pregnancy as an illness, which means as something external
which the woman receives passively. This would link up with my
interpretation of the higher 'femininity' score in the ill-adjusted
group as indicating the greater sense of passivity.
    More research would be needed to understand the social and psy-
chological elements which enable some women not to succumb to

this passive, infantile, 'ill' self concept and to be able to feel that 'woman is not an impassive container for a foetus' (Kitzinger, 1971). In our present culture, this may need a certain degree of independence from current concepts which permeate not only everyday attitudes but also scientific writings.

To come back to my findings on the Franck Drawing Completion Test, the 'femininity' scores were similar at the first testing for the well- and the ill-adjusted groups, but the number of 'passive containers and houses' was already slightly higher for the ill-adjusted women. This helps to stress the fact that here again we are faced with a complex process where past experiences, present experience and cultural stereotypes interact. I would like to suggest another possible interpretation which may be contributing to the increase in 'femininity' score in the ill-adjusted group. This refers to something I have discussed in a previous chapter. I showed that the women in the ill-adjusted group were more preoccupied postpartum with what is relevant to being a mother. In the same way as the ill-adjusted mother discriminates people more in terms of their motherliness, she depicts more objects related to the home and to what a mother ought to be thinking about (houses, interiors, etc.).

The Franck Completion Test thus appears to be, at least in part, culturally determined, although it had been thought to be culture free and its measure of femininity is partly a cultural one.[1] Indeed, how could one claim that the women who go through pregnancy and the birth of their child normally are more masculine than those who suffer various psychological and physiological disturbances?

In an exploratory study I administered the Franck Drawing Completion Test to some volunteer university students, twenty-four males and twenty-three females. I found no difference between average scores for men and women. The average score for the female student sample was more 'masculine' than that of my pregnant sample. The university sample is too small and unsystematically collected to allow any definite conclusions. However, it should be

[1] I would not recommend that the current scoring system of the Franck Drawing Completion Test be used before more thought is given to the various elements tapped by the test. The different components currently collected under the label of 'femininity' must be explored separately and reconsidered without prejudiced ideas of femininity. Content and form should be considered separately, the latter being perhaps less culturally determined than the former.

pointed out that all the women in the university group were engaged in a creative intellectual enterprise as opposed to the women in the pregnant sample, almost all of whom were only too happy to give up the jobs they were pursuing for purely financial reasons. This supports the idea that part of what is being measured by this test is an active creative element, which culturally has been defined as masculine.

Although Franck's test is, I have shown, partly culturally determined, I would like to stress that I do not thereby reject the possibility that male and female body image is partly reflected in the drawings. Only it would be necessary to tease out the cultural from the biological. I do not agree with Kate Millet (1969) who derides Erikson's stress on the importance to the woman of her 'inner space', though I would agree with her that he does fall over backwards in his idealization of the woman and her uterus.

It may be interesting to reconsider the results from a study I mentioned at the beginning of the book, in the light of my own findings and interpretation of them. I am referring to Nilsson's study of paranatal emotional adjustment: he found that 'masculine women as defined by a verbal masculinity–femininity scale (strong and self-confident for example being masculine characteristics) more often resembled their fathers, reported fewer neurotic symptoms, fewer symptoms during pregnancy and less frequently reported dysmenorrhea.' The author interprets this as a denial on the part of these supposedly 'masculine' women 'who have tended to compensate or conceal the problems which a more masculine identification must entail in connection with childbirth'. It seems necessary to question this assumption and wonder if such a masculinity–femininity scale is measuring anything besides a cultural stereotype and if the more so-called masculine women are not, in fact, better able to cope with a stressful situation (feeling strong and self-confident is a prerequisite for coping). Since the situation in question is childbearing, it is essential to reconsider the definitions of 'masculine' and 'feminine'.

There seem to be two attitudes in regard to childbearing. One of them assumes, like Nilsson, that the women with traditionally conceived masculine attitudes must encounter problems. I have shown that it is more likely to be the women with the stereotyped 'feminine' attitudes who will encounter problems. The other one, held by Freud, asserts that the woman who is having a child needs to be at this time masculine because she needs to be active (calling on her innate bi-sexuality). This is the kind of idea expressed by Marion Milner (1950) when she says: 'The urge to female passivity and receptivity in situations where a male active response is actually required is likely to bring an acute sense of personal futility.' I strongly feel that if activity is necessary in a woman for childbearing then it is absurd to call it temporary masculinity. That receptivity is more important at other times in no way diminishes the fact that this activity is an intimate part of femininity. Femininity is not composed of one attitude, emotion, self-concept but can mean different things at different times in a woman's life or moments in her life. To restrict the term as it has been done is harmful. One can only talk about masculinity in a woman when there is a sense of maleness (when the woman feels or fantasizes she has or wishes she had a male body) or when there is a wish to penetrate and impregnate. This is not the case with a normal woman having a child (which does not mean that a masculine fantasy cannot be present at times).

I think it is important when we talk of masculinity and femininity to remain at the biological level. Femininity refers to the qualities which make for a good adjustment to the female biological role, the bearing of young. It is however worth mentioning in passing that there are other situations in which the traditional feminine stereotype is maladaptive. In an unpublished study using the Repertory Grid, Ryle (1970) found that female students who consulted psychiatrically were less likely to identify with their fathers; neuroticism was associated with low instrumentality (the masculine sex role). Ryle argues that if one equates low instrumentality with relative passivity and ineffectiveness it is possible to see how the female, unlike the male, can be neurotic 'without rejecting her sex role attributes or her same sex parental model'. In other words she can be neurotic, 'feminine' and like her mother. Thus, in the same way as the 'culturally feminine' woman may be ill prepared for a good adjustment to motherhood, she may also be ill prepared for a number of other situations such as a university career (the latter is more obvious since the 'feminine' woman is not particularly expected to be intellectually oriented).

When I discussed the sense of femaleness earlier on and referred to body image, I referred to internal organs, because the genitals are what differentiate the boy and the girl. But at adolescence other body changes occur: breasts and hips in the girl, different distribution of body hair and of fat in the boy and the girl. In our society, breasts much more than the womb and vagina have come to symbolize femininity in its eroticized aspect. To such an extent that often women will not breast-feed for fear that this will spoil the shape of their breasts. Breasts have become quite split off from their maternal function. Lucie Jessner in an article entitled 'On becoming a mother' (1966) describes the feelings of a pregnant woman: 'Mrs O. was plagued by a dream: she was in an auditorium; a girl in a sexy black dress was there and Mrs O.'s husband got up to sit with the girl. The dream reminded Mrs O. that she was self-conscious of her figure and afraid of losing what had been most precious in her life: to be a woman, loved and in love. Her own feelings had become less passionate and intercourse had become a duty for her. She found some comfort in her husband's objection to breast-feeding: he said her breasts belonged to *him*. She agreed with him although she had heard that nursing a baby was the most blissful sensation. But keeping a part of herself and her beauty reserved for her husband gave her some confidence that she might be a mother and an attractive woman as well'.

In my sample, eleven out of the fifty women (21%) did not attempt to breast-feed, thirteen women breast-fed for not more than two weeks, sixteen women breast-fed for more than two weeks but less than two months, and twelve women were still breast-feeding at the time of the last interview (ten weeks postpartum). None of the six women who said during pregnancy that they did not want to breast-feed changed their minds. All the thirty-one women who firmly expressed the desire to do so breast-fed, twenty-four of them for at least a month. Of the remaining fifteen women who expressed mixed feelings or who expressed different views early from late pregnancy, or felt some outside pressure to do so (from the husband, for instance), eleven attempted breast-feeding but only four breast-fed for at least one month. These ambivalent women gave as reasons for giving up in most cases the insufficiency of milk ('the milk dried up', 'I didn't have enough milk') or the dissatisfaction of the baby ('I enjoyed it but the baby wasn't satisfied'). This type of reason was given much less frequently by the women who had definitely wanted to breast-feed; some of their reasons for stopping were bleeding, lumps in the breast or inverted nipples. Three of the women in this group who definitely wanted to breast-feed stopped because they were 'very tired', two because they 'didn't like it' and one because she said it was 'too much of a battle'; none of these latter reasons were

174 The Birth of a First Child

given by the women in the ambivalent group. This may be reflecting the fact that the women who had had mixed feelings about breast-feeding had been more likely to breast-feed because they felt they ought to and only felt justified to give up for reasons out of their control. If they were breast-feeding because it was best for the baby then they could stop because it was best for the baby (not enough milk, the baby didn't enjoy it, etc.). On the other hand the women who really had wanted to breast-feed could admit more readily that they didn't like it. Social pressures in relation to breast-feeding are actually rather interesting in that they are conflicting. On the one hand, the perfect mother is depicted as one who breast-feeds, in a blissful asexual union with the child (pain or sexual excitement are carefully forgotten). On the other hand, in many hospitals there is pressure from the medical staff for mothers to bottle-feed, making the process a more standardized sterile mechanical routine – also a way of avoiding too many feelings.

In my sample, as many women from the ill-adjusted as from the well-adjusted group never attempted breast-feeding (17% in both cases). By the time of the last interview (ten weeks after the birth) more women in the well-adjusted group (33%) than in the ill-adjusted group (11%) were still breast-feeding. It could be that the same reasons which made some women well-adjusted also made them longer breast-feeders, or it could be that because they were feeling better and were having an easy time with the baby, they were able and happy to breast-feed longer. Looking at the criteria separately I found that the increased likeliness for the well-adjusted women to be breast-feeding at the time of the last interview relates to the depression and baby criteria only. Looked at the other way around it is probably also the case that the women who, when I came for the last interview, had only fairly recently weaned their babies (which was more often the case for the ill-adjusted women since less of them were still breast-feeding) were more likely to feel depressed because of the severance, the baby more likely to be unsettled and their relationship more likely to be difficult.

Breast-feeding is obviously a feminine activity but psychoanalysts have reported that for some women breast-feeding has a masculine meaning. Melanie Klein in particular has stressed the unconscious

1 When there is an overt pressure to breast-feed, it is very often unconsciously undermined by great disapproval if it takes time for mother and baby to get used to each other and if the baby does not conform to the four hourly blue print.

equivalence between the breast and the penis (developmentally the experience of the breast is the primary one). I thought it would be interesting to see if, in my sample, the women who were still breast-feeding at the time of the last interview tended to identify more with their mothers (the feeding role) as well as more with their fathers (the phallic aspect) than the women who were no longer breast-feeding. For this I looked at the perceived similarity between themselves and each of their parents (on the Repertory Grid). Indeed, as a group, the women who were still breast-feeding tended to see themselves as being more like their mothers (though the difference is small) and also more like their fathers (to a larger extent) than did the women who were no longer breast-feeding. I also compared the women in terms of their scores on the Franck Drawing Completion Test. I made no predictions as the women who were still breast-feeding might either obtain more feminine scores (mothering element) or more masculine scores (intrusive mode). (This was, by the way, before I discovered that Franck's interpretation of the test was erroneous.) I found that there tended to be a larger spread in scores for the women breast-feeding than for the ones who were no longer breast-feeding (in other words a tendency for more extreme, both 'feminine' and 'masculine' scores on this test for the women still breast-feeding). If my interpretation of the test is correct, then one could say that this reflects a feeling of greater 'activity' and initiating (so called masculinity) in some women, and of greater 'cultural femininity' in others at the time when they are breast-feeding. This cannot however settle the question of what kind of activity we are talking about: what I would call feminine activity (when the mother feels herself to be a feeding mother involved in active giving) or masculine activity (where the breast-feeding symbolizes phallic intrusiveness). Doubtless both could be present in different women or even in the same woman.

Finally, in this area of childbearing and sexual identity it is interesting to consider what the sex of the child means to the mother. In my sample there were twenty-five male babies and twenty-six female babies. In the well-adjusted group there were twice as many boys as girls (eight boys and four girls), in the ill-adjusted group there were twice as many girls as boys (twelve girls and six boys). Since the doctor's report of pregnancy and childbirth is irrelevant here, I took a look at the difference in proportion of girls and boys in terms of the two other criteria. There is no difference in terms of the Baby Score, that is roughly half of the women who had a positive

view of their babies had girls, and roughly half of the women who
had a negative view of their babies had girls. There is however a
very large difference when we consider the depression score. 61%
of the women who gave no evidence of being depressed postpartum
gave birth to boys while only 17% of the women who were depressed postpartum gave birth to boys. In the 'depressed group'
there were only three baby boys as opposed to fourteen baby girls
(in the 'non-depressed group' there were thirteen girls and twenty-
one boys).[1] It is possible to understand this finding in terms of a
more ambivalent relationship between mother and daughter than
between mother and son. Without endorsing Freud's notion that a
woman compensates with her son for the lack of a penis (his basic
explanation for female psychology) we can retain from him the
notion that a mother's reaction to her son is 'the most free from
ambivalence of all human relationships' (1933), at least initially. As
is so often the case with Freud's generalizations, what may be partly reflected here is a cultural phenomenon, that of the greater value of
males in our society and the widespread notion that having a boy as
a first baby is preferable. This used to be concretized in laws of in-
heritance. Also a baby, in particular the first, can easily represent
what the woman would herself like to be – in our society it is often
a boy (such a preference need not only be cultural and can also be
linked to personal circumstances). Gillman (1968) found in a sample
of forty-four primiparous American women that dreams of boy
children were twice as frequent as dreams of girl children.

The greater depression in many of the women who gave birth to
baby girls then would be linked to their disappointment and con-
sequent guilt. Psychoanalysts have related depression to feelings of
guilt in relation to angry feelings. There was a tendency for the
women who gave birth to girls to respond more often positively
than did the women who gave birth to boys to the following questions: 'Do you easily lose your temper?' and 'Do you feel ashamed
for any reason?'

This preference for a male child is often not acknowledged or even

[1] Brice Pitt, in his study, did not find such a difference. However he considers
multiparous women as well as primiparae, and the psychological response to
the sex of the baby is most probably different with the first and subsequent
children. Also his depressed group included only very depressed women. The
six mildly depressed women in my sample (increase of less than six points on
the questionnaire) all gave birth to girls. Pitt did not include mildly depressed
women in his depressed group.

conscious. Many women would not express a preference during pregnancy. Out of the twenty-nine who did express a preference, sixteen said they would like a boy and thirteen a girl. Surprisingly twenty-one out of these twenty-nine gave birth to a child of the desired sex. It makes one wonder if there is in some women an unconscious knowledge of the sex of the child they are bearing. (For example the production of hormones is different when the foetus is male or female; an analysis of the amniotic fluid can reveal the sex of the baby. One could hypothesize that this difference is recorded in some part of the mother's brain.)

Actually it is difficult to know how to interpret an expressed preference. Mrs Jones, for example, expressed in late pregnancy her wish to have a girl: 'I think it will be a girl, I would like a girl. I look at girls' clothes. Perhaps it's because my mother says it will be a girl.' (She is the eldest of a large family and her mother's feeling that she will have a girl might be the wish to repeat herself through her daughter.) Mrs Jones gave birth to a boy. She said that her first reaction on seeing the baby was to cry 'because I wanted a boy so much'. This particular case illustrates the finding that, regardless of expressed preference, women were depressed less often after giving birth to boys.

I have tried to show in this chapter that in order to understand femininity it is important to look at the awareness of femininity, the acceptance of a female body and biology, and at specifically female states. Parallel to Freud's conception of the male as the prototype of the human being with the female seen as an incomplete man, there has been a tendency to consider specifically female states as illnesses. Menstruation, pregnancy, menopause are often construed as illnesses and women are encouraged to consider them as such. To equate these states with illness is dangerous and prevents a real understanding of women.

Chapter 7
Some more findings

My study was about childbearing – this includes pregnancy, child-birth and the postpartum period. Many different feelings are experienced at this time: feelings relating to present states, anticipations, conflicts, body changes, togetherness and separation, hospitals, changes in relationships, feelings relating to competency, etc. I asked each woman at our last meeting what had been to her the most significant aspect of the experience, that stuck most in her mind. It was obvious from the women's questions that they had no idea what kind of answer I expected from them. I gave no direction. I wanted to understand each woman's personal experience.

The largest proportion of experiences described related to the postpartum period and to the baby (this could partly be related to the fact that it was the closest point in time to the interview). Mrs Marsh talked about 'the way he is growing since he is born' and Mrs Cooper described her 'fear of dropping the baby'. Many women described their feeling of amazement at the creation of a new being. Mrs Pyke: 'I think it's a miracle; carrying her for nine months and then she is so perfect with eyes, nose, even her personality is special.' Mrs Cobb: 'The wonder of it all. From egg to now. Perfect fingernails, eyebrows, etc. How two ordinary people like this can produce such a perfect baby!' Mrs Hooper: 'To think that *she* came out of *me*; that nature should be so perfect – down to the fingernails and the milk for feeding. Even now I can't relate her and my pregnancy. It is so amazing.'

The second most frequent experience referred to was the actual birth. Mrs Rand said: 'The most significant experience was the birth. It was a weird experience, a shock. But it was also satisfying. I now have a lot of respect for women, women who have many children. I found it a very humiliating experience, very animal like – the things one says! Of course part of it was the drugs.' Mrs Greenson: 'the most significant experience was when the baby's head first appeared.'

Mrs Cox: 'the birth was a shock. I wasn't prepared for it. It's like an accident. Very frightening.' Mrs Dare: 'The evening of the birth: I felt so pleased with myself; as if I'd done it all myself.' Mrs Carter: 'The most significant experience was the actual birth. Feeling something hot and wet beside me. Marvellous feeling.' Mrs Goodburn: 'The most significant was the birth: the baby's head coming through. Feeling of joy.' Mrs Hunter: 'What I remember most is the beginning of labour. We had been watching a TV programme: a horror film, when the pains started. My husband was annoyed because I so often thought it was starting. I went to bed and then had to get up again.' Mrs Jones: 'Waiting for labour pains every five minutes; wondering if this was labour; it was frightening.'

Some women referred to an event during pregnancy such as being sick all the time, or waiting for the arrival of the baby. Most frequently they mentioned the first sign of life, the movements of the baby. Mrs Nelson said: 'The most significant experience was the movements of the baby. It was lovely. He was a very active baby and kicked every night. When I was in hospital after he was born, I expected he would kick till I remembered he was born. I felt so thin after he was born, I almost preferred being the way I was when I was pregnant.'

I also classified responses in terms of whether the experience related was a positive or a negative one. Slightly more than half of the responses which I could classify in this way referred to a positive experience: the baby's first smile, a feeling of fulfilment at birth, the excitement of feeling the first movements of the baby, a sense of happiness. Negative experiences often related to childbirth: 'The birth, it was like a shock, like having an accident', 'the birth, it's like a climax, it's terrible, I relive it at night', 'birth, it's a weird experience – it's animal like'. Sometimes fear, anxiety about coping with the newborn or morning sickness during pregnancy were mentioned. Positive experiences were only slightly more often expressed by women in the well- and medium-adjusted groups (this is not statistically significant).

Finally, I looked at the responses in terms of whether the experience described was self-oriented or baby-oriented. There were more self-oriented responses. I include here the comments referring to childbirth (unless it relates to the baby being born) but also more interestingly the ones concerned with the woman's own or other people's attitudes to her. Mrs Harris: 'The most significant is the fact that I'm so motherly. For example, I go down at every noise to see if the baby is OK; I didn't think that I would be like this. Also this has made me closer to my husband. I thought I would be jealous, but no. I can't believe the baby is really mine.' Mrs Daniels: 'other people's reaction to one – everybody is so friendly. You meet a lot of people. Before I didn't know anyone. Also other wives with children treat you as an equal. I can't believe she is really mine.' Mrs Tisman: 'People want to be more friendly. You make more friends. They are all waiting and doing things for you. Whereas before you are on your own.' Mrs Carter: 'being a mother, pride.' Mrs Dare: 'That evening I felt so pleased with myself, as if I'd done it all myself.' The baby-oriented responses related to the movements of the baby, to seeing the baby is born alright, to his being 'so perfect'; one woman expressed her amazement at 'having someone you are responsible for, someone who comes before you'. A few experiences related neither to herself nor to the baby but concerned the husband. Mrs Daly: 'The most significant was my husband's face when he came to see me. He was beaming . . . and he rarely smiles! He asked: "Is it all right?" "What do you mean is it all right? What's all right?" "The baby." "Of course it's all right".'

As I showed in earlier chapters, a fair amount of change occurred in this group of women. However the changes I recorded indirectly might well be different from the change actually experienced by each woman. I therefore asked each woman at our last meeting if she felt she had changed and if so how. Roughly 60% of the women felt that they had changed since the beginning of pregnancy. A lot of the changes expressed referred to such things as sense of responsibility, confidence and ability to nurture. Mrs Cobb: 'I feel more responsible, more mature. You *have* to be careful when you prepare bottles or change nappies.' Mrs Greenson: 'I have more confidence. Being married and having a child makes you feel more adequate. You must have something if you can be a wife and mother. I was very shy and self-conscious when I was younger. Now I'm OK. Also you become less modest; for instance taking a bath in front of others in hospital.' Mrs Phillips: 'Yes I have changed. There are things you *have* to do. You have more responsibilities. I feel very much more capable of coping with things than previously. One is forced into instant maturity.' Mrs Sanders: 'I feel more responsible and think less of doing housework, washing, etc., but otherwise I feel as before.' Mrs Mills: 'I think I've matured. I am more understanding, more intelligent. You have to do all the thinking for the baby, you have to have patience. It worried me since I'm quick-tempered – but I've never lost my temper with her.' Mrs Line: 'I feel I am a better person. I feel sorry for babies who for example have no fathers; I look into prams, etc. In this sense I have changed a lot.' Mrs Laing: I've changed. I used to be softer. Now I can stick up for myself. I feel better about it.'

A few women referred to the change in life-style. Mrs Boulton: 'Yes, I have changed. I'm more motherly, less ambitious. Now I'm happy to stay at home. I didn't think I would love her as much as I do. I'm not bothered if I stay home in the evenings.' Mrs Goodburn: 'now day and night is filled.' Mrs Davey: 'The main change is because I'm not working. I don't have to rush etc. Although I find certain tensions and strains directly connected with looking after the baby, these are much less than certain emotional tensions I experienced when I was working full time – mainly because I can now do things in my own time and leave them if I feel so inclined. No external pressures. The loss of personal freedom hasn't hit me too much yet although occasionally I realize it when, for example, even a short expedition out to the shops or to have my hair cut, necessitates either taking the baby or making provisions for him.' Mrs Bolt: 'I'm more housewifey. Not much change otherwise. I feel a bit tied to the home. Still go out most days.'

Some women noted the fact that now the baby comes first. Mrs Daniels: 'Yes, I've changed. You're a parent not a child anymore, with responsibilities, etc. You have to think of the child first.' Mrs Raymond: 'I've changed. I'm baby oriented. The baby comes first. I feel that I am now having to adapt to being less important than the baby in many respects. No matter how I feel, he must come first and if I must sacrifice anything I used to do, then it is only fair. We are now a complete family, and although I am very close to my own parents, my family and my way of thinking come first.'

A few women experienced childbearing as an achievement: Mrs Craft: 'I am more tolerant. I feel proud, a sense of achievement. I feel adult. People respect you more, they don't question your word.' Mrs Ramsey: 'I've changed in every way. I feel more adult. I feel I've achieved something.' Greater independence was also mentioned; Mrs Hooper: 'I've changed in the sense that I don't need other people so much. But this is more a gradual process over the last few years.' Mrs King: 'My ideas about bringing up children have changed. I

don't want advice from anyone. I want to make my own mistakes.'
Some women just referred to their feeling state. Mrs Dare: 'I feel
more content, happier, more complete.' Mrs Tisman: 'I'm more
content, I don't need to buy things all the time.' Some negative
states, too. Mrs Thomas: 'I feel depressed. My husband says that I'm
unhappy since I had the baby.' Mrs Lambert: 'I feel irritable, I
forget things.' One woman expressed the feeling, implicit in some of
the other statements, that other people's expectations or reactions to
the young mother have changed. Mrs Ward: 'I haven't changed but
other people have changed. My mother gets on much better with
me now, also with my husband.'

Amongst the women who feel they haven't changed, two feel that
they were different during pregnancy. Mrs Nelson: 'I am now the
same as before. I felt changed during pregnancy.' I asked in what
way. 'We were together, now we are separated.' Mrs Soper: 'I
haven't really changed. I have gone back to how I was before.
During pregnancy I had less energy.'

Amongst the women who feel they have not changed, Mrs Rand:
'I don't feel more mature. I must keep reminding myself that I am a
mother and responsible for someone else than myself.' Mrs Hunter:
'I haven't really changed, I often don't notice he is there, between
feeds.' Mrs Underwood: 'I don't feel I've changed; it's a part of me
that has been suppressed, having waited for many years to conceive;
I feel fulfilled.'

On the whole, the changes expressed are positive, whether the
women belong to the well- or the ill-adjusted group. Mrs Thomas
and Mrs Lambert, the two women who expressed some difficulties
(depression and irritability), belong to the intermediary group.
Similarly there is not much difference between well- and ill-adjusted
women in terms of whether they experienced change or not.

My study is concerned with the processes of change occurring at
the time of having a first child. However, tangentially, let us see if it
is possible to detect early on those women who will encounter difficulties; this is important in the area of preventive medicine. Psycho-
therapeutic help has been shown to be particularly helpful during
pregnancy.

I mentioned earlier that there was a tendency for the younger
women in the sample to experience difficulties. The seven women
who were twenty years old or younger belong to the two groups with
difficulties (five in the ill-adjusted group). None of the women in the

well-adjusted group were this young. The young age was often accompanied by premarital conception or unintentional conception. In fact there were roughly as many premarital conceptions in the group with no difficulties as the one with most difficulties – so it is probably the combination of age and premarital conception.

The fact of planning the pregnancy didn't seem to affect much its course but as I pointed out earlier, the question of 'planning' is rather more complex than it appears.

Four women in my sample experienced some problem with conceiving. One woman got pregnant after making an appointment with the fertility clinic, one woman got pregnant just after her visit to the fertility clinic, another woman one year after the visit, and the fourth woman got pregnant as she was about to adopt (the adoption had just come through). All four women experienced some difficulties (one woman was in the ill-adjusted group).

In terms of family background, I found that in the lesser-adjusted groups, eleven out of the thirty-nine women had lost a parent during childhood or up to one year before the pregnancy, as opposed to one out of the well-adjusted women. In four cases it is the loss of the mother. The one woman who's mother died when she was a child belongs to the ill-adjusted group; the two women who lost their mother during adolescence belong to the intermediary group. In the last case, the woman's mother died when she was an adult; this woman belongs to the well-adjusted group. None of the women in the well-adjusted group lost a parent during childhood, as opposed to six women in the other two groups (if we arbitrarily carry childhood up to thirteen years of age). This suggests a problem area, though the numbers are too small to draw definite conclusions.

All of the eleven women who are only children presented some difficulties (four women in the ill-adjusted group and seven in the intermediary group). There is some evidence in the psychological literature that only children experience more difficulties in various areas; in the case of childbearing it could be that the aspect of sharing is more problematic for a woman brought up as an only child (obviously here again one would need a larger sample to confirm the hunch).

A number of women lost a parent shortly before the pregnancy or during the pregnancy. This is not predictive of outcome. In fact, none of the women who suffered this kind of loss belonged to the group with most difficulties. One woman, for instance lost, two relatives during pregnancy. She described going to the funeral and feeling the movements of the baby during the ceremony; this juxtaposition of life and death gave her a painful feeling of uneasiness and she added at the bottom of the depression questionnaire, 'feeling of unreality'. Another woman lost her father while she was pregnant. Both these women belong to the well-adjusted group.

Three women had a miscarriage prior to this pregnancy; two of them experienced some difficulties with this pregnancy, the third did not.

To summarize, very tentatively, it is suggested that women who conceive when they are very young particularly if the pregnancy is premarital, women who have lost a parent in childhood or later, women who are only children and (possibly) women who have had difficulty in conceiving are more likely to experience difficulties with the birth of their first child.

The next step is to see if any of the data collected during pregnancy was predictive of difficulties. Early in pregnancy, a majority of women (78%) reported a physical symptom – mostly vomiting and nausea, also headaches and tiredness, fainting, high blood pressure. There is not much difference between the groups. Seventy-three per cent of the women in the well-adjusted group and 89% of the women in the ill-adjusted group reported such symptoms. Late in pregnancy (7 months) there is a drop to 30% of women reporting a physical symptom such as high blood pressure, sickness, trouble with kidney, bleeding, swollen legs. The proportion is similar (27%) in the extreme groups. Fourteen women said that they were feeling very well when I questioned them in late pregnancy; in fact four of them said that they had 'never felt so well'. These four women were to experience difficulties (two belong to the group with most difficulties and two to the intermediary group). It could be that these women wished to be pregnant rather than to have a child. One of them expressed this directly: 'When I was in hospital, after he was born, I expected he would kick till I remembered he was born. I felt so thin after he was born. I almost preferred being the way I was – I had put on two stones.' In fact it is more true to say that she had mixed feelings about pregnancy since she also said, 'I felt well up to the end. I never got very big – it can be so ugly.' This wish for the pregnancy more than the child is expressed by two other women (not included amongst the four who 'never felt so well' during pregnancy). Mrs Bolt had to go into hospital for a short spell during pregnancy but apart from that felt 'extremely happy and contented'.

When her baby was born and I asked her if she wished to have any more children, she said: 'probably not. It is crowded enough here. I wanted to experience childbirth and having a baby and I did. I wouldn't want any more.' (She had a very difficult childbirth.) Mrs Ramsey said in late pregnancy that she felt 'a lot calmer' than usual, though she sometimes found the movements of the baby frightening. After the birth of the baby, she said to me that she had felt much better when she was pregnant: 'perhaps I should carry all the time.'

Of the measures collected during pregnancy (the Repertory Grid measures and the different tests), two revealed a difference between the women who were to have difficulties and those who were not. First the depression questionnaire. In late pregnancy, the women who were to belong to the well-adjusted group had a *higher* depression score than did the women who were to belong to the ill-adjusted group.[1] This so-called depression questionnaire actually relates in large part to calm and self-confidence. The women who experience no difficulties with childbearing therefore express *more* feelings of anxiety and insecurity during pregnancy than do the women who experience difficulties. I interpret this finding as lending support to the notion that the awareness and expression of conflict and 'anticipatory anxiety' (that is, the expression of anxiety before a difficult event) enable a person to work through difficulties and are a sign of psychological health. The anxiety may reflect the realization that some change will have to take place in order to meet the demands of the new situation. In other words, the woman who is able, during pregnancy, to get in touch with her feelings about childbirth and about accommodating to the new member of the family will be more able to cope with these events when they take place. This was the case, for instance, with Mrs Stokes. She was in her thirties and had not wanted to have children: 'I hate children; I never thought I would have any; I went "quite mental" when I found out I was pregnant.' On her

[1] Since a decrease in the depression score is one of the three criteria of adjustment, and since the women in the group with most difficulties also include some women whose score on the depression questionnaire decreases (since inclusion in this group requires that at least two of the criteria give evidence of a problem) one would expect a difference in the means and variances of the extreme groups. However the size of the difference between the mean depression score during pregnancy of the ill- and of the well-adjusted group is not completely determined by the fact that a decrease in depression score is one of the criteria.

depression questionnaire during late pregnancy, she reported having most of the difficulties mentioned (lack of energy, inability to relax, difficulty in sleeping, etc.). Her first thought when she saw the baby was that she didn't like her much; she got very depressed and wanted to throw the baby out of the window. And yet soon things got better and she found that she could care for the baby in a way she had not expected she would. By the time I came to see her, Mrs Stokes was no longer depressed and viewed her child positively. This woman was classed amongst the women with some difficulties as she had a difficult childbirth but not as one might have anticipated, in the ill-adjusted group. This is an extreme example but illustrates the point I am trying to make that it is probably healthier in the long run to be able to express conflicts and fears. This finding is reminiscent of the previous one concerning a tendency for the women who 'never felt so well' during pregnancy to be prone to difficulties later on (if we can go by the small numbers); well tucked under the 'never so well' lie the unexplored and unfamiliar feelings.

Janis has described, in relation to surgical operations, the positive value of anticipatory fear. He found in his study that patients who displayed moderate anticipatory fear, asked and received realistic information about what was going to happen to them, were much less likely than those who were either extremely anxious or on the contrary constantly cheerful and optimistic, to display any emotional disturbance after the operation. 'This outcome clearly contradicts the popular assumption that placid people – those who are least fearful about an impending ordeal, will prove to be less disturbed than others by subsequent stress.' He also quotes a study showing that patients who were given a description of postoperative pain and told that such pain is a normal consequence of the operation, that they would be given pain-killing drugs if necessary and told how to relax their muscles in order to reduce the pain (these were abdominal operations) required less narcotics on the five days following the operation than did the patients who were not given such information. The prepared patients were also able to go home earlier than the others. Janis concludes: 'A person will be better able to tolerate suffering and deprivation if he worries about it before hand rather than remaining free from anticipatory fear by maintaining expectations of personal invulnerability. This generalization, if confirmed by research in other stress situations, might turn out to hold true for many non-physical setbacks and losses such as career failures, marital discord, and bereavement' (1969). Such 'work of worrying' I feel explains my own findings that the women in the well-adjusted group gave evidence of more expressed anxiety during late pregnancy. Similarly Yalom (1963) found a relationship between postpartum depression and less fear of labour during pregnancy.

It would be interesting to find out the effect of information given before the birth and the woman's opportunity to 'rehearse' what will be happening to her on the actual labour and delivery, the woman's tolerance of pain and on how she experiences childbirth. I have not got the data for this in my own study. I did however ask each woman in late pregnancy how she felt about labour and delivery and, post-partum, whether it had been better or worse than she had anticipated. A majority of women said ten weeks prepartum that they were not really worried; a number said that they were worried. Three women were extremely anxious about the birth. Mrs Goodburn said she was 'terrified'; she had only decided to have a child after being assured that she could have a spinal injection as she 'can't stand pain'. Mrs Rand was 'very apprehensive' and particularly afraid of losing con-trol. Both these women found it much worse than anticipated (Mrs Rand's labour and delivery were rated as easy and normal by the obstetrician, Mrs Goodburn had a forceps delivery, rated as difficult because of the patient's anxiety). The third woman, Mrs Ramsey, felt 'scared and panicky' and afraid of losing control. However, she found it easier than expected (though she had a long labour and forceps delivery).

At the other extreme, six women were strikingly unconcerned. Mrs Bolt denied any fears at all though she told me that her own mother had been extremely ill when she was born. She found it worse than expected though the labour was short and delivery straight-forward. Mrs Bridges said she had not thought much about it: 'It's like the dentist, if you've never been, you don't know what it's like so you don't worry. I think you probably worry more the second time around.' She had a difficult childbirth requiring a caesarian and found it worse than she had expected. Mrs Tisman was unconcerned and 'can't wait to get up there'; she had a fairly long labour and forceps delivery. She found it much worse than she had anticipated. Mrs Thomas also had a forceps delivery with 'maternal distress and slow progress in the second stage'. Late in pregnancy she had told me that she was quite unconcerned about the childbirth though her husband was very worried. She found it worse than expected. She is the woman who, I had felt, expressed some anxiety about the birth in the TAT story. Postpartum she said: 'The worst is when they break your water. They come at you.' This woman's way of dealing with feelings by denial is quite well expressed by her way of coping with the baby: 'I hate babies with dummies; if he cries, I shut the living-room door and the kitchen door and put the radio on and don't hear him, so it's OK.' Mrs Down said she had not thought much about the birth. She had a normal and easy labour and delivery but said that it had been much worse than she had expected. In only one of these six cases did the woman find the birth easier than expected. Mrs Greenson had not thought much about the birth. She had a normal and easy labour and delivery, and found it easier than expected.

Altogether twenty-two women found childbirth easier than they had expected while eighteen found it more difficult. Out of the twenty-two who found it easier than expected only two had shown particularly high or particularly low anxiety about it during pregnancy (9%); out of the eighteen women who found it more difficult, seven had shown particularly high or particularly low anxiety during pregnancy (38%).

The other measure which differentiates women during pregnancy is the 'femininity' score. Although the difference is not as large as it is postpartum, there is already in late pregnancy a tendency for the well-adjusted women to have more 'masculine' scores. If my inter-pretation of the results is correct (see pages 164–171) then the women who during pregnancy already are more passive are ill-prepared for the great activity required of them for childbearing and child-rearing. It definitely puts in question the passive picture of the pregnant woman which is generally depicted as 'normal'. People are prepared to accept the fact that child-rearing necessitates a certain amount of activity (though they will not necessarily agree that this says anything about femininity) but will rarely see the pregnant state as anything but passive. I would say that pregnancy is a preparatory state where the woman must go through the 'work of worrying' and reconstruct-ing relationships and also prepare herself for the demands of the new role. This requires a certain looking into the future to a time when she will need to be active, rather than a sinking into passivity and total dependency.

Chapter 8
Summary and some thoughts

Out of the mother's anguished pain he came
Fragile to touch and strangely beautiful. Elizabeth Jennings

The research which makes the core of this book was based on the assumption that a first pregnancy is an important bio-social event in the life of a woman, accompanied, if there is to be positive adjustment, by a re-appraisal of her image of herself and her relation to important people in her life. This developmental view is shared by some authors; others view pregnancy as a hurdle to be overcome in order that the woman may return to her previous psychological equilibrium. In the research literature, methods and criteria are chosen in accordance with the point of view adopted: concentrating on what remains constant in the psychological make-up in the static approach. It is therefore not the point of the study to prove that a static approach is invalid; but rather, it is an attempt to show that a process approach is possible and can yield predictable results. In view of the complexities of the postulated process and the difficulties of carrying out research in a 'real-life situation' as opposed to a laboratory situation, it is gratifying to note that the major predictions were by and large confirmed. Indeed it was possible to identify different patterns of change in a group of well- and a group of ill-adjusted women. Besides giving evidence of specific patterns of change in self perception and supporting the idea that health involves more than just the absence of symptoms, the results can be seen as supporting the notion that conflict may be expressed in a variety of ways or, at least, that similar psychological processes can relate to very different types of disturbances, be they somatic or experiential. Let me stress again that it was not my purpose to show that, for example, difficult delivery because of uterine inertia is due to emotional factors (though this may indeed be a contributing factor) but that it is possible to identify certain processes of change in women who experience difficulties at some of the different points in the childbearing process. The emphasis is on how women deal with and change through an important event in their life – with a specific interest in those women who are well adjusted to this particular situation. It is an attempt to look at an often forgotten group of people, healthy people. When all the various possible disturbances were combined the differences between extreme groups were particularly evident. The fact that none of the measures differentiated between the women who were later to experience difficulties and those who were not *in early pregnancy*, shows that we are clearly dealing with processes centering around the meaning of the birth.

The fact that women who later showed a positive adjustment to the birth of their child were able to express more anxieties in late pregnancy gives an indication of the complex processes at work. These notions of change, of 'working through', of relations between disturbances and psychological processes contribute to support a theoretical framework concerned with meanings, structuring and development, and with the notion of 'total person' where psychic structures, psyche and soma are part of a whole.

The most striking feature amongst the women who experienced most difficulties, was the split between a very idealized picture of what they felt a mother should be like (often opposed to the bad mothering they felt they had received) and the way in which they saw themselves, after the birth of the baby. Although this same picture was at times present in well-adjusted women during pregnancy, they generally modified their picture of the good mother after the birth of the baby to a more realistic one with which they were no longer at odds. At the same time as they found themselves in greater conflict with the image of the perfect selfless ideal mother they described, the ill-adjusted women were less able to admit to imperfection when the focus was on motherliness ('maternal' dimension) specifically. It is as if they had a stricter idea of what they should or should not be like and that what they should be like was more unattainable than the other women. They were also more preoccupied towards the end of pregnancy and in the postpartum period with motherhood, as evidenced by their increased use of terms relating to motherliness. They seemed, in this sense, to be stuck with the negative experience, as opposed to the well-adjusted women who were more flexible and able to maintain an openness to other experiences.

Acceptance of pregnancy, as measured by the perception of a pregnant woman in an ambiguous stimulus, was not predictive of adjustment to the experience. There was, however, some evidence of an opposite re-appraisal of familial roles, with the women who perceived pregnancy seeing their husband as taking on the role of father and being in less of a mother role than did the non-perceivers of pregnancy.

The study also attempted to contribute to an understanding of femininity. Most striking in this respect was the fact that the women who went through the experience of having a child with least difficulties, were those women who were able to feel themselves to be active, not only after the birth of the baby but also during pregnancy. Such a sense of initiation and activity is one which has often been denied women in our culture.

In sum, those women who are most adjusted to childbearing are those who are less enslaved by the experience, have more differentiated, more open appraisals of themselves and other people, do not aspire to be the perfect selfless mother which they might have felt their own mother had not been but are able to call on a good mother image with which they can identify, and do not experience themselves as passive, the cultural stereotype of femininity.

Amongst these well-adjusted women, there seem to be those who tend to be simply adjusted or resigned to a social definition of the new role and those who are more truly in harmony with themselves (the distinction is in fact never clear cut). It would be important and useful if change is to take place to look at the social situation and current life situation of these latter women. Particularly relevant would be an understanding of the husbands' images of womanhood and manhood, motherhood and fatherhood and their ability to reconsider these with the birth of their child and if necessary free themselves from past images and cultural stereotypes. Husbands' and wives' congruent and disparate images will be an important factor in their relationship and their ability to grow together with the new experience.

Appendix
Figures and statistics

The statistical analysis was done on the data collected from 50 peripartum women and 22 'control' non-pregnant women. These two groups are comparable in terms of age and length of marriage (see Table 1)

Table 1 : *Age; husband's age in relation to own age; length of marriage*

Groups	Age		Age of husband minus own age		Length of marriage	
	Mean	*Range*	*Mean*	*Range*	*Mean*	*Range*
Pregnant	24·2	18–32	3·2	−3 to +17	2 y. 1 m.	0 to 11 y.
Control	24·7	20–31	1·5	−3 to +9	2 y. 7 m.	10 m. to 9 y. 6 m.

In order to test the hypotheses, two sorts of data were required: those relating to the actual processes of change and those which enable the distinction between good and bad adjustment. The latter are referred to as the criteria of adjustment.

I will start by reporting the data relating to the criteria of adjustment[1] and will go on to set out the results relating to each of the hypotheses. Finally, I will report on some additional findings.

A. Criteria of adjustment
The three criteria were combined to distinguish three adjustment groups:

1. Well-adjusted group: composed of those women who scored positive (healthy) on all three criteria.

[1] Data here refer to 51 women. One woman whose datum is incomplete was excluded from the final analysis relating to specific hypotheses.

2. Medium-adjusted group: composed of those women who scored positive on two out of the three criteria.

3. Ill-adjusted group: composed of those women who scored positive on one or none of the criteria.

Each of the three criteria and their distribution in the population will now be described.

1. DOCTOR'S REPORT

This report is composed of three separate three-point scales relating respectively to the pregnancy period, the labour and delivery, and the health of the baby. In each case, a rating of 1 refers to a healthy adjustment; a rating of 2 to mild symptoms; and a rating of 3 to severe symptoms. This criterion (doctor's report) is scored positive (healthy) when, and only when, all three scales are scored 1. This means that, even if only a mild pregnancy symptom is recorded (pregnancy scale scored 2), the criterion is scored negatively.

Distribution of results

Twenty-three women showed a healthy adjustment on all three scales and were, therefore, rated positively on this criterion. Twenty-eight women were rated negatively. Out of these 28, 4 women had mild or severe symptoms on more than one of the three scales.

  8 women had mild or severe symptoms on the pregnancy scale. These included hypertension and haemorrhage.

17 women had mild or severe symptoms on the labour and delivery scale. These included forceps delivery, retained placenta, uterine inertia, long labour, breech delivery, prolonged second stage, postpartum haemorrhage (800 ml).

  7 women had mild or severe symptoms on the health of the baby scale. These included jaundice, sticky eye, subluxation of hip, baby light for dates, irritable baby.

2. DEPRESSION QUESTIONNAIRE

The depression questionnaire is given twice, at interview 2, that is, about 10 weeks prepartum (Depression Questionnaire 1), and at interview 3, that is, about 10 weeks postpartum (Depression Questionnaire 2.). This 'yes–no' questionnaire is made up of 24 questions.

A response denoting adjustment is scored 0, one denoting ill-adjustment is scored 2. A 'don't know' response is scored 1. Therefore, a high score relates to the reporting of ill-adjustment by the woman. Pitt, who devised this questionnaire, found that most women have higher scores during pregnancy

and that those women whose scores increase postpartum give clinical evidence of depression. The important factor is, therefore, the difference in the scores obtained at each of the two testing sessions. All women whose scores increase from time 1 to time 2, that is, when $Q.1 - Q.2 < 0$, will score negatively (ill-adjusted) on this criterion.

Distribution of results

Seventeen women increased their score from time 1 to time 2 and were, therefore, rated negatively on this criterion (ill-adjusted). The scores of the 34 other women remained the same or diminished postpartum. These women were, therefore, rated positively (well-adjusted) on this criterion.

Mean scores were as follows:

Table 2: *Means and standard deviations for the total sample:*

	Mean	Standard Deviation
Depression Q. 1.	15·46	7·97
Depression Q. 2.	13·6	9·63
Depression Score (D1–D2)	1·9	9·32

Table 3: *Comparison with Brice Pitt's results:*

A. PERCENTAGE SCORES

	Criterion + (adjusted) %	Criterion − (ill-adjusted) %
Present sample (criterion used in this study)	66	33
Present sample (Pitt's criterion)	79	21
Pitt's sample	60	40

B. MEAN SCORES

	Depression I		Depression II	
	Mean	Standard deviation	Mean	Standard deviation
Present sample	15·46	7·97	13·6	9·63
Pitt's sample	14·46	7·90	11·8	7·90

As can be seen from the figures above, using the same definition of post-partum depression as Pitt (increase in score on the questionnaire by 6 or more points), my sample yielded a smaller proportion of depressed women (21% instead of 40%). This could be due to the method of administration (home situation rather than hospital questionnaire), the fact that Pitt's sample comprised multiparous as well as primiparous women or (and this seems most likely) the fact that Pitt tested women at an earlier date postpartum (6 to 8 weeks postpartum as opposed to 10 to 15 weeks postpartum in my sample). When the women whose score increased by less than 6 points are included in the depressed group (as is the case in the present study), the percentages are roughly similar.

Principal components of the test

In order to get a better understanding of the different dimensions being tapped by this questionnaire, a principal component analysis was performed separately for time 1 and time 2. The first three components are given below with the questions recording the highest loadings ($>\cdot30$).

(a) *Depression Questionnaire: Time 1* (prepartum)[1]
  Component 1: (18·5% of the total variance)
  Q.14: Do you feel calm most of the time? ($\cdot35$)
  Q.24: Do you have confidence in yourself? ($\cdot35$)
  Component 2: (10·29% of the total variance)
  Q.19: Have you less desire for sex than usual? ($-\cdot52$)
  Q.7: Have you as much interest in sex as ever? ($\cdot51$)[2]
  Component 3: (9·59% of the total variance)
  Q.20: Have you enough energy? ($\cdot32$)
  Q.6: Do you easily forget things? ($\cdot35$)
  Q.18: Is your memory as good as it ever was? ($\cdot34$)

These components could be labelled:

  1. Anxiety and confidence.
  2. Sexual interest.
  3. Ergic tension.

---

[1] Time 1 and time 2 refer here respectively to the first time the depression questionnaire was given (in fact the second session) and the second time the depression questionnaire was given (in fact the third session).

[2] Some questions (concerning sex, food, memory) are similar to each other although not identical. These repetitions may be in part inflating their importance on certain components; it was decided to use the questionnaire without modification, however, since it had been validated on a large sample of peripartum women.

H

(b) *Depression Questionnaire: Time 2* (postpartum)
 Component 1: (25·12% of the total variance)
 Q.24: Do you have confidence in yourself? (·32)
 Component 2: (10·44 % of the total variance)
 Q.7: Have you as much interest in sex as ever? (·39)
 Q.19: Have you less desire for sex than usual? (−·38)
 Q.9: Do you feel ashamed for any reason? (·33)
 Q.16 Does food interest you less than it did? (−·32)
 Component 3: (8·5% of the total variance)
 Q.11: Can you feel the baby is really yours? (·51)
 Q.12: Do you want someone with you all the time? (−·42)
 Q.1: Do you sleep well? (·32)
 Q.4: Have you a good appetite? (−·30)

These components could be labelled:

 1. Self-confidence.
 2. Drives and shame.
 3. Acceptance of motherhood.

 The main differences between the two testing times are the association of shame with sex and food on the second component at time 2 and the composition of the third component. At time 1, the third component relates to energy and memory, whereas at time 2, it relates more to the feeling of being a mother and of coping with the situation and being the responsible one. The lost appetite could be a sign that what is now important is feeding rather than being fed although, as is the case with other questions, a hormonal factor may also be present. Also interesting to note is the increased importance of the first component relating to self-confidence.

 An analysis of the depression scores within the three adjustment groups reveals a significantly higher mean depression score for the well-adjusted as opposed to the ill-adjusted groups at time 1 (prepartum) ($p < ·02$). The opposite is true at time 2 (postpartum) ($p < ·01$).

Table 4: *Depression scores within adjustment groups:*

GROUP	Well-adjusted		Medium-adjusted		Ill-adjusted		T statistic	F ratio
DEPRES-SION	*Mean*	*Var-iance*	*Mean*	*Var-iance*	*Mean*	*Var-iance*	*(between extreme groups)*	
Time 1	18·1	8·5	16·5	97·6	12·7	49·3	2·42*	5·81**
Time 2	9·4	14·5	12·0	104·0	18·0	101·4	2·68**	7·01**

$*p < ·02$ $**p < ·01$

Since a decrease in the depression score is one of the three criteria of adjustment, and since the ill-adjusted group includes some women whose score decreases on this questionnaire (this group includes women who score positively on one of the criteria), some difference is to be expected between the means and between the variances of the extreme groups. However, the size of the difference between the mean depression score during pregnancy of the well-adjusted group and the mean depression score during pregnancy of the ill-adjusted group is not completely determined by the fact that a decrease in depression score is one of the criteria. In order to get a better understanding of this finding, analysis of the depression scores for women who were well adjusted versus those who were ill-adjusted on the two other criteria was performed. As the figures below show, although this difference is not significant, the well-adjusted women (on these two other criteria) obtain here again a higher mean depression score during pregnancy.

Table 4a: *Depression scores for extreme groups using doctor's criterion and baby criterion only:*

GROUPS:	Well-adjusted on baby and doctor criteria (N = 15)		Ill-adjusted on baby and doctor criteria (N = 9)		T statistic	F ratio
DEPRESSION SCORE:	Mean	Variance	Mean	Variance		
Time 1	18·5	58·7	16·0	59·7	0·76	1·02
Time 2	13·9	84·0	17·9	116·9	0·97	1·39

Since questions relating to calm and self-confidence have the highest loading on the first component of the depression questionnaire during pregnancy, it seems that women who are classified as well-adjusted according to the three criteria (and to a smaller extent to the two criteria) express in particular more feelings of anxiety and insecurity during pregnancy.

3. BABY QUESTIONNAIRE

This questionnaire is composed of 6 scales which the mother is asked to rate first for the 'average baby', and then for her 'own baby'. Each scale is rated on a five point scale, the lower the rating, the better the adjustment. The final score is the difference between the summed ratings for the average baby, and the summed ratings for the own baby (average baby–own baby). A positive score, therefore, reflects the mother's view of her baby as healthier than the average baby, and gives her a positive score on this criterion. When the difference is null or negative, the woman obtains a negative score on this criterion.

Distribution of results:

33 women had a positive discrepancy score on this questionnaire, that is, saw their child as healthier than the average baby. They obtained a positive score on this criterion. 18 women had a null or negative discrepancy score on this questionnaire and were, therefore, given a negative rating on this criterion.

Table 5: *a: Mean and standard deviation Baby Score (Average Baby–Own Baby)*

	Mean	Standard deviation
Discrepancy score	1·16	3·19

b: Comparison with Broussard's Sample

SAMPLE:	Present	Broussard
Percentage + discrepancy score	64·7	61·2
Percentage − discrepancy score	35·3	38·8

As can be seen from the figures above, the results are comparable with those of Broussard, even though her group of mothers was tested one month after the birth of the baby, whereas my last interview took place between two and three months postpartum. Both groups were composed only of primiparae.

Relationship between criteria of adjustment and sub-scales:

Scores on the different criterion scales and sub-scales were intercorrelated. For the doctor's criterion (Dr T) the three sub-scales (each ranging from 1 to 3) were combined (scores thus ranging from 3 to 9). Results are given in the table below.

When considering these correlations, it must be remembered that a low doctor's rating, a positive depression difference and a positive baby questionnaire score are indicative of a healthy adjustment. The interesting and significant correlations on the sub-scales are between the depression scores during pregnancy and the doctor's report. A large depression score postpartum (Q.2) is related to a difficult pregnancy and a poor health of the baby. A high depression difference (Q.2 − Q.1), indicating the absence of postpartum depression, is linked to a good labour and delivery. These results are in the expected direction.

The fact that the relationship between the three criteria (Baby Question-

Table 6: *Correlations between criterion scores and sub-scales*

	DQ.1	DQ.2	DQ.d (C)	Dr1	Dr2	Dr3	DrT (C)
BQ. (C)	·03	−·07	·10	−·17	·15	·18	−·05
DQ.1		·45‡	·39‡	·19	−·09	·16	·10
DQ.2			−·65‡	·28†	·15	·24*	·34†
DQd(C)				−·13	−·25*	−·11	−·25*
Dr1					·14	·10	·63‡
Dr2						·15	·75‡
Dr3							·55‡

*p = < ·10; 2 tailed   †p = < ·05; 2 tailed   ‡p = < ·01; 2 tailed
    C = Criterion
  BQ. = Baby Questionnaire (criterion)
DQ.1 = Depression Questionnaire 1
DQ.2 = Depression Questionnaire 2
DQ.d = Depression Questionnaire difference (criterion)
  Dr1 = Doctor Questionnaire Scale 1
  Dr2 = Doctor Questionnaire Scale 2
  Dr3 = Doctor Questionnaire Scale 3
  DrT = Doctor Questionnaire total score (criterion) 1 + 2 + 3

naire, Depression difference and Doctor's total score) are small show that different areas of difficulty are being tapped; this justifies their separate use. Indeed, combining such different criteria, different both in terms of the areas they cover and of their nature (self report and doctor's report), reflects one of the major ideas behind this study; namely, that it is possible to distinguish processes within an ill-adjusted group from those within a well-adjusted group, whatever the particular form of disturbance. Moreover, if these two groups are to be contrasted, it is important to include as many non-adaptive ways of reacting as possible.

When the criteria are combined as previously described, the following groups are defined:

Well-adjusted group (positive score on 3 criteria) N = 11
Medium-adjusted group (positive score on 2 criteria) N = 21
Ill-adjusted group (positive score on 1 or no criteria) N = 18
(Results will be calculated on these 50 women)

These three groups are broadly comparable in terms of age and length of marriage, as shown in Table 7.

Predictions were made in terms of the three criteria combined, and in particular in terms of the extreme groups. Results concerning these specific hypotheses will now be given.

Table 7

Groups	N	Age		Length of marriage	
		Mean	Variance	Mean	Variance
Well-adjusted	11	24·4	10·0	1·8	3·5
Medium-adjusted	21	24·3	12·9	2·4	7·0
Ill-adjusted	18	24·0	18·2	1·9	4·6

B. Processes of change[1]

(A) DIFFERENCES BETWEEN PREGNANT GROUPS

1. Self-concept and perception of family members
Hypothesis A1a

Taken as a group, the well-adjusted women will see themselves as becoming more like their mothers from the first (time 1) to the last interview (time 3) and the ill-adjusted women as becoming less like their mothers from time 1 to time 3. Postpartum (time 3) there will therefore be a difference between the two groups in terms of similarity between self and mother (with the greater perceived similarity for the well-adjusted women).[2]

Operational definition: The mean self-to-mother distance on the grid will decrease for the well-adjusted group, and increase for the ill-adjusted group from time 1 to time 3. At time 3, the mean self-to-mother distance will be smaller for the well-adjusted group than for the ill-adjusted group.

Results.
Table 8: *Self-to-mother distance*

GROUPS:	Well-adjusted		Medium-adjusted		Ill-adjusted	
Time	Mean	Variance	Mean	Variance	Mean	Variance
1	·81	·05	·89	·04	·84	·06
2	·86	·06	·89	·03	·90	·05
3	·75	·03	·86	·04	·92	·04

[1] Hypotheses will be tested for the extreme groups as predicted, but results on the intermediary group will also be given here.

[2] For convenience sake, the hypotheses refer to perceived similarity or to seeing oneself as 'becoming more like' a certain person. What is referred to precisely is the degree of similarity between the woman's description of herself and her description of the other person (regardless of how aware she is of the similarity).

Graph 1: *Self-to-mother distance*

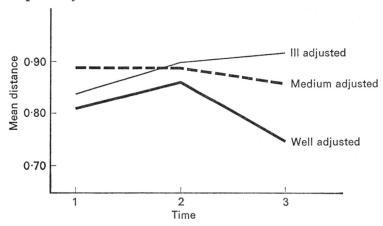

Mean self-to-mother distance decreases from time 1 to time 3 in the well-adjusted and medium-adjusted groups and increases in the ill-adjusted group as predicted, but these changes are not statistically significant. There is, however, a significant difference in means at time 3 between the extreme groups ($t = 2 \cdot 2$, $p < \cdot 02$, 1 tailed). This hypothesis is thus partially supported. The difference in means between well- and medium-adjusted groups is significant at the 10% level.

Hypothesis A₁b

If we also take account of how their own mothers are perceived, then it is predicted that the well-adjusted women, as opposed to the ill-adjusted ones will see themselves as becoming more like their own mother when the latter is perceived, or comes to be perceived as a good mother. Four different patterns of change are, therefore, predicted to be adaptive, and therefore more frequent in the well-adjusted group:

i time 1: mother seen as good mother
   time 3: mother seen as good mother
          self and mother seen as more similar than at time 1.
ii time 1: mother seen as good mother
   time 3: mother seen as bad mother
          self and mother seen as more dissimilar than at time 1.
iii time 1: mother seen as bad mother
   time 3: mother seen as good mother
          self and mother seen as more similar than at time 1.
iv time 1: mother seen as bad mother
   time 3: mother seen as bad mother
          self and mother seen as more dissimilar than at time 1

Since the 'pregnancy as development' authors talk about identification with a 'good mother image', and sometimes describe a reconciliation with own mother, the frequency of occurrence of the different adaptive patterns was hypothesized to be as follows:

i > iii > iv > ii

Four patterns are predicted to be maladaptive, and therefore more frequent in the ill-adjusted group:

a. time 1: mother seen as good mother
   time 3: mother seen as good mother
           self and mother seen as becoming more dissimilar than at time 1.
b. time 1: mother seen as good mother
   time 3: mother seen as bad mother
           self and mother seen as becoming more similar than at time 1.
c. time 1: mother seen as bad mother
   time 3: mother seen as good mother, self and mother seen as becoming more dissimilar than at time 1.
d. time 1: mother seen as bad mother
   time 3: mother seen as bad mother
           self and mother seen as becoming more similar than at time 1.

Operational definition. In the well-adjusted group, the self-to-mother distance will decrease when the mother-to-ideal mother distance on the grid is smaller or becomes smaller than 1 from time 1 to time 3, and increases when the mother-to-ideal mother distance is or becomes equal to or larger than 1 more often than in the ill-adjusted group.

The four adaptive patterns hypothesized to occur more frequently in the well-adjusted than in the ill-adjusted group are described below:

i time 1: mother-to-ideal mother distance <1
  time 3: mother-to-ideal mother distance <1
  self-to-mother distance decreases from time 1 to time 3.
ii time 1: mother-to-ideal mother distance <1
   time 3: mother-to-ideal mother distance ≥ 1
           self-to-mother distance increases from time 1 to time 3.
iii time 1: mother-to-ideal mother distance ≥ 1
    time 3: mother-to-ideal mother distance < 1
            self-to-mother distance decreases from time 1 to time 3.
iv time 1: mother-to-ideal mother distance ≥ 1
   time 3: mother-to-ideal mother distance ≥ 1
           self-to-mother distance increases from time 1 to time 3.

The frequency of occurrence of these patterns in the well-adjusted group will be as follows:

i > iii > iv > ii

The four maladaptive patterns hypothesized to occur more frequently in the well-adjusted group are described below:

a. time 1: mother-to-ideal mother distance <1
   time 3: mother-to-ideal mother distance <1
   self-to-mother distance increases from time 1 to time 3.
b. time 1: mother-to-ideal mother distance <1
   time 3: mother-to-ideal mother distance ≥ 1
   self-to-mother distance decreases from time 1 to time 3.
c. time 1: mother-to-ideal mother distance ≥ 1
   time 3: mother-to-ideal mother distance <1
   self-to-mother distance increases from time 1 to time 3.
d. time 1: mother-to-ideal mother distance ≥ 1
   time 3: mother-to-ideal mother distance ≥ 1
   self-to-mother distance decreases from time 1 to time 3.

Results.

Table 9: *Adaptive and maladaptive patterns within groups*

Groups	Adaptive pattern (i + ii + iii + iv) N	Maladaptive pattern (a + b + c + d) N
1. Well-adjusted	8	3
2. Medium-adjusted	17	5
3. Ill-adjusted	5	13

73% of the women in the well-adjusted group changed in the direction defined as adaptive as opposed to 28% of the women in the ill-adjusted group.

Table 9 gives the frequency of adaptive versus maladaptive processes within each group. A significance test was performed using the extreme groups, and revealed a difference in distribution ($x = 5.65$, $p < .02$). This hypothesis is thus confirmed.

Table 10: *Frequency of the different patterns*

PATTERNS: Groups	Adaptive patterns				Maladaptive patterns			
	i	ii	iii	iv	a	b	c	d
Adjusted	4	1	3	0	1	0	2	0
Ill-adjusted	2	0	2	1	6	0	4	3
All groups	16	2	7	5	10	0	7	4

Table 10 gives the frequency of the different adaptive patterns in the extreme groups and for the total sample. With the well-adjusted group, the frequency of the patterns differs slightly from the predicted one: i > iii > ii >iv instead of i > iii > iv > ii. Looking at the two groups together, we find that the order of adaptive patterns is as predicted: i > iii > iv > ii. The ordering of the maladaptive patterns within the ill-adjusted group alone as well as in the total sample is: a > c > d > b. This ordering reflects a tendency for pregnant women to see their mothers as good mothers (i + ii + a + b = 28> iii + iv + c + d = 23) and the tendency for women to see their mothers as being better mothers after the birth of their child, whatever group they belong to[1] (in patterns i and iii, and a and c, own mother is seen as a good mother at time 3).

Hypothesis A1c
The well-adjusted women will see themselves as becoming more similar to their notion of what a mother should be like from time 1 to time 3 (this would reflect both the reappraisal of the ideal image and the modification of the self image). The ill-adjusted women will see themselves as becoming more dissimilar to their notion of what a mother should be like from time 1 to time 3. At time 3 there will be a difference between the groups in terms of perceived similarity between self and ideal mother (with the greater similarity for the well-adjusted women).

Operational definition. The mean self-to-ideal mother distance on the grid will decrease from time 1 to time 3 for the well-adjusted group and increase from time 1 to time 3 for the ill-adjusted group. At time 3, the mean self-to-ideal mother distance will be smaller for the well-adjusted than for the ill-adjusted group.

Results.

The mean self-to-ideal mother distance, in the well-adjusted group, decreases; and in the medium and ill-adjusted groups, increases; but the changes are not statistically significant. There is, however, a significant difference in means at time 3 between the extreme groups ($t = 1.75$, $p = .02$, 1 tailed). This hypothesis is thus partially supported.

[1] Mean mother-to-ideal mother distance:

GROUPS: Time	Well-adjusted	Medium-adjusted	Ill-adjusted
1	0·93	0·94	1·00
3	0·83	0·88	0·91

Table 11 : *Self-to-ideal mother distance*

GROUPS:	Well-adjusted		Medium-adjusted		Ill-adjusted	
Time	Mean	Variance	Mean	Variance	Mean	Variance
1	·85	·04	·83	·04	·90	·06
2	·86	·07	·88	·04	·89	·07
3	·79	·02	·85	·03	·95	·06

Graph II : Self-to-ideal mother distance

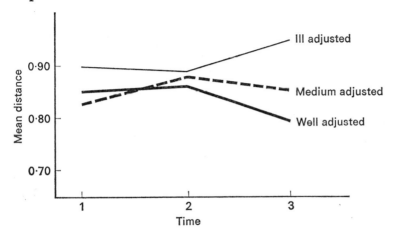

Hypothesis A1d

If one considers not only the pattern of change involving similarity of self with mother and perception of mother (hypothesis (*b*)) but also the perception of the self in relation to the ideal mother (hypothesis (*c*)) it will be possible to discriminate better between the groups than if only pattern (*b*) is considered.

Operational definition. It will be possible to increase the differentiation between well-adjusted and ill-adjusted groups if the direction of change in self-to-ideal mother distance is considered in combination with the pattern of change involving self-to-mother in relation to mother–ideal mother distance (hypotheses (*b*) + (*c*).

Results.

Table 12: *Adaptive patterns of change considering self-to-mother and mother-to-deal mother, or self-to-mother, mother-to-ideal mother and self-to-ideal mother distances*

Groups	Prediction (b) Adaptive patterns		Prediction (b) + (c) Adaptive patterns	
	N	%	N	%
Well-adjusted (N = 11)	8	73	7	64
Medium-adjusted (N = 21)	17	77	10	45
Ill-adjusted (N = 18)	5	28	2	11

This hypothesis considers the patterns of adjustment described in hypothesis A1b (involving the distance of self-to-mother, depending on whether mother is seen or comes to be seen as a good or a bad mother) along with the self-to-ideal mother distance described in hypothesis A1c. In this case, the direction of change will be considered here for the latter. 'Adaptive patterns $b + c$' in the table above, therefore, refers to those women who both changed according to one of the adaptive patterns described on page 203, but also saw themselves as becoming more similar to what they felt a mother ought to be like. This was true of 64% of all the women in the well-adjusted group as compared with 11% of those in the ill-adjusted group. This discrimination is slightly better than when hypothesis A1b is considered alone. A significance test was performed, using the extreme groups. From an χ^2 of 5·65 ($p < ·02$) when pattern b alone is used, the χ^2 is equal to 8·86 ($p < ·01$) when the pattern $b + c$ is considered. This hypothesis is thus confirmed.

Using this additional measure, the number of adaptive patterns decreases for all groups, but particularly for the medium-adjusted group which now takes on the appearance of an intermediary group.

Hypothesis A1e
In view of the fact that some women use the mechanism of denial in the face of conflict, whilst others succumb to excessive rumination, the ill-adjusted women will be either more or less satisfied with themselves as mothers at time 3 than the well-adjusted women.

Operational definition. The spread in self-to-ideal mother distances on the grid will be greater for the ill-adjusted group than for the well-adjusted group at time 3.

Results. As can be seen from Table 11, there is no increase in variance from time 1 to time 3 in the ill-adjusted group, but there is a significant difference between the extreme groups in the variance at time 3 (F ratio = 2·6, $p < ·05$, I tailed). As predicted, the spread is greater for the ill-adjusted group. This hypothesis is thus partially supported.

Hypothesis A1f
The well-adjusted women, as opposed to the ill-adjusted ones, will perceive the increased differentiation in role between self and husband from time I to time 3 and will, therefore, perceive themselves to be more dissimilar to him after the birth of the child than will the ill-adjusted women.

Operational definition. The mean self-to-husband distance on the grid will increase for the well-adjusted group and decrease for the ill-adjusted group from time I to time 3. At time 3, the mean self-to-husband distance will be larger for the well-adjusted group.

Results.

Table 13: *Self-to-husband distance*

GROUPS:	Well-adjusted		Medium-adjusted		Ill-adjusted	
Time	Mean	Variance	Mean	Variance	Mean	Variance
I	·80	·02	·84	·04	·82	·02
2	·95	·04	·78	·04	·83	·05
3	·92	·06	·85	·04	·80	·01

Graph III: *Self-to-husband distance*

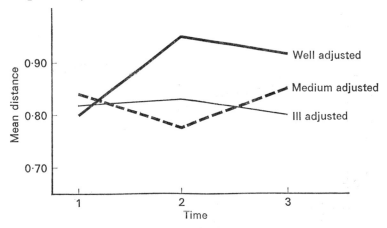

The direction of change is confirmed for both groups although the change is not statistically significant. There is, however, a significant difference in the predicted direction at time 3 between the extreme groups ($t = 1·84$, $p < ·05$, 1 tailed). The results also show that there is a significant difference between the variances of these groups at time 3, the well-adjusted group having a larger spread of scores ($F = 4·5$, $p < ·01$, 2 tailed). This difference also exists between the medium and ill-adjusted groups, the latter having the smaller variance ($p < ·02$). This hypothesis is partially supported.

Hypothesis A1g
The well-adjusted women will be more prepared to accept their new situation as mothers after the birth of the baby than will the ill-adjusted women. This will be reflected by their greater taking into account of the new situation.

Operational definition. There will be a greater use of motherhood-relevant constructs (i.e. the number of constructs having a correlation of ·67 or more with the 'maternal construct')[1] in the well-adjusted group than in the ill-adjusted group at time 3.

Results.

Table 14: *Number of motherhood-relevant constructs*

| GROUPS: | Well-adjusted | | Medium-adjusted | | Ill-adjusted | |
Time	Mean	Variance	Mean	Variance	Mean	Variance
1	3·8	3·4	5·0	6·4	4·0	4·0
2	3·1	1·5	4·7	7·5	4·7	6·9
3	3·4	6·2	3·9	4·9	5·2	5·5

Graph IV: *Number of motherhood-relevant constructs*

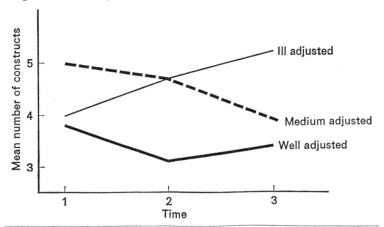

[1] The 10% level of significance was arbitrarily chosen.

The results are opposite to prediction. The ill-adjusted group increased their use of motherhood-relevant constructs. The difference between the groups is significant at time 2 ($p < \cdot 10$, 2 tailed) and time 3 ($p = \cdot 05$, 2 tailed)

Hypothesis A1h
These different predictions (a to g) are expected to occur to an even greater extent if we consider the perceptions of self in relation to important others in the area of motherhood only.

Operational definition. Predictions (a to g) will occur to an even greater extent on the partial grid.

Results. As the following Tables, 15–18 will indicate, this hypothesis is not supported.

1. *Self-to-mother distance*

Table 15: *Self-to-mother distance (partial grid): extreme groups*

Time	GROUPS: Well-adjusted Mean	Ill-adjusted Mean	t statistic
1	·722	·891	1·14
2	·835	·929	0·67
3	·695	·842	·157*

*$p < \cdot 10$

Self-to-mother distances decrease in all three groups. The difference at time 3 between the extreme groups is significant and in the predicted direction.

2. *Pattern of change involving self-to-mother and mother-to-ideal mother distances*

Table 16: *Patterns of change (partial grid)*

Pattern	GROUPS: Well-adjusted N	Medium-adjusted N	Ill-adjusted N
+	4	16	10
−	7	5	8

The results are opposite to prediction since the well-adjusted pattern is more frequent in the medium- and ill-adjusted groups.

3. *Self-to-ideal mother distance and spread in scores*

Table 17: *Self-to-ideal mother distance (partial grid)*

GROUPS:	Well-adjusted		Medium-adjusted		Ill-adjusted	
Time	Mean	Variance	Mean	Variance	Mean	Variance
1	·807	·078	·950	·176	1·050	·308
2	·846	·157	·952	·099	·986	·125
3	·998	·197	·810	·076	1.001	·164

Changes take place in the opposite direction to the prediction and to changes on the total grid: self-to-ideal mother distance increases from time 1 to time 3 in the well-adjusted group and decreases in the ill-adjusted and the medium-adjusted groups. At time 3, the distance is only slightly smaller in the well-adjusted group than in the ill-adjusted group. The distance is smallest in the medium-adjusted group and significantly different from that in the ill-adjusted group ($p < ·10$, 2 tailed). The variance is also significantly different in these two groups ($p < ·05$) as well as between well-adjusted and medium-adjusted groups ($p < ·05$).

4. *Self-to-husband distance*

Table 18: *Self-to-husband distance (partial grid)*

GROUPS:	Well-adjusted		Medium-adjusted		Ill-adjusted	
Time	Mean	Variance	Mean	Variance	Mean	Variance
1	·783	·082	·720	·101	·825	·184
2	·828	·099	·701	·072	·699	·100
3	·795	·084	·762	·123	·782	·063

Although the changes are in the predicted direction, increase in mean distance for the positive- and medium-adjusted groups, and decrease for the ill-adjusted one, none of these differences is statistically significant.

2. Changes in sense of femininity

Hypothesis A2
The well-adjusted women, as opposed to the ill-adjusted ones, will develop a greater sense of their own femininity with the birth of the baby. There will, therefore, be a difference between well- and ill-adjusted groups at time 3 in terms of femininity (with the well-adjusted women having a greater sense of femininity).

Operational definition. Mean FDCT scores will increase (more feminine scores) for the well-adjusted group from time 1 to time 3. At time 3, the mean FDCT scores will be higher for the well-adjusted group than for the ill-adjusted group.

Results.

Table 19: *FDCT scores*

	GROUPS:	Well-adjusted		Medium-adjusted		Ill-adjusted	
Time		Mean	Variance	Mean	Variance	Mean	Variance
1		19·1	14·5	17·4	12·2	19·4	12·4
2		17·9	6·7	19·2	11·7	20·1	10·1
3		16·9	7·9	18·2	11·5	20·6	13·8

Graph V: *FDCT Scores*

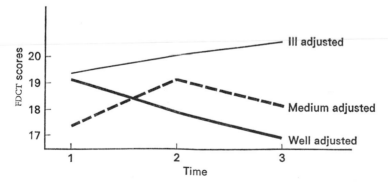

As can be seen on the graph, the well-adjusted group shows a decrease in mean score from time 1 to time 3, while the ill-adjusted group shows an increase in mean score. The well-adjusted group thus obtains more masculine scores than the ill-adjusted group at time 2 ($p<\cdot$10, 2 tailed) and time 3 ($p<\cdot$01, 2 tailed).

3. Acceptance of pregnancy

Hypothesis A3
There will be more women in the well-adjusted group than in the ill-adjusted one who accept their pregnancy.

Operational definition. More women in the well-adjusted than in the ill-adjusted group will report the woman to be pregnant on the TAT card presented at time 2.

Results.

Table 20: *Percentage of women perceiving the pregnant woman*

GROUPS:	Well-adjusted	Medium-adjusted	Ill-adjusted
% of perceived pregnant woman	64	62	67

This hypothesis is not supported. There is no difference between the groups in the percentage of women who perceive the woman as pregnant on the TAT card.

(B) DIFFERENCES BETWEEN PREGNANT AND NON-PREGNANT GROUPS

Hypothesis B1
1. As a group, the pregnant women will see themselves as more similar to their mothers, and more like their mothers than their fathers, than will the non-pregnant ones, at all three times. This would give evidence for the beginning of the process of identification with own mother during the first few months of pregnancy, or for the process which led to a decision to conceive.

Operational definition. At all three times, the mean self-to-mother distance will be smaller for the pregnant than for the non-pregnant group, and self-to-father minus self-to-mother distance will be larger for the pregnant than for the non-pregnant group.

Results.

1. *Total grid*

Table 21: *Self-to-mother distance*

GROUPS:	Pregnant		Control		T statistic
Time	Mean	Variance	Mean	Variance	
1	·86	·05	·94	·03	1·52*
2	·89	·04	·89	·02	·02
3	·86	·04	·96	·03	2·07†

$*p < ·10$, 1 tailed $†p < ·02$, 1 tailed

The difference in mean self-to-mother distance between the total pregnant group and the control group is statistically significant at time 1 $(p < ·10)$ and 3 $(p < ·02)$.

Table 22: *Self-to-mother minus self-to-father distance*

GROUPS:	Pregnant		Control		T statistic
Time	Mean	Variance	Mean	Variance	
1	·09	·08	·05	·09	0·52
2	·01	·08	·05	·12	0·51
3	·09	·07	·02	·08	0·99

The pregnant women do not see themselves as more like their mother than like their father as measured on the total grid.

2. *Partial grid*

Table 23: *Self-to-mother distance*

GROUPS:	Pregnant		Control		T statistic
Time	Mean	Variance	Mean	Variance	
1	·81	·13	1·00	·14	2·2†
2	·82	·10	1·00	·26	2·0†
3	·78	·10	·96	·15	2·0†

$†p < ·02$, 1 tailed

The difference in self-to-mother distance between total pregnant and control groups is statistically significant at all 3 times, and larger than on the total grid.

Table 24: *Self-to-mother minus self-to-father distance*

GROUPS:	Pregnant		Control		*T* statistic
Time	Mean	Variance	Mean	Variance	
1	·14	·24	—·22	·22	2·9†
2	·03	·20	—·12	·50	1·1
3	·09	·25	—·19	·36	2·0*

*p < ·02, 1 tailed   †p < ·01, 1 tailed

The pregnant women see themselves as more similar to their mother than their father at all three times; the opposite is true for the control group. The difference is statistically significant at time 1 ($p < ·01$) and 3 ($p < ·02$).

Hypothesis B2
The changes within the non-pregnant group will be random for the group as a whole, and there will, therefore, be no changes over time in the different areas considered under A1 and A2.

Operational definition. There will be no changes in the variables mentioned under A1 and A2 from time 1 to time 3 for the non-pregnant group.

Results:
Table 25: *T statistic between variables at time 1 and time 3*

Variables	*T*
Self-to-mother	0·32
Self-to-ideal mother	1·41
Self-to-husband	1·41
FDCT	0·92

None of the differences between times on the relevant variables are statistically significant. This hypothesis is thus supported.

Hypothesis B3

There will be a difference at time 3 between the non-pregnant group and the well-adjusted pregnant group in the different areas mentioned under A, that is, for the well-adjusted pregnant group, there will be a greater perceived similarity between self and mother, between self and ideal mother; a greater perceived dissimilarity between self and husband; a greater concern with motherhood and a greater sense of femininity than for the non-pregnant group. (This difference would reflect the hypothesized changes occurring in the well-adjusted group from time 1 to time 3.)

Operational definition. At time 3, mean self-to-mother distance, mean self-to-ideal mother distance will be smaller for the well-adjusted pregnant group than for the non-pregnant group; self-to-husband distance will be larger for the well-adjusted pregnant group than for the non-pregnant group; number of motherhood relevant constructs and mean FDCT scores will be larger for the well-adjusted than for the non-pregnant group.

Results.

Table 26: *Variables at time 3 on the total grid*

Groups:	Well-adjusted pregnant		Control		*T statistic*
Variables	Mean	Variance	Mean	Variance	
Self–mother	·75	·03	·96	·03	3·29‡
Self–mother⎫ Self–father ⎬	·17	·05	·02	·03	1·49*
Self–ideal mother	·79	·02	·77	·04	0·44
Self–husband	·92	·06	·86	·05	0·87
Number of maternal constructs	3·46	6·25	4·38	17·50	0·70
FDCT	16·9	7·99	18·7	7·1	1·79†

*p < ·10 1 tailed   †p < ·05, 1 tailed   ‡p < ·001, 1 tailed

This hypothesis is confirmed for the self-to-mother distance and the self-to-mother minus self-to-father distance. It is not confirmed for the self-to-ideal mother and self-to-husband distances. The 'femininity' score is significantly different between the groups in the opposite direction to that predicted, the more masculine scores belonging to the well-adjusted pregnant group (in line with the difference between well- and ill-adjusted groups). The well-adjusted pregnant group does not use more 'motherhood constructs' than the control group at time 3, and the difference between pregnant groups is thus due to an increase in the use of such constructs by ill-adjusted women.

FURTHER ANALYSIS AND ADDITIONAL FINDINGS

1. Hypotheses supported

The main hypotheses concerning opposite changes between well- and ill-adjusted groups, differentiated on a multiple criteria measure, in the perception of the self in relation to own mother and to husband, and in the satisfaction with self as a mother (in terms of identification with 'good mother' image and in terms of similarity to the 'ideal mother') were confirmed in terms of the direction of changes and the significant differences at time 3 between these two groups. The predicted changes within these groups from time 1 to time 3 were not statistically significant. The small number of women

Table 27: *Mean grid measures, F ratio and T statistic between well- and ill-adjusted women on the perception of baby criterion only*

GROUPS:	Well-adjusted		Ill-adjusted		F	T
Variables (distances)	Mean	Variance	Mean	Variance		
Self–mother						
Time 1	0·83	0·04	0·89	0·05	1·21	0·80
Time 2	0·89	0·04	0·90	0·04	1·16	0·19
Time 3	0·83	0·03	0·90	0·06	1·95†	1·05
Self–ideal mother						
Time 1	0·83	0·03	0·94	0·07	2·26‡	1·74*
Time 2	0·84	0·04	0·97	0·08	2·32‡	1·96†
Time 3	0·85	0·03	0·92	0·07	2·38§	1·21
Self–husband						
Time 1	0·82	0·02	0·82	0·03	1·49	0·00
Time 2	0·84	0·05	0·83	0·04	1·36	0·14
Time 3	0·86	0·05	0·83	0·02	2·33†	0·48
FDCT						
Time 1	18·33	13·7	18·9	12·48	1·10	0·50
Time 2	18·9	9·1	19·9	12·5	1·37	1·05
Time 3	18·2	10·2	19·9	18·4	1·81*	1·47

$*p \leqslant ·10$ $†p \leqslant ·05$ $‡p \leqslant ·02$ $§p \leqslant ·01$
(1 tailed for predicted hypotheses, otherwise 2 tailed)

in each group, and particularly the extreme ones ($N = 11$ and $N = 18$) is probably a large contributing factor. The fact that mean scores are similar between extreme groups at time 1 and very different at time 3 supports the hypothesized notion of process. The intermediary position of the medium-adjusted group at time 3 gives additional support to the results and to the tripartite grouping.

Individual criteria

The three criteria are different in nature and in timing. Two of them are based on questionnaires, one on a doctor's notes. The latter refers to the pregnancy, the birth and the baby's health after the birth; the baby criterion refers mainly to the third month postpartum and the depression criterion compares pre- and postpartum. Taken separately, each criterion yields a

Table 28: *Mean grid measures, F ratio and T statistic between well- and ill-adjusted women on the depression criterion only*

GROUPS:	Well-adjusted		Ill-adjusted		F	T
Variables (distances)	Mean	Variance	Mean	Variance		
Self–mother						
Time 1	0·90	0·04	0·78	0·04	1·02	1·90*
Time 2	0·90	0·04	0·86	0·04	1·14	0·77
Time 3	0·85	0·04	0·87	0·03	1·38	0·29
Self–ideal mother						
Time 1	0·86	0·05	0·86	0·05	1·07	0·05
Time 2	0·87	0·04	0·91	0·08	1·84*	0·54
Time 3	0·83	0·03	0·95	0·06	1·71†	1·97†
Self–husband						
Time 1	0·83	0·03	0·80	0·02	1·33	0·65
Time 2	0·86	0·05	0·79	0·04	1·06	1·05
Time 3	0·88	0·04	0·79	0·02	2·00*	1·64†
FDCT						
Time 1	18·2	13·1	19·0	13·5	1·04	0·75
Time 2	18·8	10·1	19·9	10·3	1·02	1·15
Time 3	18·3	14·0	19·6	11·2	1·25	1·21

*$p \leqslant ·10$ †$p \leqslant ·05$ (1 tailed for predicted hypotheses, otherwise 2 tailed)

different proportion of adjusted women. The largest proportion of ill-adjusted occurs for the doctor's criterion (52%) as opposed to 34% for each of the other two criteria. These differences justify a separate analysis. Since the medium-adjustment group was a result of combining criteria, we will here, of course, have only two groups with each criterion.

Table 29: *Mean grid measures, F ratio and T statistic between well- and ill-adjusted women on the doctor's sheet criterion only*

GROUPS:	Well-adjusted		Ill-adjusted		F	T
Variables (distances)	Mean	Variance	Mean	Variance		
Self–mother						
Time 1	0·83	0·04	0·88	0·05	1·08	0·74
Time 2	0·88	0·05	0·89	0·03	1·51	0·17
Time 3	0·81	0·04	0·91	0·04	1·01	1·94†
Self–ideal mother						
Time 1	0·84	0·04	0·88	0·06	1·49	0·70
Time 2	0·89	0·05	0·87	0·06	1·06	0·22
Time 3	0·84	0·02	0·90	0·06	3·31‖	0·96
Self–husband						
Time 1	0·81	0·04	0·83	0·02	1·93*	0·52
Time 2	0·84	0·05	0·83	0·04	1·23	0·06
Time 3	0·87	0·05	0·83	0·02	2·59§	0·72
FDCT						
Time 1	18·0	14·4	19·9	12·0	1·20	0·90
Time 2	18·7	11·4	19·6	9·2	1·24	1·00
Time 3	17·9	12·6	19·5	13·0	1·03	1·56

$*p \leqslant ·10$ $†p \leqslant ·05$ $§p \leqslant ·01$ $‖p \leqslant ·001$
(1 tailed for the predicted hypotheses, otherwise 2 tailed)

Self-to-mother distance

Change in mean self-to-mother distance is in the predicted direction for all three criteria, i.e. an increase for the negative scoring group and a decrease for the positive scoring group. At time 3, all the differences are in the predicted direction, but the doctor's criterion only differentiates significantly at the 5% level.

Self-to-ideal mother distance

The difference in direction of change between negative and positive scoring groups is as predicted for the depression and for the doctor's criteria. At time 3, the difference, in the predicted direction for all three criteria, is significant for the depression criterion only.

Self-to-ideal mother spread in scores

At time 3, the negative group has a significantly larger variance within each of the criteria.

Self-to-husband distance

Differential direction of change between positive and negative scoring groups is in the predicted direction for the depression and for the doctor's criteria. At time 3, the difference in means is in the predicted direction for all three criteria and reaches statistical significance for the depression score.

FDCT

At time 3, the mean score for the positive group within each of the criteria is lower than that of the negative group. None of these differences reaches statistical significance.

Each of the criteria discriminates groups at time 3 in the same direction, but the differences are larger when the criteria are combined, thus confirming the usefulness of the multiple criteria and the tripartite distinction employed.

As hypothesized, similar psychological processes can relate to different types of disturbances, be they somatic or experiential.

DEPRESSION SCORE + BABY SCORE

A further analysis was performed combining the two more obviously psychological measures (Baby score and Depression score). The well-adjusted group now includes 24 women (+ + group); the ill-adjusted group 8 women (− − group); and the mixed group 18 women (+ − group).

Distances self-to-mother, self-to-ideal mother and self-to-husband change in the predicted directions from time 1 to time 3 for the extreme groups. At time 3, the differences are in the predicted direction but only reach statistical significance for the self-to-ideal mother distance ($p < ·01$) when the variance is also smaller for the well-adjusted group ($p < ·05$). As with the three criteria combined, the FDCT means are opposite to prediction but the difference does not reach statistical significance.

Table 30: *Mean grid measures, F ratio and T statistic between extreme groups (depression and baby criteria combined)*

GROUPS: Variables (distances)	Well-adjusted		Ill-adjusted		F	T
	Mean	Variance	Mean	Variance		
Self–mother						
Time 1	0·87	0·04	0·78	0·04	1·06	1·06
Time 2	0·88	0·04	0·87	0·03	1·53	0·15
Time 3	0·81	0·03	0·85	0·03	1·15	0·48
Self–ideal mother						
Time 1	0·84	0·04	0·93	0·10	2·26*	0·96
Time 2	0·85	0·04	1·04	1·12	3·09	1·91*
Time 3	0·83	0·03	1·06	0·08	2·40†	2·58§
Self–husband						
Time 1	0·84	0·02	0·76	0·01	2·51	1·34
Time 2	0·86	0·04	0·79	0·04	1·10	0·94
Time 3	0·89	0·05	0·81	0·01	3·90†	1·03
FDCT						
Time 1	17·9	12·7	18·7	11·6	1·09	0·55
Time 2	18·4	7·6	19·7	9·9	1·31	1·11
Time 3	17·5	8·1	19·4	8·5	1·06	1·60

$*p \leqslant \cdot 10$ $†p \leqslant \cdot 05$ $§p \leqslant \cdot 01$ (1 tailed where predicted)

The mixed group is similar to the positive group for the self-to-ideal mother distance and different from the ill-adjusted group at time 3 ($p = \cdot 01$). It is similar to the negative group on the self-to-mother and self-to-husband variables and the FDCT, and significantly different from the positive group at time 3 on self-to-mother, self-to-husband and FDCT measures.

The previous results show that all three criteria contributed to confirming the hypotheses; their combination proved more discriminative than any one of them considered separately. Even the combination of the two self-report measures was not as useful as the tripartite classification using all criteria; only the self-to-ideal mother difference became larger this way.

Table 31: *Mean grid measures, F ratio and T statistic between well-adjusted and mixed group (depression and baby criteria combined)*

GROUPS:	Well-adjusted		Mixed group		F	T
Variables (distances)	Mean	Variance	Mean	Variance		
Self–mother						
Time 1	0·87	0·04	0·88	0·06	1·62	0·20
Time 2	0·88	0·04	0·90	0·05	1·17	0·38
Time 3	0·81	0·03	0·92	0·06	2·02*	1·59*
Self–ideal mother						
Time 1	0·84	0·04	0·86	0·03	1·10	0·29
Time 2	0·85	0·04	0·86	0·04	1·02	0·04
Time 3	0·83	0·03	0·85	0·03	1·29	0·36
Self–husband						
Time 1	0·84	0·02	0·83	0·04	1·84	0·11
Time 2	0·86	0·04	0·81	0·05	1·23	0·85
Time 3	0·89	0·05	0·80	0·03	1·56	1·48
FDCT						
Time 1	17·9	12·7	19·2	14·8	1·17	1·05
Time 2	18·4	7·56	20·0	13·6	1·80	1·55
Time 3	17·5	8·09	20·2	19·0	2·35†	2·45‡

$^\star p \leqslant \cdot 10$ $\dagger p \leqslant \cdot 05$ $\ddagger p \leqslant \cdot 02$ (1 tailed where predicted)

Table 32: *Mean grid measures, F ratio and T statistic between mixed and ill-adjusted groups (combining depression and baby criteria)*

GROUPS:	Mixed		Ill-adjusted		F	T
Variables (distances)	Mean	Variance	Mean	Variance		
Self–mother						
Time 1	0·88	0·06	0·78	0·04	1·53	0·98
Time 2	0·90	0·05	0·87	0·03	1·80	0·42
Time 3	0·92	0·06	0·85	0·03	1·76	0·70
Self–ideal mother						
Time 1	0·86	0·04	0·93	0·10	2·48★	0·73
Time 2	0·86	0·04	1·04	0·12	3·16†	1·73★
Time 3	0·85	0·03	1·06	0·08	3·10†	2·33‡
Self–husband						
Time 1	0·83	0·04	0·76	0·01	4·63†	0·93
Time 2	0·81	0·05	0·79	0·04	1·35	0·23
Time 3	0·80	0·03	0·81	0·01	2·50	0·14
FDCT						
Time 1	19·2	14·8	18·7	11·6	1·28	0·26
Time 2	20·0	13·6	19·7	9·9	1·37	0·17
Time 3	20·2	19·0	19·4	8·5	2·22	0·50

★$p \leqslant ·10$ †$p \leqslant ·05$ ‡$p \leqslant ·02$ (1 tailed where predicted)

2. Results opposite to prediction and hypotheses not confirmed

(A) TAT CARD 7

Perception of the pregnant woman on card 7 of the TAT card was not predictive of adjustment, as measured by the three criteria.

Davids and DeVault (1962) report that a greater proportion of women in their normal group as compared with their abnormal group perceived the woman as pregnant on this card. Davids' and DeVault's abnormal group, however, comprised only 'abnormal delivery-room records' (including such things as baby's subluxation of hip). I therefore attempted to use a similar criterion to split my sample into two groups: one composed of women who scored more than 1 (mild or severe symptoms) on either the doctor's scale relating to labour or delivery, or on the one relating to the health of the baby; the other composed of women who were well-adjusted on these two scales.

This new distinction was not more effective: 65% of the 23 women in the newly defined abnormal group and 62% of the 27 women in the newly defined normal group perceived the woman as pregnant on the TAT card. There was, however, a relationship between seeing the woman as pregnant on the TAT card and short labour time ($r = \cdot 24$), light weight of baby at birth ($r = \cdot 26$) and low Apgar Rating[1] ($r = \cdot 26$)[2]

A possible explanation for these findings could be given in terms of anxiety, with the more anxious women during pregnancy being less likely to perceive the pregnant woman. McDonald, Gynther and Christakos (1963) found a positive correlation between anxiety scores (IPAT Anxiety scale) and labour times, and Davids' and DeVault's normal group obtained significantly lower mean anxiety scores during pregnancy (MAS scale). McDonald et al. also found a positive relationship between anxiety and birth weight ($p < \cdot 01$). The inverse relationship with Apgar Rating is difficult to explain. In any case, these figures should be taken with caution as a large number of correlations were performed, thus increasing the chances of type B error.

One can also argue that acceptance of the pregnancy should entail a reappraisal of roles within the family and, in particular, a modified perception of the husband in his new role of father. The new similarity in roles should appear on the grid as a decrease in husband-to-father distance. This is indeed the case (see Tables 33 and 34 and Graph VI). On both total and partial grids

---

[1] Apgar Rating: numerical expression of the condition of a newborn infant 50 seconds after birth; it is the sum of points gained on assessment after birth of the heart rate, respiratory effort, muscle tone, reflex irritability and colour. The higher the rating, the healthier the baby.

[2] Correlations of $\cdot 24$ and $\cdot 26$ are significant at the 10% level (2 tailed) with $N = 50$.

Table 33: *Husband-to-father distances on the total grid*

GROUPS:	Perceivers		Non-perceivers		T statistic
Time	Mean	Variance	Mean	Variance	
1	·97	·03	1·06	·04	1·8*
2	·92	·05	1·11	·04	2·9‡
3	·90	·03	1·14	·06	3·9§

*$p < ·10$ ‡$p < ·01$ §$p < ·001$

Graph VI: *Husband–father distance:*

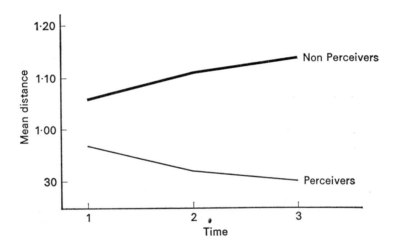

Table 34: *Husband-to-father distances on the partial grid*

GROUPS:	Perceivers		Non-perceivers		T statistic
Time	Mean	Variance	Mean	Variance	
1	0·88	0·88	1·01	0·24	1·22
2	0·80	0·11	1·20	0·17	3·75§
3	0·77	0·10	1·08	0·17	2·92‡

‡$p < ·01$ §$p < ·001$

there is an opposite trend, husband-to-father distance decreasing for perceivers and increasing for non-perceivers, leading to a very significant difference at times 2 and 3.

One could also expect the women who accept pregnancy to differentiate more between male and female roles than the other women. If this is so, there should be a greater husband-to-ideal mother distance on the grid for the former. This is indeed the case for the partial grid at times 1 and 3, and the total grid at all three times.

Table 35: *Husband-to-ideal mother distance on the partial grid*

	GROUPS: Perceivers	Non-perceivers	
Time	Mean	Mean	T statistic
1	1·00	0·75	2·69‡
2	0·92	0·78	1·26
3	1·12	0·79	2·82‡

‡$p < ·01$

Table 36: *Husband-to-ideal mother distance on the total grid*

	GROUPS: Perceivers	Non-perceivers	
Time	Mean	Mean	T statistic
1	0·93	0·85	1·60†
2	0·95	0·83	1·89†
3	0·97	0·86	1·57*

*$p < ·10$ †$p < ·05$

These findings give support to the idea that the defence mechanism of denial is present in the non-perception of the pregnancy on the TAT card since it is linked to another situation where denial seems to be taking place, that of the non-perception of the newly acquired similarity in roles between father and husband.

(B) NUMBER OF 'MATERNAL CONSTRUCTS'

Opposite to prediction, the ill-adjusted group increased the number of motherhood constructs used ($p < ·10$) from the first to the last interview. At time 3, they gave more such constructs than did the well-adjusted group ($p < \cdot 05$). A separate analysis for each criterion measure revealed that the difference was due to the depression criterion.

Table 37: *Number of maternal constructs used by depressed and non-depressed women*

GROUPS:	Non-depressed		Depressed		F ratio	T statistic
Time	Mean	Variance	Mean	Variance		
1	4·09	4·96	5·00	4·87	1·02	1·37
2	3·82	5·90	5·29	5·72	1·03	2·04★
3	3·61	4·62	5·59	5·63	1·22	2·98†

★$p < \cdot 05$ †$p < \cdot 01$

(C) DRAWING COMPLETION TEST

In an effort to understand the significant difference found on the Drawing Completion Test (more 'masculine' scores for the well-adjusted group at time 2 and, especially, 3), I looked at the different scoring categories separately. There are 23 scoring categories, 10 of which are considered male responses. Six of the 'male' categories and 8 of the 'female' categories refer to formal properties of the drawings, the rest describe content.

Formal properties of the drawings do not differentiate well-adjusted and ill-adjusted women. A large difference, however, exists at time 3 between the extreme groups for the two main female content categories. These two categories ('passive containers' and 'houses, furniture', etc.) are closely linked since houses could be considered to be a sub-category of passive containers. The difference in use of these two categories combined between the extreme groups is statistically significant at time 3 ($p < \cdot 10$).

Table 38: *Mean score in 'passive containers' + 'houses' categories on the FDCT*

GROUPS:	Well-adjusted	Ill-adjusted
Time	Mean	Mean
1	1·27	2·72
2	1·69	4·12
3	1·17	4·15

3. Additional results

(c) SEX OF THE BABY

There were 25 male babies and 26 female ones. The proportion differs within groups. In the well-adjusted group there were twice as many boys as there were girls; this proportion is exactly reversed in the ill-adjusted group. A X^2 significance test reveals a difference ($X^2 = 3 \cdot 2$, $p < \cdot 10$). The proportion is about equal for the medium-adjusted group.

Table 39: *Number of boys and girls to each group*

Sex	GROUPS: Well-adjusted	Medium-adjusted	Ill-adjusted
Girls	4	10	12
Boys	8	11	6

Since the delivery score is irrelevant when considering the psychological implications of the sex of the child, it is important to look at the two other criteria. There is no difference in terms of the Baby Score: 15 out of 32 women who scored positive on this criterion had boys; 9 out of 19 who scored negative had boys. There is, on the other hand, a significant difference between non-depressed and depressed women. 61% of the non-depressed women had boys as opposed to 17% of the depressed ones ($X^2 = 8 \cdot 82$, $p = \cdot 005$).

Table 40: *Number of boys and girls to depressed and non-depressed women*

Sex	GROUPS: Non-depressed	Depressed
Girls	13	14
Boys	21	3

The probability of obtaining such a difference through chance alone is less than 1%.

BREAST-FEEDING

In their study, the Newsons (1963) report that 54% of mothers were still breast-feeding at one month as reported to the Health Visitor, 39·5% as reported to the University Visitor. In this sample, 46·1% were still

I

Table 41: *Distribution of breast-feeders and non-breast-feeders*

BREAST-FEEDING:	Never	≤ 2 weeks	> 2 weeks ≤ 1 month	> 1 month ≤ 2 months	At the time of the last interview
Number	11	13	6	10	12
Percentage	21		56		23

breast-feeding at one month; distortion is likely to be less than in the Newsons' study which relied on retrospective interviews when the child was one year old.

Breast-feeding was related in my sample to expressed desire to do so during pregnancy. None of the 6 women who firmly said that they did not want to breast-feed attempted to do so. All the 31 women who firmly expressed the desire to breast-feed did so, 24 of them for one month or more. Of the 15 women who expressed ambivalence or who expressed opposite views at interviews 1 and 2, or who felt that they ought to or that their husbands would like them to, 11 attempted breast-feeding, but only 4 breast-fed for one month or longer.

Breast-feeding and adjustment

Table 42: *Percentage of women breast-feeding at different times within adjustment groups*

GROUPS:	Ill-adjusted	Medium-adjusted	Well-adjusted
Breast-feeding	%	%	%
Never	17	24	17
≤ 2 weeks	33	24	25
> 2 weeks ≤ 2 months}	39	28	25
At time of interview 3	11	24	33

As the above figures show, breast-feeders do not differ from non-breast-feeders in terms of adjustment. There are, however, more women breast-feeding at the time of the last interview in the well-adjusted group than in the ill-adjusted group, with the medium-adjusted group falling in the intermediate position.

Looking at the criteria separately, there was equally no difference between breast-feeders and non-breast-feeders. The increased likeliness for the well-adjusted women to be breast-feeding at the time of the last interview relates to the depression and baby criteria. The women who were still breast-feeding then tended to have a more positive view of their baby and to be less depressed. This probably reflects an interaction rather than a causal relationship.

Breast-feeding and grid measures

It seemed likely that there would be a difference between women who never attempted breast-feeding, women who breast-fed for less than two months and women who were still breast-feeding at the time of the last interview. I thought that these latter women would see themselves at time 3 as (a) more like their mothers (feeding role) and (b) more like their fathers (active partner) than either of the other groups.[1] They would also see themselves as (c) more like the ideal mother at time 3 than the group of 'unsuccessful feeders' (that is, who breast-feed for less than two months)[2] but not than the non-feeders (who probably do not see it as a necessary attribute of being a good mother). The group of unsuccessful feeders, would have (d) a larger spread in self-ideal mother scores than the successful feeders at time 3, as some women would be expressing their dissatisfaction with themselves, while others would be attempting to regain their self-esteem.

(a) Although the successful feeders do see themselves as more like their mothers at time 3, the differences are not statistically significant.
(b) The successful feeders see themselves as more like their fathers than do either of the other two groups. The difference between the mean self-to-father distance for the successful feeders and the non-successful feeders is statistically significant ($p < .05$, 1 tailed).

---

[1] Breast-feeding can be seen as combining feminine and masculine elements. In his article on maternal love, Lomas (1962) describes the woman who 'is able to combine the feminine quality of receptivity, which enables her to "hold" the baby, with functions which can easily symbolize masculine activity – for example, breast-feeding sometimes has the unconscious meaning of a phallic activity'.
[2] 'Unsuccessful' is used as a short-hand term, since this group includes women who breast-fed for a number of weeks. Women were often imprecise as to the length of time they had breast-fed (social desirability probably biasing their answers) and it seemed more legitimate to group together those women who were not breast-feeding at the time of the last interview than to choose a different cut-off point.

Table 43: *Mean grid measures at time 3 in groups distinguished in terms of breast-feeding*

	Successful breast-feeders (N = 11)		Breast-fed for 2 months (N = 28)		Never breast-fed (N = 11)	
DISTANCE:	M	V	M	V	M	V
Self–mother	·81	·02	·87	·05	·86	·04
Self–father	·87	·04	·99	·04	·89	·06
Self–ideal mother	·83	·02	·92	·06	·82	·03

(c) The successful feeders do see themselves as more like the ideal mother at time 3 than do the non-successful feeders, though not significantly so. It is worth noting that the mean score decreases for successful feeders from time 1 to time 3, whereas it increases for unsuccessful feeders during this time.

(d) The unsuccessful feeders obtain a larger spread in scores at time 3 for the self-to-ideal mother distance than do the successful feeders ($F = 3·6$; $p < ·01$, 1 tailed).

A comparison was made of FDCT measures between breast-feeders and non-breast-feeders. The direction of difference was not predicted as there are arguments in favour of both more feminine (mothering element) and more masculine (intrusive mode) scores for the breast-feeders. Results show that there is no difference in means but a difference in variance, giving an F ratio of $2·77$ ($p < ·10$, 2 tailed), the larger variance being for the group of women who were still breast-feeding. Thus, it seems possible that both components are present. As shown previously, FDCT scores may have to be interpreted differently. If this new interpretation is correct, the larger spread in scores for breast-feeders may be reflecting an 'activity' component and a 'cultural femininity' component.

STRUCTURE OF THE CONSTRUCT SYSTEM

There is some evidence that the complexity of the construct system is related to neuroticism, psychiatric patients using a simpler construct system to discriminate significant people (Ryle and Breen 1972). The idea was, therefore, explored that cognitive complexity would be greater in the well-adjusted group at time 3 than in the ill-adjusted group as measured by the importance of the first component, and that there would be, at time 2, a peak (simpler system) for the group as a whole, due to the increased anxiety experienced during pregnancy.

Table 44: *Percentage of the variance accounted for by the first component*

Time	GROUPS: Well-adjusted % variance	Ill-adjusted % variance	T	Total group % variance
1	48·4	48·9	0·12	50·0
2	47·7	52·7	1·19	51·4
3	47·1	53·8	1·63*	50·5

*$p < ·10$

Results are as expected, with a significant difference at time 3. It should be noted that there is a decrease from time 1 to time 2 in the well-adjusted group, the opposite occurring in the ill-adjusted group. Although this is not statistically significant, there is a peak at time 2 for the pregnant group taken as a whole.

This finding concerning adjustment groups is probably related to the one concerning an increased use of 'motherhood' constructs in the ill-adjusted group. These women are, in a sense, 'imprisoned' in a narrow view of the world and stuck with the experience.

OTHER FACTORS

A number of women mentioned the death of a relative, and I wondered if this additional stress might be a factor in difficulties to adjust.

Table 45: *Effect of death of a parent, planning of pregnancy, and marital status on adjustment groups*

GROUPS:	Well-adjusted (N = 11) N	Medium-adjusted (N = 21) N	Ill-adjusted (N = 13) N
Death of a parent during childhood and up to 1 year before interview	1	8	3
Death of a parent during interviewing time and up to 1 year before	4	1	0
Planned pregnancy	6	13	12
Single status at conception	2	0	4

The death of a relative during pregnancy or up to a year before was not predictive of outcome. In fact, none of the women who experienced this kind of loss belonged to the ill-adjusted group.

Eleven of the 39 women belonging to the less-adjusted groups had only one parent living a year before the first interview as opposed to 1 of the well-adjusted women. These numbers are, however, too small to lead to any conclusions.

Planning of pregnancy (discussed at the first interview) did not seem to affect the outcome, although social desirability and interpretation of the terms 'planned, unplanned' probably yield misleading figures. 54% of the women in the well-adjusted group as opposed to 67% in the ill-adjusted group said that their pregnancy had been planned. The slightly larger proportion for the latter group should not surprise, as it is the more secure woman who can admit the ambivalence about having a child. Two women in the well-adjusted group and 4 women in the ill-adjusted group became pregnant before getting married.

Glossary

Definitions for some words have been taken from the following books. In some cases only part of the definition has been included. Bracketed numbers after definitions indicate sources.

1. C. Rycroft, *A Critical Dictionary of Psychoanalysis*, Nelson, 1968.
2. S. Kitzinger, *Giving Birth*, Sphere Books, 1971.
3. H. Morten, *The Nurses's Dictionary* (revised by P. J. Cunningham), Faber and Faber, 1962.
4. *Dictionary of Pregnancy, Childbirth and Contraception*, Mayflower Books, 1971.

Abortion: This is the general term for the ending of a pregnancy after implantation and before the end of the twenty-eighth week. (4)

Albumen: Protein which appears in the urine. It can be a sign of preeclampsia. (2)

Amenorrhea: Abnormal absence of menstruation.

Amniotic fluid: The liquid in which the baby is floating in the bag of waters inside the uterus. (2)

Anaemia: A deficiency of haemoglobin in the blood. There may or may not be a deficiency in the number of red corpuscles. (3)

Apgar rating: Numerical expression of the condition of the newborn infant 50 seconds after birth; it is the sum of points gained on assessment after birth of the heart rate, respiratory effort, muscle tone, reflex irritability and colour. The higher the rating, the healthier the baby.

Autonomic nervous system: Includes all those parts of the nervous system which innervate plain muscular tissue and glands. Although it is not under the control of the will it is closely correlated to the central nervous system.

Breech presentation: This means that the breech (or buttocks of the baby) is 'presenting', that is, coming first, in the pelvis, instead of the normal head presentation. (4)

Caesarean section (Caesarean, Caesarean operation, Caesarean birth): This important and safe operation is employed whenever vaginal delivery would be hazardous for either the mother or the baby. . . . Caesarean section is usually performed under a general anaesthetic but may be under an epidural anaesthetic. An incision is made in the abdominal wall below the umbilicus or tummy button. (4)

Caudal: One kind of epidural anaesthesia. (2)

Cervix: The neck of the uterus which dilates during labour.

Clitoris: The female organ which lies about an inch in front of the opening of the urethra, where the labia minora join and enclose it. It has a very sensitive tip, continuous with its shaft or body, which is of variable size and fades away into the surrounding tissues. During sexual stimulation it becomes distended with blood and increases in size as does the male penis. It is the focal point of a woman's feelings of sexual pleasure. (4)

Colostrum: The pre-milk fluid secreted in the breasts during pregnancy. This is the first food the baby gets from the mother after birth. It contains antibodies which are part of his defence system against infection. The true milk does not come into the breasts until about the third day. (4)

Congenital: Existing at birth. (3)

Defence: 'A general designation for all the techniques which the ego makes use of in conflicts which may lead to neurosis' – Freud (1922). The function of defence is to protect the ego, and defences may be instigated by (a) anxiety due to increases in instinctual tension; (b) anxiety due to a bad conscience (super-ego threats); or (c) realistic dangers. (1)

Denial: Defence mechanism by which either (a) some painful experience is denied; or (b) some impulse or aspect of the self is denied. (1)

Dynamic: Psychoanalysis is a dynamic psychology since its concepts of process, instinct, and development imply movement; in contrast to static psychologies such as faculty psychology which merely enumerate and define attributes of the mind. (1)

Dysmenorrhea: Difficult or painful menstruation.

Ego: A structural and topographical concept referring to the organized parts of the psychic apparatus, in contrast to the unorganized id. '. . . The ego is that part of the id which has been modified by the direct influence of the external world. The ego represents what may be called reason and common sense, in contrast to the id, which contains the passions . . .' – Freud (1923). For analysts who do not subscribe to the notion of an undifferentiated id out of which the ego develops, the ego is either (a) the whole psyche: 'The pristine personality of the child consists of a unitary dynamic ego' – Fairbairn (1952); (b) that part of the personality which relates to objects and/or is formed by introjection of objects; or (c) that part of the personality which is experienced as being oneself, which one recognizes as 'I'.

Ego and self are often confused; they probably belong to different frames of references, the ego belonging to an objective frame of reference which views the personality as a structure and self belonging to a phenomenological frame of reference which view personality as experiences. (1)

Embryo: The developing baby from two weeks after fertilization to the twelfth week of pregnancy when formation of all the organs is completed. It is then called a foetus.

Endocrine: The term used in describing the ductless glands giving rise to an internal secretion. Some of the internal secretion organs have both an internal and an external secretion, and so may have ducts. (3)

Epidural: An injection in the spine which causes loss of sensation from the waist down. The amount of movement lost varies with the anaesthetic used. Uterine action is slowed for the first ten minutes, but in a difficult labour the uterus then relaxes better between contractions, thus improving its blood supply. The mother does not want to bear down and the bladder must be emptied by catheter. Forceps are necessary for delivery. (2)

Episiotomy: A cut in the perineum to facilitate delivery. (2)

Fallopian tubes: The tubes branching out from either side of the uterus in which fertilization takes place. (2)

Foetal distress: Means there is evidence that the foetus may not be getting enough oxygen through the placenta for its continued safety.

Foetus: The baby in the uterus from the third month until delivery. (2)

Forceps delivery: This is now a safe and valuable technique for assisting delivery of the baby. Forceps are in two pieces which fit neatly together as they are applied, and are rather like scissor-type salad servers. The spoon-shaped ends slip easily into the pelvis and gently but securely grip the baby's head. The commonest reason for their use is to add a little extra pull when the mother's pushing ability and strength of the womb contractions are not enough to deliver the baby . . .

Forceps can be used to deliver the baby quickly if foetal distress develops, to protect the head of a small premature baby or to shorten the second stage of labour when the mother is not well. (4)

Haemorrhage: A flow of blood. (3)

Hormone: A substance produced in one organ, which excites functional activity in another organ. (3)

Hyperemisis: Persistent vomiting in pregnancy. (2)

Hypertension: Raised blood pressure. A few women have hypertension before pregnancy and then need special care in pregnancy, but more often it arises late in pregnancy. (4)

Hypotension: Low blood pressure. (3)

Identification: The process by which a person either (a) extends his identity

238 Glossary

into someone else, (b) borrows his identity from someone else, or (c) fuses or confuses his identity with someone else. (1)

Induction of labour: Starting labour artificially instead of waiting for the natural onset. Usually this is done in the interests of the baby, when it is considered less safe for him to stay longer in the womb. In most cases this is because there is reason to believe that the function of the placenta in supplying nourishment and oxygen to the baby is declining towards a dangerously low level. Sometimes the reason for starting labour is that continuing pregnancy would present a hazard to the mother. This might apply when toxaemia of pregnancy is fairly severe or in some cases of antepartum haemorrhage.

The usual method of induction is by breaking the membranes and allowing liquor (water) to escape. This alters the pressure relationships and usually triggers off labour. Breaking the membranes is quite painless but in order to reach them the cervix may need to be stretched. This may be quite uncomfortable or painful . . . As a rule, provided the patient relaxes well, no drugs are necessary. Often a pain-relieving injection is given beforehand and very rarely a general anaesthetic is necessary. (4)

Inertia: Insufficient uterine activity. Primary inertia means weak contractions from the beginning of labour. Secondary inertia means a weakening or complete cessation of uterine contractions before the baby is delivered. (2)

Introjection: The process by which the functions of an external object are taken over by its mental representation, by which the relationship with and object 'out there' is replaced by one with an imagined object 'inside' . . . The super-ego is formed by introjection of parental figures and it may be analysed into a number of component introjects (the GOOD (BAD) INTERNAL FATHER (MOTHER)). Introjection is both a defence and a normal developmental process; a defence because it diminishes separation anxiety, a developmental process because it renders the subject increasingly autonomous. (1)

Jaundice: About a third of new-born babies go a bit yellow between the second and fifth days of life. This is even more likely if they are premature. It is called 'physiological jaundice' and there is no cause for concern. Sometimes, however, babies are jaundiced (and this usually happens a few minutes after delivery) signalling that something is wrong, and this may be associated with rhesus incompatibility. (2)

Labour, normal: The uterine contractions of late pregnancy are not really different from those of labour. Some women find the one merging imperceptibly with the other, while for others there is a fairly abrupt change . . .

During the first stage the uterus contracts and relaxes rhythmically for an average of twelve to twenty hours until the cervix is fully open . . .

The second stage – the part where (the woman) pushes down with contractions and delivers the baby – lasts fifteen minutes to two hours with a first baby but often only a few minutes to half an hour with a later baby. The third stage is the delivery of the placenta. (4)

Labour, premature: When labour starts before the completion of thirty-seven weeks of pregnancy. (4)

Labour, prolonged: It is often difficult to measure the length of labour as the onset may be quite indefinite. What is much more important than the length of labour is to relate the progress in labour (as measured by dilation of the cervix and descent of the baby through the pelvis) to the strength and frequency of the contractions. If contractions are infrequent and weak it would be normal to make slow progress, whereas if contractions are strong and frequent, slow progress might indicate to the doctor that there is too tight a fit between the baby and the pelvis, in these circumstances a caesarean section might be considered. (4)

Let down reflex: A conditioned reflex stimulated by the feeling of the baby at the breast or his cries, or even simply thinking about feeding the baby. When it occurs the breasts tingle and feel warm, the nipples become erect, and the milk is secreted into the ducts. (2)

Membranes: Within the uterus the foetus lies in the liquor contained by a double layer of clear, thin but fairly tough tissue. It is called the bag of waters or the bag of membranes. The membranes usually break late in labour but sometimes at the start or several days or weeks before. (4)

Menarch: The onset of menstruation.

Menopause: The cessation of the periods.

Menstrual cycle: The series of changes occurring each month in the adolescent or woman between the menarch and the menopause. . . . The cycle is controlled by hormones from the pituitary gland which have two effects. The first is to cause the egg (ovum) in the ovary to produce further hormones (the female sex hormones oestrogen and progesterone) which act on the lining of the uterus to prepare the very delicately balanced conditions necessary to receive a fertilized ovum and nourish it into forming the placenta and foetus.

If a fertilized ovum does not settle into the uterine lining, these special conditions cannot be maintained and the shedding of this lining begins fourteen days after ovulation, ready to allow it to be freshly prepared again in the next cycle. Blood is one of the readily available fluids in the body and it is used to wash off the lining . . .

Apart from the effect on the uterus, these female sex hormones have effects on every part of the body. They keep up the general female body characteristics, cause the breasts to swell a little each cycle and are responsible for the mood changes women experience in the menstrual cycle. (4)

Miscarriage: This term is often used for an abortion occurring naturally. (4)

Movements (quickening): The time when the mother first feels the baby's movements. This is usually between 16 weeks and 20 weeks. (2)

Multigravidae or Multiparae: A woman who is bearing her second or subsequent child.

Natural childbirth: A general term referring to the movement started by the Englishman Grantly Dick Read some forty years ago, whereby much more effort is made to recognize that the pregnant or labouring woman is a person and to care for her accordingly. (4)

Oedema: Fluid retained in the tissues causing puffiness. It may be a sign of pre-eclampsia. Sometimes it occurs in the legs simply because the mother is hot and tired. (2)

Oestrogen: Hormone of the ovaries which incites menstruation. It is also present in the blood and urine of pregnant women. (3)

Os: The mouth. External os: the opening of the cervix into the vagina. Internal os: opening of the cervix into the uterine cavity. (3)

Ovaries: The female egg cell 'factory' and storage house situated at the end of the fallopian tubes. (2)

Ovulation: The process of liberation of the egg (ovum) from the ovary. This usually occurs about two weeks before the next menstrual period, as a response of the ovary to stimulation by the pituitary hormones. (4)

Parity: The number of children a woman has borne. (3)

Perineum: The soft tissues on the outside around the vagina and anus. These stretch and fan out with the descent of the baby's head, and open up with a warm, tingling sensation when the head is 'on the perineum'. (2)

Pituitary gland: This is quite small and situated at the base of the brain. It produces hormones which control the other glands of the body such as the ovaries and the thyroid. (4)

Placenta: The after-birth. It is through the placenta that the baby is nourished and receives his oxygen from the mother's bloodstream, and through it, too, he excretes waste products. The placenta has been called the 'tree of life' for the baby. It is constructed like a sponge, with blood filling the spaces. The mother's blood does not actually mix with the baby's blood, but is separated from it by a thin membrane. The placenta looks like a large piece of raw liver. (2)

Postpartum: After labour. Postpartum haemorrhage is excessive vaginal bleeding occurring either immediately after the birth of the baby or within a few days. (2)

Precipitate labour: Very rapid labour – under five hours in a woman having her first baby. There are also precipitate first and second stages. (2)

Pre-eclampsia: Toxaemia of pregnancy. Symptoms are: raised blood pressure, albumin in the urine, puffiness of the fingers, ankles and legs, and a sudden excessive weight gain. (2)

Premature: An international classification consisting of any babies under 5½ lb in weight. (2)

Presentation: A description of the way in which the baby is lying in terms of the part of the baby which is down in the cervix. The most common is a vertex presentation. (2)

Primigravidae (or primiparae): Means those pregnant for the first time (though often earlier miscarriages are ignored). (4)

Progesterone: The hormone of the corpus luteum which causes secretory changes in the uterine mucous in pregnancy and during the menstrual cycle. (3)

Projective test: Psychological tests which attempt to ascertain personality traits by inviting the subject to interpret pictures or indeterminate shapes such as ink-blots in the light of his imagination. (1)

Prolonged pregnancy (post-maturity): Means that the length of pregnancy is known and has continued more than fourteen days (some doctors say ten days) past the expected delivery date. In these circumstances induction of labour is usual because of the possibility that the placenta may no longer be able to nourish the baby adequately. (4)

Proteinuria: Protein in the urine. (3)

Psychical reality: This refers to mental phenomena: images, thoughts, fantasies, feelings. (1)

Puerperium: The six weeks after childbirth when the mother's body is returning to its pre-pregnancy state. (2)

Repression: The process (defence mechanism) by which an unacceptable impulse or idea is rendered unconscious. (1)

Second stage of labour: The time from full dilation of the cervix until delivery. This is the expulsive stage. (2)

Spinal: An injection into the spine causing complete paralysis of the lower part of the body. There is no bearing-down sensation. (2)

Spontaneous delivery: The mother giving birth to the baby herself, without mechanical assistance from her attendants. (2)

Suturing: Sewing up.

Toxaemia of pregnancy: This is a disorder found only in pregnancy and is present when two of the following three features are found by the doctor's or midwife's examination: a rise in blood pressure (hypertension), protein in the urine and generalized swelling. (4)

Uterus: The womb. A muscular, hollow, pearshaped organ normally situated in the pelvis. It consists of two parts – the cervix or neck, one inch long, which is the lower part, and projects into the vagina; and the corpus, or body, two inches long, in which the fertilized ovum is retained for 250 days in a normal pregnancy. The uterus is enclosed within the two broad ligaments, and from its upper corners spring the two Fallopian tubes. (3)

Vagina: The rather elastic organ designed to receive the penis during sexual intercourse so that semen is deposited in the woman. The sperms can then pass up through the cervix into the uterus and to the tube to fertilize the ovum. (4)

Vaginismus: Spasmodic contraction of the vagina whenever the vulva or vagina is touched. (3)

Vertex: The top of the baby's head, when still inside the mother. (2)

Bibliography

ABRAMSON, J. H., SINGH, A. R. and MBAMBO, V. (1969). 'Antenatal Stress and the Baby's Development', *Archs. Dis. Childh.* **37,** 42–9.

AINSWORTH, M. (1969). *Some Contemporary Patterns of Mother–Infant Interaction in the Feeding Situation.* Ambrose. *Stimulation in Early Infancy.* London and New York, Academic Press.

ALEXANDER, F. (1943). 'Fundamental Concepts of Psychosomatic Research: Psychogenesis, Conversion, Specificity', *Psychosom. Med.* **5,** 205–10.

ANASTASI, A. and SCHAEFER, C. B. (1971). 'The Franck Drawing Completion Test as a Measure of Creativity', *J. Genet. Psychol.* **115,** 3–12.

ANDERSON, E. (1967). 'A study of the Relationship between Depression and Interpersonal Conflict in the Postpartum', *Diss. Abstr.* **28,** 6.

ANDRIEUX, C. (1961). 'Association de quelques Variables Socio-Culturelles avec la Représentation du Role de la Mère', *Psychol. Fr.* **6** (2), 126–36.

ASTRACHAN, J. M. (1965). 'Severe Psychologic Disorders of the Puerperium', *Obstet. and Gynaec.* **25** (1), 13–25.

AULAGNIER-SPAIRANI, PIERA (1967). 'Remarques sur la féminité et ses avatars' in *Le Désir et la Perversion,* edited by P. Aulagnier-Spairani and others. Paris, Le Seuil.

BAIRD, D. (1952). 'Cause and prevention of difficult labour', *Am. J. Obstet. Gynaec.* **63** (6), 1200–1212.

BALINT, E., (1972). 'Fair shares and mutal concern', *Int. J. of Psychoanalysis,* **52,** 61–5.

BALINT, M., 'The Basic Fault; therapeutic aspects of regression (Tavistock Publications).

BARKER-BENFIELD, B., (1972). 'The spermatic economy: a nineteenth-century view of sexuality', *Feminist Studies,* vol. 1.

BEACH, S. R., HENLEY, K., PETERSON, A. and FARR, M. (1955). 'Husbands of women with postpartum psychosis', *J. Psych. Social Work,* April 1955, 165–9.

BARDWICK, J. M. AND BEERMAN, S. J. (1967). 'Investigation into the effects of anxiety, sexual arousal and menstrual cycle phase on uterine contractions', *Psychosomatic Medicine,* 1967, **29** (5), 468–82.

BENEDEK, T. (1949). 'The Psychosomatic Implications of the Primary Unit: Mother–Child', *Am. J. Orthopsychiat.* **19,** 642–54.

—— (1952). 'Infertility as a Psychosomatic Defense', *Fert. Steril.* **3,** 527–41.

BENEDEK, T. (1956). 'Psychobiological Aspects of Mothering', *Am. J. Orthopsychiat.* **26**, 272.

—— (1960). 'The Organisation of the Reproductive Drive', *Int. J. Psycho-Analysis* **51** (1), 1–15.

BEZDEK, W. and STRODTBECK, F. L. (1970). 'Sex Role Identity and Pragmatic Action'. *Am. Sociol. Rev.* **35** (5), 491–502.

BIBRING, G. (1959). 'Some Considerations of the Psychological Processes in Pregnancy', *Psychoanal. Study Child* **14**, 113–21.

BIBRING, G. L., DWYER, T. F., HUNTINGTON, D. S. and VALENSTEIN, F. (1961). 'A Study of the Psychological Processes in Pregnancy and of the Earliest Mother–Child Relationship', *Psychoanal. Study Child* **16**, 9–72.

BIELIAUSKAS, V. J. (1965). 'Recent Advances in Psychology of Masculinity and Femininity', *J. Psychol.* **60**, 255–63.

BIELIAUSKAS, V., MIRANDA, S. and LANSKY, L. (1968). 'Obviousness or Two Masculinity–Femininity Tests', *J. Consult. Clin. Psychol.* **32** (3), 314–18.

BILLER, H. (1969). 'Maternal Salience and Feminine Development in Young Girls', *Proceedings of the 77th Annual Conference APA*, 259–60.

BLAU, A., SLAFF, B., BASTON, D., WELKOWITZ, J., SPRINGBARN, J. and COHEN, J. (1963). 'Psychogenic Etiology of Premature Births', *Psychosom. Med.* **25**, 201–11.

BONAPARTE, M. (1953). *Female Sexuality*. New York, International Universities Press.

BONARIUS, J. J. (1965). 'Research in the Personal Construct Psychology', in B. Maher (ed.), *Progress in Experimental Personality Research*. London and New York, Academic Press.

BONNAUD ET REVAULT D'ALLONES (1963). 'Vécu Psychologique des Premiers Movements de l'Enfant', *Bulletin Officiel de la Société de Psychoprophylaxie Obstetricale* **15**, 43–7.

BOWLBY, J. (1953). 'The Roots of Parenthood'. Convocation Lecture of the National Children's Home. London, National Children's Home.

—— (1969). *Attachment and Loss*. London, Hogarth Press.

BOYD, D. (1942). 'Mental Disorders Associated with Childbearing', *Am. J. Obstet. and Gynaec.* **43** (19), 148–63; **43** (2), 335–49.

BRECHER, R. and BRECHER, E. (1968). *An Analysis of Human Sexual Response*. London, Panther Books.

BREEN, C. (1971). 'Liberation and Pregnancy: A Nine Month Diary'. Unpublished.

BREW, M. F. and SEIDENBERG, R. (1950). 'Psychotic Reactions Associated with Pregnancy and Childbirth', *J. Nerv. Ment. Dis.* **111** (5), 408–23.

BROUSSARD, E. and HARTNER, M. (1969). 'Maternal Perception of Neonate as Related to Development'. Paper Delivered at the American Psychiatric Association, Miami.

BROWN, F., CHASE, J. and WINSON, J. (1961). 'Studies in Infant Feeding Choices of Primiparae', *J. Project. Tech.* **25**, 412–21.

BROWN, L. (1964). 'Anxiety in Pregnancy', *Br. J. Med. Psychiat.* **37**, 27–57.

BUTTS, H. F. (1968). 'Psychodynamic and Endocrine Factors in Postpartum Psychoses', *J. Natn. Med. Ass.* **60** (3), 224–7.

BYRNE, D. (1964). 'Repression–Sensitisation as a Dimension of Personality', in B. Maher (ed.), *Progress in Experimental Personality Research.* New York, Academic Press.

CAINE, T. M. and SMAIL, D. J. (1967). 'Personal Relevance and the Choice of Constructs for the Repertory Grid Technique', *Psychiatry* **113**, 517–20.

California Manual for the Drawing Completion Test: Obtainable from Dr L. Lansky, University of Cincinnati, Ohio, U.S.A.

CALIGOR, L. (1951). 'The Determination of the Individual's Unconscious Conception of his own Masculinity–Femininity Identification', *J. Project. Tech. and Person. Assessment* **15**, 494–509.

CALL, J. D. (1959). 'Emotional Factors Favoring Successful Breast Feeding in Infants', *J. Pediat.* **55**, 485–98.

CAMPBELL, D. and STANLEY, J. C., (1966). *Experimental and Quasi Experimental Designs for Research.* Chicago, Illinois, Rand McNally.

CAPLAN, G. (1962). 'Emotional Implication of Pregnancy and Influences on Family Relationships', in *The Healthy Child,* ed. H. C. Stuart and J. G. Prugh. Cambridge, Mass., Harvard University Press.

—— (1964). *Principles of Preventive Psychiatry.* New York, Basic Books.

CAPPON, D. (1954). 'Some Psychodynamic Aspects of Pregnancy', *Canad. Med. Ass. J.* **70** (2), 147–56.

CARLEBACK, J. (1966). 'Tribal Customs Associated with Pregnancy', *Mother and Child* **36** (12), 9–12.

CHAPPLE, P. A. and FURNEAUX, W. D. (1964). 'Changes of Personality in Pregnancy and Labour', *Proceedings of the Royal Society of Medicine* **57**, 260–1.

CHASSEGUET-SMIRGEL, J. (1964). *Recherches Psychanalytiques sur la Sexualité Feminine.* Paris, Payot.

CHERTOK, L. (1966). *Feminité et Maternité.* Paris, Desclée de Brouwer.

CHERTOK, L., MONDZAIN, M. L., BONNARD, M. (1963) 'Vomiting and the Wish To Have a Child', *Psychosom. Med.* **25** (1), 13–18.

CLIFFORD, E. (1962). 'Expressed Attitudes in Pregnancy of Unmarried Women and Primigravidae and Multigravidae', *Child Dev.* **33**, 945–51.

COCHET-DENIAU, M. (1969). 'Creativité et moi Corporel Imaginaire', *Bull. Soc. Rech. Psychotherap. Langue Fr.* **7** (1), 27–8.

COHEN, R. L. (1966). 'Some Maladaptive Syndromes of Pregnancy and the Puerperium', *Obstet. and Gynec.* **27** (4), 562–70.

COMPTON, N. H. (1969). 'Body Perception in Relation to Anxiety among Women', *Percept. Mot. Skills* **28** (1), 215–19.

COPPEN, A. (1958). 'Psychosomatic Aspects of Pre-eclamptic Toxemia', *J. Psychosom. Res.* **2**, 241–65.

—— (1958). 'Uterine Dysfunction during Labour', *Lancet* i, 209.

CORBIN, H. R. N. (1948). 'Emotional Aspects of Maternity', *Am. J. Nurs.* **48**, 20–2.

CORNELL, M. (1969). 'Psychological Variables in the Mother Related to Infant Feeding Patterns', *Diss. Abstr.* **29** (9–B), 3479.

COTTLE, T. J., EDWARDS, C. N. and PLECK, J. (1970). 'The Relationship of Sex Role Identity and Social and Political Attitudes', *J. Personality* **38** (3), 435–52.

CRAMOND, H. (1954). 'Psychological Aspects of Uterine Dysfunction', *Lancet* ii, 1241–5.

CRAWFORD, M. I. (1969). 'Physiological and Behavioural Cues to Disturbances in Childbirth', *Diss. Abstr.* **29** (7–B), 2504.

CROWTHER, P. (1965). 'Psychological Aspects of Motherhood', *Child Welfare* **7**, 365–76.

DALTON, K. (1971). 'Perspective Study into Puerperal Depression', *Br. J. Psychiat.* **118**, 689–92.

DANIELS, R. S. and LESSOW, H. (1964). 'Severe Postpartum Reactions, an Interpersonal View', *Psychosomatics* **5** (1), 21–6.

DAVIDS, A. (1968). 'A Research Design for Studying Maternal Emotionality before Childbirth and after Social Interaction with the Child', *Merrill Palm. Q.* **14** (4), 349–54.

DAVIDS, A. and DEVAULT, S. (1960). 'Use of the TAT and Human Figure Drawings in Research on Personality, Pregnancy and Perception', *J. Project. Tech.* **24** (4), 362–5.

—— (1962). 'Maternal Anxiety during Pregnancy and Childbirth Abnormalities', *Psychosom. Med.* **24** (5), 464–70.

DAVIDS, A., DEVAULT, S. and TALMADGE, M. (1961). 'Psychological Study of Emotional Factors in Pregnancy: a Preliminary Report', *Psychosom. Med.* **23** (2), 93–103.

DAVIDS, A. and ROSENGREN, W. (1962). 'Social Stability and Psychological Adjustment during Pregnancy', *Psychosom. Med.* **24** (6), 579–83.

DAVIDS, A., HOLDEN, R. H. and GRAY, G. B. (1963). 'Maternal Anxiety during Pregnancy and Adequacy of Mother and Child Adjustment Eight Months Following Childbirth', *Child Dev.* **34**, 993–1001.

DAVIDS, A. and HOLDEN, R. (1970). 'Consistency of Maternal Attitudes and Personality from Pregnancy to Eight Months following Childbirth', *Developmental Psych.* **2** (3), 364–6.

DERSHIMER, P. (1936). 'The Influence of Mental Attitudes in Childbearing', *Am. J. Obstet. Gynec.* **31**,

DEUTSCH, H. (1945). *The Psychology of Women*. New York, Grune and Stratton.

—— (1949). 'An Introduction to the Discussion of the Psychological Problems of Pregnancy', *Josiah Macy Jr. Foundation* 11.

DOLTO, F. (1967). 'La Genèse du Sentiment Maternel', *Bulletin de la Société Française de Psychoprophylaxie Obstétricale*, 32, 43–55.

DOTY, B. (1967). 'Relation among Attitudes in Pregnancy and other Maternal Characteristics', *J. Genet. Psychol.* 111 (2), 203–17.

DOUGLAS, G. (1963). 'Puerperal Depression and Excessive Compliance with the Mother', *Br. J. Med. Psychol.* 36 (3), 271–8.

—— (1968). 'Some Emotional Disorders of the Puerperium', *J. Psychosom. Res.* 12 (1), 101–6.

DUNBAR, G. (1946). *Emotions and Bodily Changes*. New York, Columbia University Press.

DUNHAM, E. C. (1951). 'Premature Births as a World Health Problem', *Pediatrics* 7 (2), 262–8.

DYER, B. (1963). 'Parenthood as a Crisis: a Restudy', *Marriage and Family Living* 25, 196–201.

ENGSTRÖM, L., AFGEITERSTAM, G., HOLMBERG, N. G. and UHRUS, K. (1964). 'A prospective study of the relationship between psycho-social factors and course of pregnancy and delivery', *Journ. Psychosmatic Research*, 8, 151–5.

ERIKSEN, C. W. and LAZARUS, R. S. (1952). 'Perceptual Defense and Projective Tests', *J. Abnorm. Soc. Psychol.* 47, 302–8.

ERIKSON, E. (1968). *Identity, Youth and Crisis*. New York, Norton.

ESCALONA, S. K. (1945). 'Feeding Disturbances in Very Young Children', *Am. J. Orthopsychiat.* 15, 76–80.

EVANS, T. N. (1955). 'Prolonged Labour', *Obstet. Gynec.* 6, 522–31.

FABRE, H. (1960). *La Maternité Consciente*. Paris, Denoel.

FARADAY, A. (1972). *Dream power*. London, Pan Books.

FERREIRA, A. J. (1960). 'The Pregnant Mother's Emotional Attitude and its Reflexion upon the Newborn', *Am. J. Orthopsychiat.* 30 (3), 553–62.

FIGGE, M. (1932). 'Some Factors in the Etiology of Maternal Rejection', *Smith Coll. Stud. Soc. Work.* March 2, 237–60.

FJELD, S. P. and LANDFIELD, A. W. (1961). 'Personal Construct Consistency', *Psychol. Rep.* 8, 127–9.

FOUNDEUR, M., FIXSEN, C., TRIEBEL, W. A. and WHITE, M. A. (1957). 'Postpartum mental illness', *Am. Med. Assoc. Archives Neurol. and Psychiatry.* 77 (5), 503–12.

FOX, H. (1958). 'Narcissistic Defenses during Pregnancy', *Psychoanal. Quarterly* 27, 340–58.

FOX, W. I. (1964). 'Psychological Factors in Childbirth', *Diss. Abstr.* 27, 4122B.

FRANCK, K. (undated). *Manual for Franck Drawing Completion Test*. Published by Australian Council for Educational Research, Frederick Street, Hawthorn, Victoria, 3122.

FRANCK, K. (1946). 'Preference for Sex Symbols and their Personality Correlates', *Genet. Psychol. Monogr.* **33**, 73–123.

FRANCK, K. and ROSEN, E. (1948). 'Projective Test of Masculinity–Femininity', *J. Consult. Psychol.* **13**, 247–56.

FREEMAN, M. (1932). 'Factors Associated with Length of Breast Feeding', *Smith Coll. Stud. Soc. Work.* March 2, 274–82.

FREUD, A. (1947). 'The Psychoanalytic Study of Infantile Feeding Disturbances', *Psychoanal. Study Child* **II**, 119–32.

FREUD, S. (1925). 'Some Psychical Consequences of the Anatomical Distinction Between the Sexes', Vol. 19, *Standard Edition*, 243. London, Hogarth Press.

—— (1931). 'Female Sexuality', Vol. 21, *Standard Edition*, 223. London, Hogarth Press.

—— (1933). 'The Psychology of Women' in *New Introductory Lectures in Psychoanalysis* Vol. 22, *Standard Edition*. London, Hogarth Press.

—— 'The Economic problem in Masochism', *Collected Papers*, **2** (Hogarth, 1922), Chap. 22.

FRIES, M. (1944). 'Psychosomatic Relation between Mother and Infant'. *Psychosom. Med.* **6**, 159–63.

GARNER, A. and WENER, C. (1959). *The Mother Child interaction in Psychosomatic Disorders.* Illinois, U. of Illinois Press.

GILLESPIE, W. H. (1969). 'Concepts of Vaginal Orgasm', *Int. J. Psychoanal.* **50**, 495–7.

GILLMAN, R. (1968). *Am. J. Orthopsychiat.* **30**

GIORGI, A. (1970). *Psychology as a Human Science.* New York, Harper and Row.

GLUCK, I. and WRENN, M. (1959). 'Contribution to the Understanding of Disturbances of Mothering', *Br. J. Med. Psychol.* **32**, 171–81.

GOODRICH, F. W. (1961). 'Psychosomatic Aspects of Obstetrics', *Psychosomatics* **2**, 194.

GORDON, J. and THOMAS, C. (1959). 'Psychosis After Childbirth: Ecological Aspects of a Single Impact Stress', *Am. J. of the Medical Services* **238** (3).

GORDON, R. E. and GORDON, K. K. (1959). 'Social Factors in the Prediction and Treatment of Emotional Disorders of Pregnancy', *Am. J. Obstet. and Gynaec.* **77** (5), 1074–83.

—— (1960). 'Social Factors in Prevention of Postpartum Emotional Problems', *Obstet. Gynaec.* **15**, 433–8.

—— (1967). 'Factors in Postpartum Emotional Adjustment', *Am. J. Orthopsychiat.* **37** (2), 359–60.

GORDON, R. E., KAPOSTINE, E. E. and GORDON, K. K. (1965). 'Factors in Postpartum Emotional Adjustment', *Obstet Gynaec.* **25** (2), 158–66.

GOUGH, H. G. (1952). 'Identifying Psychological Femininity', *Educ. and Psychol. Measurement* **12**, 427–39.

GOZALI, J. and DEMAREST, A. (1970). *A Review of the Literature on Postpartal Mental Disorders.* Milwaukee, Jewish Vocational Service.

GREENACRE, P. (1944). 'The Predisposition to Anxiety in Contemporary Psychopathology', ed. S. S. Tomkins. Cambridge, Mass., Harvard Univ. Press.

GREENBERG, N. H., LOESCH, J. G. and LAKIN, M. (1959). 'Life Situations Associated with the Onset of Pregnancy', *Psychosom. Med.* **21**, 256–310.

GUNTER, L. (1963). 'Psychopathology and Stress in the Life Experience of Mothers of Premature Infants', *Am. J. Obstet. Gynaec.* **86**, 333–40.

GUNTRIP, H. (1971). *Psychoanalytic Theory, Therapy and the Self.* London, Hogarth Press.

HALL, J. (1972). 'At the Mercy of the Institution', *Children's Rights*, No. 3. London Children's Rights Publications Ltd.

HAMILTON, J. A. (1962). *Postpartum Psychiatric Problems.* St. Louis, Mosby.

HAMILTON, M. (1960). 'A Rating Scale for Depression', *J. Neurol. Neurosurg. Psychiat.* **23**, 560.

HANFORD, J. M. (1968). 'Pregnancy as a State of Conflict', *Psychol. Rep.* **22** (3), 1313–42.

HARFORD, T. C., WILLIS, C. H. and DEABLER, H. L. (1967). 'Personality Correlates of Masculinity–Femininity', *Psychol. Rep.* **21** (3), 881–5.

HARDING, E. M. (1933). *The Way of All Women.* London, Longmans.

HARTEMANN, J., RIBON, M. and DELLESTABLE, P. (1962). 'Les Effets de l'Attraction de la mère et de l'Enfant sur l'Entretien de l'Allaitement', *Bull. Société Nationale de Gynec. et Obstet. de France.* Nov. 1962, 770–3.

HAYMAN, A. (1962). 'Some Aspects of Regression in Non-Psychotic Puerperal Breakdown', *Br. J. Med. Psychol.* **35** (2), 135–45.

HAYNAL, A. (1968). 'Le Syndrome de Couvade', *Annales Médico-Psychol.* **I** (4), 539–71.

HEILBRUN, A. B. (1965). 'An Empirical Test of the Modelling Theory of Sex Role Learning', *Child Develop.* **36**, 789–99.

HEINMANN, P. (1955). 'A Contribution to the Re-evaluation of the Oedipus Complex – the Early Stages', in *New Directions in Psychoanalysis.* London, Tavistock Publications.

HEINSTEIN, M. (1963). 'Behavioural Correlates of Breast Bottle Regimes under Varying Parent–Infant Relationships', Monograph Serial No. 88, **28** (4). The Society for Research in Child Development.

——(1967). 'Expressed Attitudes and Feelings of Pregnant Women and their Relation to Physical Complication of Pregnancy', *Merrill Palmer Quarterly* **13** (3), 217–36.

HELPER, M. M., COHEN, R. L., EATON, L. F. and BEITENMANET, J. (1968). 'Life Events and Acceptance of Pregnancy', *J. Psychosom. Res.* **12**, 183–8.

HEMPHILL, R. E. (1952). 'Incidence and Nature of Puerperal Mental Illness.' *Br. Med. J.*, **2**, 1232–5.

HETZEL, B., BRUER, B. and POIDEVIN, J. D. S. (1961). 'Survey of Relation between Certain Common Antenatal Complications in Pregnancy and Stressful Life Conditions during Pregnancy', *J. Psychosom. Res.* **5**, 175–82.

HOBBS, D. (1963). 'Parenthood as a Crisis: a Third Study', *J. of Marriage and the Family* **27** (3), 367–72.
—— (1968). 'Transition to Parenthood. A Replication and Extension' *J. of Marriage and the Family* **30** (3), 413–18.
HONZIK, M. P. (1951). 'Sex Differences in the Occurrence of Materials in the Play Constructions of Preadolescents', *Child Develop.* **22** (1), 15–36.
HOOK, D. and MARKS, P. L. (1962). 'MMPI Characteristics of Pregnancy'. *J. Clin. Psychol.* **18**, 316–17.
HORNEY, K. (1926). 'The Flight from Womanhood: The Masculinity-complex as viewed by Men and Women', *Int. J. Psychoanal.* **7**, 324–39.
—— (1933). 'Maternal Conflicts'. *Am. J. Orthopsychiat.* **3**, 455–63.
—— (1933). 'The Denial of the Vagina', *Int. J. Psychoanal.* **14**, 57–70.
—— (1939). 'Feminine Psychology' in *New Ways on Psychoanalysis*. New York, Norton.
HYTTEN, F. E., YORSTON, J. E. and THOMSON, A. M. (1958). 'Difficulties Associated with Breast Feeding', *Br. Med. J.* **1**, 310–15.
IVEY, M. E. and BARDWICK, J. M. (1968). 'Patterns of Affective Fluctuation in the Menstrual Cycle', *Psychosom. Med.* **30** (3), 336–45.
JACOBS, B. (1943). 'Aetiological Factors and Reaction Types in Psychoses following Childbirth', *J. Ment. Sci.* **89**, 242.
JACOBSON, L., KAIJ, L. and NILSSON, A. (1965). 'Postpartal Mental Disorders in an Unselected Sample: Frequency of Symptoms and Predisposing Factors', *Br. Med. J.* **2** (5451), 1640–3.
JAHODA, M. (1958). *Current Concepts of Positive Mental Health*. Monograph Series No. 1 New York, Basic Books.
JANIS, I. L. (1958). *Psychological Stress*. New York, Wiley.
—— (1968).'When Fear is Healthy', *Psychology Today* **1**, 46–9, 60–1.
—— (ed.) (1969). *Personality: Dynamics, Development and Assessment*. New York, Harcourt Brace.
JANSSON, B. (1964). 'Psychic Insufficiencies Associated with Childbearing', *Acta Psychiat. Scand.* **33**, Supply No. 172.
JARRACHI-ZADEK, A., KANE, F. J., VANDE CASTLE, R. L., LACHEN-BRUCH, P. A. and EWING, J. A. (1969). 'Emotional and Cognitive Changes in Pregnancy and Early Puerperium', *Br. J. Psychiat.* **115**, 797–805.
JEFFCOATE, J. (1951) in Sir Eardley Lancelot Holland and A. W. Bourne, (eds.), *British Obstetric and Gynaecological Practice*. 2 Vols. Vol. 1, *Obstetrics*, edited E. Holland. London, Heinemann.
JESSNER, L. (1966). 'On Becoming a Mother', *Conditio Humana*, 102–15. Baeyer and Griffith.
JOFFE, J. M. (1969). *Prenatal Determinants of Behaviour*. Oxford, Pergamon Press.
JONES, E. (1942). 'Psychology and Childbirth', *Lancet* i, 695–6.

JONES, R. E. (1961). 'Identification in Terms of P.C.; Reconciling a Paradox in Theory', *J. Consult. Psychol.* **25**, 276.

KAIJ, L., JACOBSON, L. and NILSSON, A. (1967). 'Postpartum Mental Disorders in an Unselected Sample: Influence of Parity', *J. Psychosom. Res.* **10** (4), 317–25.

KANE, F. (1968). 'Postpartum Psychosis in Identical Twins', *Psychosomatics* **9** (5), 278–81.

KAPLAN, D. M. and MASON, B. A. (1960). 'Maternal Reaction to Premature Birth', *Am. J. Orthopsychiat.* **30**, 539–52.

KARACAN, L. (1968). 'Sleep and Dreaming During Late Pregnancy and Postpartum', *Psychophysiology* **4** (3), 378.

KARTCHNER, F. D. (1950). 'A study of the Emotional Reactions during Labour', *Am. J. Obstet. Gynec.* **60** (1), 19–29.

KEAR-COLWELL, J. J. (1965). 'Neuroticism in the Early Puerperium', *Br. J. Psychiat.* **3**, 1189–92.

KELLY, G. A. (1955). *The Psychology of Personal Constructs*, New York, Norton.

KELMAN, H. C. (1968). *A Time to Speak: on Human Values and Social Research*. San Francisco, Jossey-Bass.

KITZINGER, S. (1971). 'The Woman on the Delivery Table' in M. Laing, *Woman on Woman*. London, Sidgwick & Jackson.

—— (1971). *Giving Birth*. London, Sphere Books.

KLEIN, H., POTTER, H. W. and DYKE, R. B. (1950). *Anxiety in Pregnancy and Childbirth*. New York and London, Harper and Row.

KLEIN, M. (1948). *Contributions to Psychoanalysis 1921–1945*. London, Hogarth Press.

KLINE, C. L. (1955). 'Emotional Illness Associated with Childbirth', *J. Obstet. Gynaec.* **69** (4), 748–57.

KLINE, P. (1972). *Fact and Fantasy in Freudian Theory*. London, Methuen and Co.

KOGAN, W. S., BOE, E. E. and VALENTINE, B. L. (1965). 'Changes in the Self-Concept of Unwed Mothers', *J. Psychol.* **59**, 3–10.

KOGAN, W. S., BOE, E. E. and GOCKA, E. F. (1968). 'Personality Changes in Unwed Mothers Following Parturition', *J. Clin. Psychol.* **24** (1), 2–11.

KNOBEL, M. (1967). 'Preventive Psychotherapy in Pregnancy', *Psychother. and Psychosom.* **15** (1), 34.

LACEY, B. and VAN LEHEM, R., BATEMAN, D. E. (1953). 'Autonomic Response Specificity: an Experimental Study', *Psychosom. Med.* **15**, 8–21.

LAING, R. D. (1961). 'The Coldness of Death. The Phenomenology of a Puerperal Psychosis', in *The Self and Others*. London, Tavistock Publications.

LAKIN, M. (1957). 'Assessment of Significant Role Attitudes in Primiparous Mothers', *Psychosom. Med.* **19** (1), 50–60.

LANDFIELD, A. W. (1965). 'Meaningfulness of Self, Ideal and Other as Related to Own Versus Therapist's Personal Construct Dimensions', *Psychol. Rep.* **16**, 605–8.

LANGER, M. Reviewed by RACANICS, P. C. (1953). 'Apropos de *Maternité et Sexe* de Marie Langer', *Evolution Psychiatrique* **3**, 559–65.

LANSKY, L. M. (1960). 'Mechanism of Defense: Sex Identity and Defenses Against Conflict', in D. R. Miller and G. Swanson, *Inner Conflict and Defense*. New York, Holt, 272–88.

—— (1964). 'The Family Structure also Reflects the Model: Sex Role Identification in Parents of Pre-School Children', *Merrill Palmer Quarterly* **10** (1).

LEVY, L. H. (1956). 'Personal Constructs and Predictive Behaviour', *J. Abnorm. Soc. Psychol.* **53**, 54–8.

LEWIS, A. (1951). *An Interesting Condition: the diary of a pregnant woman*. London, Odhams.

LOESCH, J. G. and GREENBERG, N. H. (1962). 'Areas of Conflict Observed During Pregnancy', *Am. J. Orthopsychiat.* **32**, 624–36.

LOMAS, P. (1959). 'The Husband–Wife Relationship in Cases of Puerperal Breakdown', *Br. J. Med. Psychol.* **32**, 117–23.

LOMAS, P. (1960). 'Defensive Organisation and the Puerperal Breakdown', *Br. J. Med. Psychol.* **33**, 61–6.

—— (1960). 'Dread of Envy as an Aetiological Factor in Puerperal Breakdown', *Br. J. Med. Psychol.* **33**, 105–12.

—— (1962). 'The Concept of Maternal Love', *Psychiatry* **25** (3), 256–62.

—— (1966). 'Ritualistic Elements in the Management of Childbirth', *Br. J. Med. Psychol.* **39**, 207–13.

—— (1972). 'The significance of Post-partum Breakdown', in *The Predicament of the Family*. London, Hogarth Press.

MCCONNELL, O. L. and DASTON, P. G. (1961). 'Body Image in Pregnancy', *J. Proj. Technique* **25**, 451–6.

MCDONALD, R. L. (1965). 'Fantasy and the Outcome of Pregnancy', *Archs. Gen. Psychiat.* **12**, 602–6.

—— (1968). 'The Role of Emotional Factors in Obstetric Complications: A Review', *Psychosom. Med.* **30** (2), 222–34.

MCDONALD, R. L. and CHRISTAKOS, S. C. (1963). 'Relationship of Emotional Adjustment during Pregnancy to Obstetric Complications', *Am. J. Obstet. Gynaec.* **86**, 341–8.

MCDONALD, R. L. and GYNTHER, M. D. (1965). 'Relations between Self and Parental Perceptions of Unwed Mothers and Obstetric Complications', *Psychosom. Med.* **25**, 31–8.

MCDONALD, R. L., GYNTHER, M. D. and CHRISTAKOS, A. C. (1963). 'Relations Between Maternal Anxiety and Obstetric Complications', *Psychosom. Med.* **25**, 357–63.

MCDONALD, R. L. and PARHAM, K. J. (1964). 'Relation of Emotional

Changes During Pregnancy to Obstetric Complications in Unmarried Primigravidae', *Am. J. Obstet. Gynaec.* **90**, 195–201.

MCNAIR, F. E. (1952). 'Psychosis Occurring Postpartum: Analysis of 34 Cases', *Canadian Medical Assoc. J.* **67** (6), 637–41.

MALMQUIST, A., KAIJ, L. and NILSSON, A. (1969). 'Psychiatric Aspects of Spontaneous Abortion – A Matched Control Study of Women with Living Children', *J. Psychosom. Res.* **13**, 45–51.

MARKHAM, S. (1961). 'A Comparative Evaluation of Psychotic and Non-Psychotic Reactions to Childbirth', *Am. J. Orthopsychiat.* **31**,565–78.

MASLOW, A. H. (1969). 'Towards a Humanistic Biology', *Am. Psychol.* **24**, 724–35.

MASTERS, W. H. and JOHNSON, V. E. (1962). 'The Sexual Response Cycle of the Human Female', *West. J. Surg. Obst. and Gynec.* **70**, 248–57.

MEAD, M. (1950). *Male and Female.* London, Victor Gollancz.

MEISEL, P. J. (1969). 'Cognitive Structure and Construct Change', *Dissert. Abstr.* **29** (7B), 2637.

MELGES, F. T. (1968). 'Postpartum Psychiatric Syndromes', *Psychosom. Med.* **30** (1), 95–108.

MENNINGER, K. A. (1939). 'Somatic Correlations with the Unconscious Repudiation of Femininity in Women', *J. Nerv. Ment. Dis.* **89**, 514–27.

MENNINGER, W. C. (1943). 'The Emotional Factors in Pregnancy', *Menninger Clinic Bull.* **7**, 15–24.

MILLER, D. and SWANSON, G. (1960). *Inner Conflict and Defense.* New York, Holt.

MILLET, K. (1970). *Sexual Politics.* New York, Doubleday.

MILNER, M. (1950). *On Not Being Able to Paint.* London, Heinemann.

NEWMAN, D. K. (1956). 'A study of Factors Leading to Change Within the Personal Construct System'. Ph.D. Thesis, Ohio State University.

NEWTON, N. (1955). *Maternal Emotions.* Jackson, Mississippi. Phronia Craft.

—— (1958). 'The influence of the Let Down Reflex in Breast Feeding on the Mother Child Relationship', *Marriage and Family Living* **20**, 18.

—— (1959). 'Biological Femininity Versus Cultural Femininity', *Child Family Digest* **18** (1), 37–44.

—— (1963). 'Emotions of Pregnancy', *Clin. Obstet. Gynec.* **6**, 639–65.

NEWTON, N. and NEWTON, M. (1950). 'Relations of Ability to Breast Feed and Maternal Attitudes towards Breast Feeding', *Pediatrics* **5**, 869–75.

—— (1962). 'Mothers' Reactions to their Newborn Babies', *J. Am. Med. Ass.* **181**, 206–10.

NEWTON, N., PEELER, D. and NEWTON, M. (1968). 'Effect of Disturbance on Labour', *Am. J. Obstet. Gynec.* **101** (8), 1096.

NICHOLS, R. C. (1962). 'Subtle, Obvious and Stereotype Measures of Masculinity–Femininity', *Educ. and Psych. Measurement* **22**, 449–62.

NILSSON, A. (1970). 'Para-natal Emotional Adjustment. A Prospective Investigation of 165 Women', *Acta Psychiat. Scand.* Suppl. 220.

254 Bibliography

ORR, D. W. (1941). 'Pregnancy Following the Decision to Adopt', *Psychosom. Med.* **3**, 441.

—— (1968). 'Anthropological Notes on Female Sexual Role', *J. Am. Psychoanal. Ass.* **16**, 601–12.

OSTWALD, P. F. and REGAN, O. F. (1957). 'Psychiatric Disorders Associated with Childbirth', *J. Nerv. Ment. Dis.* **125** (2), 153–65.

OTTINGER, D. R. and SIMMONS, J. E. (1964). 'Behaviour of Human Neonates and Prenatal Maternal Anxiety', *Psychol. Rep.* **14**, 391–4.

OURTH, L. and BROWN, K. (1961). 'Inadequate Mothering and Disturbance in the Neonatal Period', *Child. Dev.* **32**, 287–94.

PAFFENBERGER, R. S. (1961). 'The Picture Puzzle of the Postpartum Psychosis', *J. Chron. Dis.* **13** (2), 161–73.

—— (1964). 'Epidemiological Aspects of Parapartum Mental Illness', *Br. J. Prev. Soc. Med.* **18** (4), 189–95.

PATTERSON, U., BLOCK, J., BLOCK, J. and JACKSON, D. (1960). 'The Relationship between Intention to Conceive and Symptoms during Pregnancy', *Psychosom. Med.* **22**, 373–6.

PAYNE, S. (1936). 'A Concept of Femininity', *Br. J. Med. Psychol.* **15**, 18–33.

PERLMAN, H. H. (1968). *Personal Social Role and Personality.* Chicago, University of Chicago Press.

PIKER, P. (1939). 'Psychoses Complicating Childbearing', *Am. J. Obstet. Gynec.* **35.**

PITT, B. (1968). 'Atypical Depression Following Childbirth', *Br. J. Psychiat.* **114**, 1325–35.

POTTER, H. W. and KLEIN, H. R. (1957). 'On Nursing Behaviour', *Psychiatry*, **20**, 39–46.

PROTHEROE, C. (1969). 'Puerperal Psychoses: a Long Term Study 1927–1961', *Br. J. Psychiat.* **115** (518), 9–30.

RACAMIER, P. C. (1953). 'A Propos de *Maternité et Sexe* de Marie Langer', *Evolution Psychiatrique* **1**, 559–65.

—— (1955). 'Mythologie de la Grossesse et de la Menstruation', *Evolution Psychiatrique* **2**, 285–97.

—— (1961). 'La Mère et l'Enfant dans les Psychoses du Postpartum', *Evolution Psychiatrique* **10**, 525–70.

—— (1967). 'Troubles de la Sexualité Feminine et du Sens Maternel', *Bulletin Officiel de la Société Fr. de Psychoprophylaxie Obstétricale* **432**, 1–40.

RANK, B., PUTNAM, M. C. and ROCHLIN, E. (1948). 'The Significance of the "Emotional Climate" in Early Feeding Difficulties', *Psychosom. Med.* **10**, 279–83.

RAPAPORT, R. (1963). 'Normal Crises, Family Structure and Mental Health', *Family Process* **2** (1), 68–80.

REVAULT D'ALLONNES, C. (1961). 'L'Accouchement est un Fait Culturel', *Bulletin de la Société Internationale de Psychoprophylaxie Obstetricale* **111** (3).

—— (1968). 'Vécu Psychologique des Premiers Mouvements de l'Enfant', *Bulletin de la Société Fr. Psychoprophylaxie Obstétricale* **15**.

RHEINGOLD, J. (1964). *The Fear of Being a Woman*. New York, Grune and Stratton.

RIBBLE, M. (1941). 'Disorganizing Factors of Infant Personality', *Am. J. Psychiat.* **38** (3), 459–63.

RICHARDSON, S. and GUTTMACHER, A. F. (ed.) (1967). *Childbearing: Social and Psychological Aspects*. Baltimore, Williams and Wilkins.

RINGROSE, C. (1961). 'Psychosomatic Influence in the Genesis of Toxaemia of Pregnancy', *Canadian Med. Assoc. J.* **84**.

ROBIN, A. (1962). 'Psychological Changes of Normal Parturition', *Psychiatric Quarterly* **36**, 129–50.

ROBINSON, M. (1943). 'Failing Lactation – A study of 110 Cases', *Lancet* Vol. 1, 66–8.

ROGERS, S. C. (1965). 'Depression Following Childbirth', *Practitioner* **195** (2), 257–60.

ROSBERG, J. and KARON, B. P. (1959). 'A Direct Analytic Contribution to the Understanding of Postpartum Psychosis', *Psychiatric Quarterly* **33**, 296–304.

ROSENGREN, W. R. (1961). 'Social Sources of Pregnancy as Illness or Normality', *Social Forces* **39**, 260.

—— (1961). 'Some Social Psychological Aspects of Delivery Room Difficulties', *J. Nerv. Ment. Dis.* **132** (6), 515–21.

RUBIN, R. (1967). 'Attainment of the Maternal Role. Processes. Models and Referrants', *Nursing Research* **16**, 237–45 and 342–6.

RYCROFT, C. (1968). *A Critical Dictionary of Psychoanalysis*. London, Nelson.

RYLE, A. (1961). 'The Psychological Disturbances Associated with 345 Pregnancies in 137 Women', *J. Ment. Sci.* **107**, 249–86.

RYLE, A. and BREEN, D. (1972). 'Some Differences in the Personal Constructs of Neurotic and Normal Subjects', *Br. J. Psychiat.* **120**, 558, 483–9.

SALZBERGER-WITTENBERG, I. (1970). *Psychoanalytic Thought and Relationships: a Human Approach*. London, Routledge and Kegan Paul.

SANDLER, B. (1968). 'Emotional Stress and Infertility', *J. Psychosom. Res.* **12** (1), 51–60.

SANTAYANA, G. (1968). *The Birth of Reason and Other Essays*. New York, Columbia University Press.

SARBIN, C. N. (1963). 'Feminine Identity', *J. Am. Psychoanal. Ass.* **11**.

SCHAEFER, E. and MANHEIMER, H. (1960). 'Dimensions of Perinatal Adjustment'. Paper read at Eastern Psychol. Ass., New York, April 1960.

SCHMIEDEBERG, M. (1946). 'Some Neurotic Difficulties in Nursing Mothers', *Psychiat. Quarterly* **20**, 147–55.

SCOTT, E. and THOMPSON, A. (1956). 'Psychological Investigation of Primigravidae', *J. Obstet. Gynaec. Brit. Emp.* **63**.

SEAGER, C. (1960). 'A Controlled Study of Postpartum Mental Illness', *J. Ment. Sci.* **106** (442), 214–30.

SHAINESS, N. (1969). 'Images of Women Past and Present, Overt and Obscured', *Am. J. Psychother.* **23** (1), 77–97.

SHEPLER, B. (1951). 'A Comparison of Masculinity–Femininity Measures', *J. Consult. Psychol.* **15**, 484–6.

SIM, M. (1968). 'Psychiatric Disorders of Pregnancy', *J. Psychosom. Res.* **12**, 95–100.

SINGER, I. (1973). *The Goals of Human Sexuality*. London, Wildwood House.

SLATER, P. (1969). 'Theory and Technique of the Repertory Grid', *Br. J. Psychiat.* **115**, 1287–96.

—— (1964). *The Principal Components of a Repertory Grid*. Obtainable from Dr Slater, Institute of Psychiatry, Denmark Hill, London S.E.5.

SOICHET, S. (1959). 'Emotional Factors in Toxaemia of Pregnancy', *Am. J. Obstet. Gynec.* **77**, 1065–73.

SONTAG, L. W. (1941). 'Significance of Foetal Environmental Differences', *Am. J. Obstet. Gynec.* **42**, 996–1003.

—— (1950). 'The Genetics of Differences in Psychosomatic Patterns in Childhood', *Am. J. Orthopsychiat.* **20**, 479–89.

SQUIER, R. and DUNBAR, F. (1946). 'Emotional Factors in the Course of Pregnancy', *Psychosom. Med.* **8**, 161–75.

STEIN, R. F. (1967–8). 'Social Orientations to Mental Illness in Pregnancy and Childbirth', *Int. J. Soc. Psychiat.* **14** (1), 56–64.

STERN, K. (1966). *The Flight from Woman*. London, Allen & Unwin.

STEWART, A. H., LEIDER, A. R., MANGHAM, C. A., HOLMES, T. H., RIPLEY, H. S. and WEILAND, I. H. (1954). 'Excessive Infant Crying (colic) in Relation to Parent Behaviour', *Am. J. Psychiat.* **110**, 687–94.

STOLLER, R. (1968). *Sex and Gender*. London, Hogarth Press.

—— (1973). 'The Male Transsexual as Experiment', *Int. J. Psychoanal.* **54**, Part 2.

SUTTIE, I. and J. (1932). 'The Mother: Agent or Object', *Brit. J. of Med. Psychol.* **XII**, Part III, 199–233.

TETLOW, C. (1955). 'Psychoses of Childbearing', *J. Ment. Sci.* **101**, 629–39.

THOMAS, C. L. and GORDON, J. E. (1959). 'Psychoses After Childbirth: Ecological Aspects of a Single Impact Stress', *Am. J. Med. Sci.* **238**, 363–88.

THOMPSON, C. (1943). 'Penis Envy in Women', *Psychiatry* **6**, 123–5.

TIPPETT, J. S. (1959). 'A Study of Change Process During Psychotherapy'. Doctoral Dissertation. Ohio State University.

TOBIN, S. M. (1957). 'Emotional Depression During Pregnancy', *Obstet. Gy bnaec.* **10**, 677–81.

TREADWAY, C. R., KANE, F. J., JARRAHI-ZADEH, A. and L., and MORRIS, A. (1969). 'A Psychoendocrine Study of Pregnancy and the Puerperium', *Am. J. Psychiat.* **125** (10), 480–6.

TURNER, B. K. (1956). 'The Syndrome in the Infant Resulting from Maternal Emotional Tension During Pregnancy', *Med. J. Australia* 1, 222–3.

URBINA, S., HARRISON, J. B., SCHAEFFER, C. E. and ANASTASI, A. (1970). 'Relationship Between Masculinity, Femininity and Creativity as Measured by the FDCT', *Psychol. Rep.* 26 (3), 799–804.

VAN DE CASTLE, R. L. (1968). 'Dream Content During Pregnancy', *Psychophysiology* 4 (3), 374–5.

VANDEN BERGH, R. L., TAYLOR, E. S. and DROSE, V. (1966). 'Emotional Illness in Habitual Aborters Following Suturing of the Incompetent Cervical Os', *Psychosom. Med.* 28 (3), 257–63.

VERMELIN, H. and RIBON, M. (1961). 'Conduite et Résultats de l'Allaitement Maternel à la Maternité de Nancy', *Rev. Fr. Gynec. Obstet.* 2, 119–29.

VICTOROFF, V. M. (1952). 'Dynamics and Management of Parapartum Neuropathic Reactions', *Diseases of the Nervous System* 13 (10), 291–8.

VISLIE, H. (1956). 'Puerperal Mental Disorders', *Acta Psychiatrica et Neurologica Scandinavia* 31, Suppl. 3, 3–42.

VARBLE, D. L. and LANDFIELD, A. W. (1969). 'Validity of the Self-Ideal Discrepancy as a Criterion Measure for Success in Psychotherapy', Journal of Counseling Psychology. 16 (2), 150–6.

WAGNER, E. and SLOMBASKI, J. (1968). 'Psychological Reactions of Pregnant Unwed Women as Measured by the Rorschach', *J. Clin. Psychol.* 24 (4), 467–9.

WAINWRIGHT, W. H. (1966). 'Fatherhood as a Precipitant of Mental Illness', *Am. J. Psychiat.* 123, 40–4.

WALLEN, P. and RILEY, R. (1950). 'Reactions of Mothers to Pregnancy and Adjustment of Offspring in Infancy', *Am. J. Orthopsychiat.* 20, 616–22.

WALSER, H. and DETROIT, M. 'Fear, an important etiological Factor in obstretrical problems', *Am. J. Obst. and Gynacol.* 55, 799.

WATSON, A. (1959). 'A Psychiatric Study of Idiopathic Prolonged Labour', *Obstet. and Gynaec.* 13, 589.

WENNER, N. K., COHEN, M. B., WEIGERT, E. V., KVARNES, R. G., CHANESON, E. M. and FEARING, J. M. (1969). 'Emotional Problems in Pregnancy', *Psychiatry* 32 (4), 389–410.

WIEDORN, W. S. (1954). 'Toxaemia of Pregnancy and Schizophrenia', *J. Nerv. Ment. Dis.* 120, 1.

WINER, F. (1961). 'The Relationship of Certain Attitudes Towards the Mother to Sex Role Identity'. Unpublished Ph.D. Thesis. New York University.

WINNICOTT, D. W. (1968). 'Breast-Feeding as a Communication'. One day Conference on Breast-Feeding Organised by the National Childbirth Trust, Nov. 1968.

—— (1971). *Playing and Reality*. London, Tavistock Publications.

—— (1971). 'The Concept of a Healthy Individual', in J. D. Sutherland, *Towards Community Mental Health*. London, Tavistock Publications.

WINOKUR, G. and WERBOFF, J. (1956). 'The Relationship of Conscious

Maternal Attitudes to Certain Aspects of Pregnancy', *Psychiat. Q. Suppl.* **30**, 61–73.

WINTER, S. (1969). 'Characteristics of Fantasy while Nursing', *J. Personal.* **37** (1), 58–72.

WYLIE, R. (1961). *The Self Concept: a Critical Survey of Pertinent Research Literature.* Lincoln, University of Nebraska Press.

YALOM, I. D., LUMDE, D. T., MOSS, R. H. and HAMBURG, D. A. (1968). 'Postpartum Blues Syndrome', *Archs. Gen. Psychiat.* **18** (1), 16–27.

ZEMLICK, M. J. and WATSON, D. (1953). 'Maternal Attitudes of Acceptance and Rejection during and after Pregnancy', *Am. J. Orthopsychiat.* **23**, 570–84.

ZILBOORG, G. (1928). 'Malignant Psychoses related to Childbirth', *Am. J. Obstet. Gynec.* **15**, 145.

—— (1929). 'The Dynamics of Schizophrenic Reactions Related to Parenthood'. *Am. J. Psychiat.* **8** (4), 733–67.

ZUCKERMAN, M., NURNBERGER, J., GARDINER, S., VANDIVEER, J., BARRETT, B., DEN BREEIJEN, A. (1963). 'Psychological correlates of somatic complaints in pregnancy and difficulty in childbirth', *Journ. Consulting Psych.* **27**, 4.

Index

260   Index